Underground

Comedia
Series editor: David Morley

UNDERGROUND

THE LONDON ALTERNATIVE PRESS 1966–74

Nigel Fountain

A Comedia book
published by Routledge
London and New York

First published in 1988 by
Routledge
a division of Routledge, Chapman and Hall
11 New Fetter Lane, London EC4P 4EE

Published in the USA by
Routledge
a division of Routledge, Chapman and Hall, Inc.
29 West 35th Street, New York NY 10001

Typeset by Columns of Reading
Printed and bound by Richard Clay Ltd
Chichester, Sussex

British Library Cataloguing in Publication Data
Fountain, Nigel
   Underground: the London alternative
   press 1966–74. – (A Comedia book).
   1. London. Underground press, 1966–1974
   I. Title
   070.5′9

   ISBN 0 415 00727 5
        0 415 00728 3 Pbk

Library of Congress Cataloging in Publication Data
Fountain, Nigel.
   Underground: the London alternative press, 1966–74/Nigel
   Fountain.
   p. cm. – (A Comedia book)
   Bibliography: p.
   Includes index.
   ISBN 0 415 00727 5. ISBN 0–415 00728 3 (pbk.)
   1. Underground press – England – London – History – 20th century.
   2. London (England) – Intellectual life – 20th century. I. Title.
   PN5124.U5F68 1988
   072′.1 – dc1988–4382

Contents

Introduction

This is a book about a lucky generation. Lucky because they had missed the war, and grew up in a world where the expansion of affluence seemed infinite. With the typical gratitude of the young, they responded with protest, argument, and what their parents regarded as deviant behaviour. In Britain, the United States, in Europe – west and, to an extent, east – they developed what became known as an underground culture. In the east, of course, where Herbert Marcuse's formulation of 'repressive tolerance' was more often substituted with straight repression, the stakes were rather higher.

But the stakes were high in the west too. The long boom that followed the Second World War brought plenty, and raised plenty of questions. Affluence enabled the United States to wage war on south-east Asia while expanding living standards at home. Affluence enabled people to enjoy *things* – and then wonder just what the things were for, and ask why they had been denied them for so long. For many, such questions were merely lingering doubts pushed to the back of the mind; for an increasing number of the young, the questions were central.

The underground, as Jeff Nuttall wrote in his pioneering *Bomb Culture* back in 1968, happened everywhere, but in Britain it first developed in London in the early 1960s. Hundreds, and then thousands, and then tens of thousands, of people – young and old – began to enter it, whether for a weekend or a decade. However long the stay was, some method of communication that ditched mainstream preoccupations of Fleet Street and their official youth offshoots was bound to develop. Sometimes it was movies, sometimes word of mouth, but crucially it was the underground press.

That press didn't just argue with the established order, it polemicized furiously within itself: generating exciting, crazy, repetitive, and innovative language and design. For once it seemed too that the barrier between the producers of the words and images and the consumers was breaking down. Anyone could work for the underground press, and many took up the opportunity with varying results. And those who didn't write could still feel that they were part of a movement for change.

Where the change was going was something else. For some it was simple hedonism, if hedonism is ever simple; for some it was anarchism, redefined for the times, or Marxism. There too the barriers broke down, people who in earlier and later decades wouldn't have passed the time of day, or night, with each other were forced into contact, coalition, and confrontation. By the time of its peak in the late 1960s the underground had developed a network across Britain and across the English Channel and the Atlantic.

I hope in concentrating on the London underground press that this book can explain something of that movement within the city and outside. There are many deliberate omissions. It does not deal with the press of the organized far left, except where it touches on the underground press. It does not deal with the papers which began to emerge out of the black community in the late 1960s. And it does not deal with the wave of community papers partly triggered by the example of the underground. Nor do excellent papers like *Inside Story* which attempted to redefine radical reportage find a place. But in the papers I have concentrated on I trust that readers will get a flavour of the turmoil, excitement, and occasional farce that they generated.

I also hope that this book will not be seen as an exercise in nostalgia. A lot of people had a very good time in those days, some of them didn't live to remember them, but the issues the underground press raised have not been settled. In colder times they may have frosted over, but as long as individuals and groups seek to take control of their own lives the experiences of those times contain information that can and must be used.

This book couldn't have been written without the assistance of the people who worked on the papers, from whom I gathered information and opinions. The mistakes are all mine.

Particularly I would like to thank the following for giving generously of their time and insights: Richard Adams, Jerome Burne, Tony Elliott, Alison Fell, Louise Ferrier, Jonathon Green, John Hoyland, Roger Hutchinson, Phil Kelly, John Lloyd, Pearce Marchbank, Alan Marcuson, Jane de Mendelson, Miles, Richard Neville, Dick Pountaine, David Robins, Sheila Rowbotham, Marsha Rowe, Sue Small, Michelene Wandor, David Widgery, Mark Williams, and an American Yorkshireman who perhaps started it all, John Wilcock. Thanks also to David Pallister, Margaret Busby, to Comedia and particularly the long-suffering Dave Morley, Judith Williamson, and for her support and encouragement, Laura Cotton.

Chapter 1

Almost tomorrow

The generation above us had a hard time.
(Miles, co-founder of *International Times*)

I feel the hints, the clues, the whisper of a new time coming.
There is a universal rebellion in the air, and the power of the two
colossal superstates may be, yes, may just be ebbing, may be
failing in energy even more rapidly than we are failing in energy,
and if that is so, then the destructive, the liberating, the creative
nihilism of the Hip, the frantic search for potent change may
break into the open with all its violence, its confusion, its ugliness
and horror.
(Norman Mailer, *Village Voice*, 1956)

In October 1955 Jimmy Young's 'The man from Laramie' was at
number one in the British hit parade. It was a domestic cover
version of an American record from an American film. The
Communist Party of Great Britain was still mourning the death of
Joseph Stalin. The Conservative Party was celebrating the election
of another administration.

By the end of 1956 the Communist Party was mourning its lost
membership. The Conservative Party was reeling, with its leader
stricken in the aftermath of the Suez debacle. Nine days into 1957
Anthony Eden quit, having consigned Britain's role as the world's
third power to the bottom of the Canal together with President
Nasser's block ships.

With the dreams of 1945's Labour victory long gone, and the
pretensions of the Conservatives painfully exposed it was the hour
for the group of young meritocrats who had done well out of the
peace, the Angry Young Men. Kingsley Amis's *Lucky Jim* was
popular. A woolly-jumpered Colin Wilson was photographed for
the press in his Notting Hill bedsit and under the tree in Hampstead
Heath where he had worked on his best-seller *The Outsider*, a paean
to the existential rebel Wilson wished to be. John Osborne's *Look
Back In Anger* added to the chorus from the lost boys of the lower
middles. With the titans of 1945 gone, the stumbling old guard of
the Conservative Party finally tripped up: it was the chance for the
lower orders of the middle classes to bite back.

And they would not be choosing the Communist Party. Earlier that year it had been uneasily digesting the Soviet leader Nikita Khrushchev's secret speech denouncing the excesses of the Stalin era. Meanwhile in Hungary the reform-minded Communist leader Imre Nagy responded to popular pressure and began liberalization. The process had accelerated by the autumn into revolution. Within the small but industrially and intellectually significant British party dissatisfaction with the leadership had already been growing before the Soviet Union provided its response to the Hungarian events. From Budapest that November the *Daily Worker*'s correspondent Peter Fryer provided pro-revolution and anti-Stalinist reports until they were suppressed. Later he was ousted from the CPGB, but with Hungary, the party split wide open. In the dissident Communist *New Reasoner* magazine historian Edward Thompson asked: 'Where is my party in Hungary? Was it in the broadcasting stations or on the barricades?'

Between 1956 and 1958 the Communist Party lost 10,000 people, some 30 per cent of its membership. The Party's role on the left of British politics had far outweighed its size, and the fall-out from that explosion threw new clusters of groups, causes, and concerns into British politics. They met head on with elements of that teenage army that had also emerged from 1956.

In 1955, while Jimmy Young and Dickie Valentine's ersatz American crooning dominated the milk bars of Britain, Bill Haley, the John the Baptist of rock 'n' roll, took four records into the Top Twenty. *Blackboard Jungle*, that portrait of minor-league delinquency in a New York school, with Haley's 'Rock around the clock' on the soundtrack, opened, and briskly closed cinemas.

And after Haley came Presley, Little Richard, and Fats Domino, laying a freeway through popular culture that outraged left and right alike, and down which successive generations of youth were to drive for the next three decades.

The impact of rock 'n' roll went everywhere, including the debating society of my Southampton grammar school, debating, as 1956 closed, that the new music should be deplored. While Eden manques wrestled with the finer points of parliamentary style a wild man struggled to his feet from the bottom stream of the fifth form. His blazer studded with drawing pins in homage to Presley's cloth of gold, he cut through the verbiage with a revolutionary cry for the times. 'All I gotta say', he proclaimed to wild applause, 'is *don't knock the rock!*'

In Liverpool John Lennon, aged 16, bought Lonnie Donegan's 'Rock island line' and a guitar. Beat was hot and cool, rock was hot. Drink, junk, poetry, Stalin's legacy, Eden's folly, Presley's charisma, Brando's (unseen in Britain) *Wild One* filtered into the consciousness of the young. The hip could experiment and buy

Coltrane, the mass market could buy Johnny Dankworth's modern jazz pastiche, 'Experiments with micc', in cnough numbcrs to make it seven in the April 1956 hit parade. With class war anaesthetized by the Cold War and affluence, the generation gap and teenagers became a subject for serious observation.

Amongst the books, tracts, poetry, and pamphlets that the young would-be intellectuals began to absorb was the new writing from the United States, that accompaniment to the modern jazz that survived alongside rock into the 1960s. But one Englishman at least was experiencing it all first hand.

In 1946 a 19-year-old Yorkshireman, John Wilcock, got a lucky break, his first job in journalism on the *Sheffield Morning Telegraph*. Three years later he switched to the *Daily Mirror*; he was still based in Yorkshire, covering the local beat. By 1952 the attraction of America was tugging on the young journalist. But America wasn't easy to get into. He picked up a copy of *Time* magazine, the cover story was about Canada; maybe the British Dominion would be the compromise. He made inquiries and discovered that for just £19 he could get to Ontario. Wilcock set off for the New World. Jobs weren't easy but eventually he fixed a slot as a night wire man at a Toronto press agency. He made contacts which brought him in touch with Jack Kent Cook who ran *Saturday Night Magazine*. Cook had done well, Wilcock heard, making a fast million working with the Canadian newspaper magnate Roy Thomson. And Cook was impressed by the young man from Sheffield. He took him on.

It was a literary weekly with an upfront section modelled on the *New Yorker*. Wilcock stayed for a year before briefly taking off for a job in Nassau. It was a wonderful place, he thought, but the money, the job, the office were awful. Within six months he was back in Toronto. Thanks to Cook's intervention he got a job on *Liberty* magazine, and Wilcock began working on its 'Screwball' column. It was a downmarket job; he'd report on reactions to his attempts to change a $1000 bill, sit in a lion's cage at the local zoo, or clean windows on the twenty-eighth floor of a skyscraper. It paid the rent.

He was crazy about New York and went there for long weekends. It was where he wanted to be. After a year he made the move. Money was bad, but he was still working for *Liberty* and picked up work on *Pageant* magazine. Things got better, he even got commissioned to visit Hollywood and interview Rock Hudson, Milton Berle, Marlene Dietrich, and Marilyn Monroe. It beat the *Sheffield Morning Telegraph* but Hollywood was far from New York and Greenwich Village. The Village, thought the Yorkshireman, was the centre of the universe.

By 1955 the star of Senator Joe McCarthy, the red baiter, was waning. And even at the zenith of his power Greenwich Village had remained a place shielded from some of his excesses, open to the pull of Europe, a haven for the dissident, the Bohemian, the drop-out. Allen Ginsberg was writing his first major work *Howl* that summer in the Village. His contemporary Gregory Corso's first book *The Vestal Lady On Brattle* had just been published. The coffee shops and bars, little theatres and jazz made the Village quite different from small-town America, quite different from Eisenhower's other America.

But it had one thing missing – a proper paper. There *was* a paper, the *Villager*, but a parish pump periodical wasn't really what the place needed. Wilcock put a notice up in a bookshop. Would anyone like to get together about starting a paper, it said, if so, meet with Wilcock. People did, and people met, and nothing came of it.

But the meetings had shown there was interest. One day in a bar he ran into two of the people who'd attended the meetings, Dan Wolf and Ed Fancher. Fancher had some money, at last. Did Wilcock want to come in? He did. Fancher put in $5,000, and persuaded Norman Mailer, a friend of Wolf's girlfriend, to do the same. Long sessions followed. What was it to be called? Eventually a title was suggested by Mailer, and it was agreed – the *Village Voice*.

Wilcock was doing all right at *Pageant*, taking home $100 a week, but he quit the job to become the *Village Voice*'s news editor, at $25. He did lay-out, editing and writing. On 26 October 1955 the first issue hit the news-stands. Their friends told them they were crazy, it sold for a nickel and nobody, they discovered, had the curiosity to buy it although it did make all the local Greenwich Village news-stands.

Maybe the paper was too literary but, whatever the reasons, the 'Weekly newspaper designed to be read', targeted to sell 10,000 a week, sold, maybe, 2,000 that first week, and began losing $1,000 a week. Yet it survived. It wasn't very radical, it wasn't very intellectual, but it caught a mood of dissent in mid-1950s America, just edging away from the excesses of McCarthyism, still immersed in the Eisenhower years. Never was it to be regarded as 'under-ground', but it was the straw in the wind.

On Wilcock's suggestion the *Voice* had approached a distin-guished critic with the *New York Times Book Review*, Gilbert Seldes. The young man from the *Voice* had met Seldes in Canada where, curiously ahead of his time, he was lecturing on television. Since the publication of his *The Seven Lively Arts* in the 1920s Seldes had been a linchpin of New York's arts scene. To recruit the veteran on the *Voice*'s rates would be unlikely, they realized.

Intriguingly, Seldes agreed, on one condition – that he had a column, and it appeared every week. The *Voice* accepted and Wilcock learned a lesson he was to remember: the value of a column, the value of control over one's work. A column was the rubric under which the writer could put anything at all. Wilcock was to spend the next thirty years attempting to put it into practice.

Hearing Ginsberg's tumultuous reading of *Howl* spurred Lawrence Ferlinghetti to ask for permission to publish it under his City Lights imprint in San Francisco. In 1956 it came out, and Ferlinghetti had opened the City Lights Bookshop in that city. The publishing house and the shop became a focus for the new writing born in the aftermath of the Second World War, the Beats and their associates, Jack Kerouac, William Burroughs, Kenneth Rexroth, Gregory Corso, and the poets, surrealists, and film-makers of San Francisco.

It was a movement whose history went back into the Second World War, into the New York clubs that had bred Charlie Parker, Dizzy Gillespie, and the new jazz of be-bop. But 1957 was its year, with the publication of Jack Kerouac's *On the Road*. Suddenly its author became the 'King of the Beats', and his milieu the stuff of headlines, cover features, and money.

In 1958 came another sign of the US emergence from the McCarthyite age with the debut of Paul Krassner's *The Realist*. An early contributor was Wilcock. In 1956 he had quit the *Voice* full-time, settled into writing his weekly column, 'The Village Square' for the paper, and taken a job with the *New York Times* travel section. It was to ensure that throughout the years that lay ahead he would remain on the road. *The Realist*, meanwhile, provided Wilcock with a vehicle for his own essays into experimental writing.

That year Allen Ginsberg paid his first – and largely unnoticed – visit to England and read his poetry in Oxford. Back in London, in February, at Central Hall Westminster, a movement that was to provide fertile soil for his work was launched. The great and good from the liberal/left establishment – A.J.P. Taylor, the historian, James Cameron, the journalist, and key organizers Peggy Duff and Canon John Collins – sat on the platform as the Campaign for Nuclear Disarmament was launched. The attendance was so large that five overflow halls had to be used. A movement was born that provided for the next four years the reference point for the left, and for artists and what passed for Britain's Beats. It was a key part of what Jeff Nuttall was to label 'bomb culture'.

Soon after, at the offices of *Peace News*, the pacifist paper that had provided, and was to provide into the 1960s, the key radical voice of the new movement, the first Aldermaston March was organized by the Direct Action Committee against Nuclear War. That year was special, the marchers marched *to* the British atomic research centre in Berkshire. From 1959 it changed: their target, each Easter, was to be London.

Chapter 2

The biggest place in town

The underground happened everywhere simultaneously: it was simply what you did in the H-bomb world if you were, by nature, creative and concerned for humanity as a whole. . . . The nineteenth-century artists were faced with the collapse of Christianity and the end of Hellenism. We are faced with the end of man.

(Jeff Nuttall, *Bomb Culture*)

The 1956 vintage of the independent left was one of extraordinary potential, numbering many thousands of experienced cadres from the Communist Party crisis, hundreds of Labour lefts bursting from their party prison, contingents of determined and defiant pacifists and, within a short while the Children's Crusade of teenagers from all classes.

(Peter Sedgwick, *The Left In Britain*)

Amongst those who watched and then joined that route from Berkshire to central London was the future co-founder of *International Times*, Barry Miles from Cheltenham.

He was 16 in 1959, and just entering a local arts college still run on quasi-Victorian lines. The son of parents 'in service' in Gloucestershire, Miles – as he was to be known universally within the underground and after – had interests which moved rapidly across from art into poetry. CND provided the trigger, setting up a network of connections across the country.

Through an Oxford commune he met Michael Horovitz. His vital and pioneering poetry magazine, *New Departures*, had first been published in late 1959. And Miles met a musician, trumpeter Pete Brown. Also in his first year at Cheltenham, a copy of a poem by Gregory Corso came into his hands. The most contemporary poet he had until then encountered was Siegfried Sassoon. At the bottom of the poem was an address, City Lights Bookshop, San Francisco. He wrote for a catalogue, and they sent him back a list of ten titles. He had heard of none of them, but his eye was caught by Ginsberg's *Howl*. 'Through the bank I ordered one dollar, two dollars maybe, and sent off for it. The book came back and I was amazed. It absolutely knocked me out.'

Literature had that effect on other people too. In 1960 Penguin Books published D.H. Lawrence's *Lady Chatterley's Lover*. The company expected legal action, and it got it. The case was to set a stamp on the decade, and one question from prosecuting counsel Mervyn Griffiths-Jones was to mark the period as precisely as Neville Chamberlain's 'Peace in our time' had done in 1938. The difference was that it took a year before Chamberlain's words came back to haunt him. For Griffiths-Jones the lag was the time it took his words to leave his mouth and hit the pages of the newspapers.

'Is it a book that you would even wish your wife or your servants to read?

Is it *what*? asked everybody under 40. Why, there were graduate wives now, soon Margaret Drabble was to make a comfortable living writing about such people in her novels. And where were these servants? Where had Griffiths-Jones *been*? Had he taken no note of changing employment patterns, from 1945 to 1960? Did he not know that 33 per cent of married women were going out to work, and that didn't mean they were competing to do Mrs Griffiths-Jones' dishes?

But the barrister wasn't the only person in Britain affronted by its publication. In Edinburgh, autumn 1959, another co-founder of *International Times*, Louisiana-born Jim Haynes, soon after winning an early discharge from the US Airforce at the nearby Kirknewton base, opened his Paperback Shop in Charles Street, off George Square. It became a centre for the young, the radical, and the literati of that city. It also, in 1960, shifted a lot of copies of *Lady Chatterley*. It shifted even more when a former missionary from Africa came in, bought a copy, took it out on the end of a pair of coal tongs, and set fire to it. A conveniently placed photographer ensured that the story made national, and international, news.

Amongst the younger generation the arrival of the book in the wake of Penguin's successful defence met with an enthusiasm which rarely survived a thumbing of its pages. For male adolescents *Lady Chatterley* was hardly even a competitor with the modest pornographic magazines of the period. But, for the young, she was loose, roaming the public domain, flaunting sex *and* intellectual respectability, a companion for Simone Signoret in *Room at the Top*, Shirley-Anne Field in *Saturday Night and Sunday Morning*, and Alberto Moravia. It was one in the eye for the old order.

The show that underlined changing days was the Oxford review, *Beyond The Fringe*, with its mild demolition job on national pretensions which had been the Conservatives' stock-in-trade since 1951. Peter Cook, Jonathan Miller, Alan Bennett, and Dudley Moore came from public and grammar schools, juvenile mandarins of the meritocracy, they provided a show lodged in the half-way house between the angries of 1956 and the arts labs and tepees of the later 1960s, and, unlike much of what was to follow, it was very English. In May 1961 the show opened in London to a rapturous welcome.

By Autumn 1961 Miles had begun to visit London. At the Whitechapel Art Gallery he could see the American abstract impressionists whose work provided in paint what be-bop and Beat aimed for in music and words. And he began to connect to the nascent counter-culture, visiting Pete Brown's home in Oppidans Road, Primrose Hill. The house was shared by designer Mal Dean, the future underground press writer Felix de Mendelsohn and an avant-garde sax player, George Kahn. But the place to crash was further west, with John 'Hoppy' Hopkins, in Westbourne Terrace – Hopkins, future instigator of the London Free School, photo-journalist, and another founder of *It*. It was easy to see the place was cool, thought Miles, there was always a copy of *The Naked Lunch* on the table. The book, by Ginsberg and Kerouac's associate William Burroughs, was still illegal at the time.

Another of Burroughs's acquaintances was the Glasgow poet, writer and junkie author of *Cain's Book*, Alex Trocchi. In nearby Powis Square he was running a book-cum-record shop with John Michel, whose semi-mystic writing was to become a feature of *It* five years later. And the bookshop also brought another figure of the future on to the perimeter of the circle, Michael de Freitas, later Michael X, and Michael Abdul Malik, then a frontman for the racketeering landlord Peter Rachman.

Separate worlds brushed against each other in those early 1960s days. Another visitor too was Aloysius 'Lucky' Gordon. That autumn, while a youthful Mick Jagger was enrolling at the London School of Economics, Gordon met Christine Keeler at Notting Hill's Rio Cafe, and Keeler was in mid-affair with John Profumo, the Conservative Government's Secretary of State for War. Gordon was to be a key element in Profumo's downfall, the event that dragged the Conservatives into an unwelcome part of the modern world.

Unlike that unfortunate, notorious heroine of the mid-1950s, Ruth Ellis, Keeler didn't ape Tory style. She looked natural, in *time*. Two years later, when the scandal peaked and middle-aged mobs shouted abuse at her as she sped away in large cars, it seemed less outraged morality they were proclaiming than outrage at being left behind in the 1950s. She too became a victim, but to many of the young, observing from out in the sticks, far even from the world of CND, she was a victor. In a collision between the furtive sex of the old order and the impression of freer sex of the young, the Tories – like the doomed professor in *The Blue Angel* three decades earlier – had come off worse. The Tories did it, but didn't want to talk about it. Why not just do it?

The Profumo affair had been perfectly timed for the beneficiaries of the *Beyond the Fringe* satire boom. On 25 October 1961, the first issue of *Private Eye*, all 5,000 copies of it, was published. Produced by public schoolboys, with public schoolboy tastes, and public schoolboy humour, the magazine had, within eighteen months, circulated to the schools of the land, crossed oceans, irritated politicians, and helped bring down Profumo. Never of the underground, and despising, and despised by it, it was the link between mainstream and fringe publishing, between the small magazines of the poets, the politicos, and the despised conglomerates of Fleet Street.

At the core of the paper in its early days were Peter Usborne, Christopher Booker, and Richard Ingrams. With Paul Foot, Booker and Ingrams had been at Shrewsbury in the early 1950s. Oxford in the late 1950s brought together a coterie, which, after graduation, and without much else on, led to *Private Eye*. Booker had been working at *Liberal News* and, after receiving a letter from Usborne, whose proto-satirical magazine *Mesopotamia* at Oxford had centred around Foot, Ingrams, and John Wells, the product hit the streets – or rather those streets in South Kensington to which Andrew Osmond, another Oxford contemporary, chose to distribute it. After ten issues the magazine was selling around 18,000; within a year, as the satire boom celebrated the collapse of Macmillan's reign, it had climbed to 35,000.

Another key to *Private Eye*'s success, and one that was not to be lost on the underground, was its use of offset litho printing. The paper could be pasted up by amateurs, and set on a typewriter. Hot metal would last another two decades in Fleet Street. For the underground it was to be almost unknown.

Out of *Private Eye*, too, came, briefly, the Establishment Club, set up in the week of the magazine's launch, capitalizing on the upsurge and faintly echoing Greenwich Village's more vibrant nightlife. The club was to nearly kill the magazine as its losses accumulated, but it also provided a link with the United States which was to snap as the magazine moved towards Little England-ism, or Little Londonism. It provided a venue for Lennie Bruce.

Back in New York, John Wilcock was still writing his column, still hanging out with the *Realist*'s Paul Krassner, and had moved from *New York Times* travel writing to travel books, indeed an opus on Mexico had begun to open – or dilate – his eyes to drugs. One evening at the Village Vanguard Krassner introduced Wilcock to the comedian whose black humour pushed comedy beyond any of the mild Eisenhower era limits of Shelley Berman and Bob Newhart. The Yorkshireman explained that he lived around the corner, if Bruce needed to rest between gigs. The comedian took up the offer. Wilcock, with a lifelong affinity for cultural outlaws was intrigued by Bruce, even if alarmed that the jacket pocket spilling out with hypodermics would get them both busted. He had, he told him, to write a *Voice* column about him, and his act. 'You wanna do it now?' asked Bruce. 'Bring the typewriter into the kitchen.'

Bruce went into the bathroom, put on his tie, and stuck the needle that was to plague his remaining years into his arm. He shouted out questions – and answers – to Wilcock. Within ten minutes the journalist had his story.

But when the Establishment booked a return visit for the comedian for 8 April 1963 it had problems. The then Home Secretary, a man notorious even in an unloved job, Henry Brook, banned his entry. The week before in New York Bruce had been arrested backstage by the New York police for giving an 'indecent performance'. The snatch had taken place at Greenwich Village's Café à Go Go and it was Wilcock and fellow *Voice* journalist Nat Hentoff who provided the backbone of the 'Emergency Committee Against the Harassment of Lennie Bruce'. The comedian never made it to England again, and was soon to die. But tangentially he was part of that transatlantic wave shaping the British 1960s, with Ginsberg, Laurence Ferlinghetti, Corso, and Burroughs – cult figures amongst the milieu spilling out of CND.

Private Eye's inception had drawn on other foreign influences. One had been Paris's satirical daily, *Le Canard Enchainé*. The France of the period, in its memories, movies, and residual expatriate culture, still pulled strongly on radical America and Britain. In 1958 William Burroughs had moved to Paris, where Allen Ginsberg had helped set up the 'Beat Hotel' that persisted into the early 1960s. Alex Trocchi had escaped Glasgow for the city, and release from Calvinism. It was still the city of the existentialists, of Jean-Paul Sartre and Simone de Beauvoir, Jaques Brel and Juliette Greco. The New Wave was sweeping through the cinema. And the bars didn't close at half past ten.

One tripper on 1960 had been the future *Black Dwarf* journalist, feminist and socialist, Sheila Rowbotham, fresh out of Yorkshire Methodist boarding school and en route to Oxford. The influences that had pressed on her adolescent consciousness began to come together that summer in the French capital with her arts school boyfriend, Bernie from Bermondsey. Earlier, holidaying in the less exotic Yorkshire resort of Filey she had picked up the American Beat anthology *Protest*, one of the volumes triggered by the 'on the road' boom after 1957. Back in her home town of Leeds she patronized the local cinema which alternated art and porno movies. A lot of the clientele, she noted, didn't seem to discriminate between the two. There she had seen Jean Cocteau's *Orphee*. Under Bernie's influence she shifted to Beat, black sweaters, black stockings, shades from Woolworth's for two and sixpence, layers of ripped T-shirts and old jeans – fifteen years pre-punk. In Paris fifty years of radical arts movement, Dada, surrealism, danced with American hip and jazz. Unnoticed too in those years, and out of Marx and surrealism, another movement for the 1960s began to take shape. In 1962 the International Situationists began to impinge on the wilder fringes of Gallic politics, with the publication of Raoul Vaneigem's *Totality For Kids*. Five years would pass before the Sits' days would come.

Across the globe in that year, 1962, 21-year old Richard Neville was taking his first step into journalism, editing the University of New South Wales student paper, *Tharunka*. By the following year he was working on his second and more notorious venture into magazine publishing, *Oz*, with Richard Walsh from Sydney University, and a gifted young student graphic designer, Martin Sharp. The Australia of the early 1960s still seemed secure and stultified with the apparently eternal regime of Robert Menzies. Under his rule the old English-fashioned elite rubbed uneasy shoulders with a new 'classless' middle-class youth sold on American music. On April Fool's Day 1963 came the first issue of *Oz*. All its 6,000 print run sold out. It fired at God, Royalty, the upper crust, politicians and the new pop culture, using cartoons, lampoons, and interviews. Some labelled it an Australian *Private Eye*, but there was more to it than that. The young Australian had sensed other places, and other moods. In the university library he had happened on a copy of the *Village Voice*. He was intrigued, and particularly by John Wilcock's 'Village Square' column. Neville wrote to ask Wilcock, could he reproduce the column? 'He wrote back an absolutely charming letter', he remembers, 'saying don't worry about the money, of course you can reproduce it, and don't worry about the copyright.' Which is why, suggests Neville, to this day Wilcock has remained a poor, and honest, man. Through Wilcock, too, he came into contact with another American, Tuli Kupferberg, whose poetry and cartoons astonished him, and with Paul Krassner and his *Realist*. In the second issue, echoing the 1950s' *Realist*, *Oz* gave a sympathetic interview to a practitioner of that then outrageous operation, abortion. In the sixth issue – and what was to be the most famous Australian *Oz* – the magazine reprinted a Lennie Bruce feature from the *Realist*, providing a print debut for the comedian in Sydney.

The first issue also netted its editors \$40 fines for obscenity. Having started on a shoestring, the paper built itself a circulation of 40,000 and also got itself, with the sixth issue in February 1964, its big Australian obscenity charge. Sydney's latest new building, and its pride was the P&O block. Part of its appeal stemmed from the Tom Bass fountain inset into its wall, a long thin crack in the stone. To some – notably the three *Oz* editors – it bore an irresistible resemblance to a urinal. Thus were they photographed, their backs to the camera, their fronts, in the traditional male pose, to the fountain. The picture adorned *Oz*'s cover, and outraged polite society. Charged with obscenity the magistrates gave them six months hard labour each. They appealed, and eventually the sentences were revoked.

Early in 1964 the magazine gained another recruit. Marsha Rowe was part-timing at university and working in a dead-end secretarial job. Seeing an ad for a secretary on *Oz* she went along. 'The editors noticed a kindred spirit and were dazzled', wrote Richard Neville two decades later of the tousle-haired 20-year old. Rowe made a joke about *Oz*'s pension scheme and they both laughed. It was the beginning of an on-off professional relationship that was to persist into the 1970s, by which time, in London, Neville would even write for Rowe's new magazine, *Spare Rib*.

Feminism was some way away. Her erstwhile Bohemian boy-friend advised firmly against such a *risqué* job. So did her parents, her father announcing that should she work for *Oz* he wouldn't speak to her any more. She was on the point of abandoning the plan when a neighbour, a solicitor who had been advising the magazine, explained that Neville and company were respectable young men really, from decent backgrounds – after all, his father had been a colonel in the Australian Army. She took up with *Oz* at £14 a week.

But her generation and its immediate elders were beginning to move north. Rowe, the loyal Australian, stayed put, but a group of Australians whose influence on London and the underground was to be crucial had started the shift, including Neville, Sharp, and Germaine Greer.

The country they arrived in, after the Profumo affair, was hearing a mild hurrah for the dissidents of 1956, as Harold Wilson's brand of socialism without class or pain, and with industrial modernization and assorted 'plans', edged towards power. In October 1964 the Labour Party buried the Conservatives of Sir Alec Douglas-Home in a shallow grave, and the talk, briefly, was of a 'Kennedy-style' new broom in Downing Street.

The orthodox left, the *Daily Mirror*, *New Statesman*, and *Tribune*, celebrated. And, briefly, in university bedsits more backward undergraduates added the new Prime Minister to collections of newly-fashionable photo-posters, alongside such Beat heroes as Brando and Dean.

Others were more sceptical – the far left, and the dissidents and pacifists of *Anarchy* and *Peace News*. The latter, during those days, was edited by Theodore Roszak, the American whose *The Making of the Counter Culture* (1970) was to be a key work of the early 1970s. With the clean, sanserif layout pioneered as a classic 1960s design by the *Observer*, *Peace News* stood at the crossroads of mid-

1960s dissident culture. From the United States came reports of the battles on campus and in the south, and writers like jazz critic and *Village Voice* columnist Nat Hentoff; from London came a critique of Wilson's first stumbling days of power, a concern with the new politics of ecology, the black movement, Vietnam, Algeria, Cuba – by then in the sixth year of revolutionary rule – the seizure of Burroughs's *The Naked Lunch* by the Director of Public Prosecutions, R.D. Laing on 'Violence Masquerading as Love', the campaign to legalize marijuana. Under the editorship of Roszak, and subsequently Rod Prince, *Peace News* trailed the bulk of the preoccupations for the next half-decade.

And it was selling to an audience that, with the change in mass pop culture after the rise of the Beatles in 1963 was expanding, in London and elsewhere. A flood of new bands, from the north and around London, had emerged, fed by the influences of the blues, the bomb, CND. In March 1962 Alexis Korner had opened his blues club in Ealing Broadway, by July that year the Rolling Stones were debuting at the Marquee. By the following winter Michael Horovitz's *New Departures* magazine had advanced so far as to put on a live performance at the same venue. Horovitz was to be vital to the underground's birth. In Soho the Partisan coffee bar, founded by the *New Left Review* – which had grown out of the *New Reasoner* in 1960 – was attracting a far more Bohemian and disreputable crowd than the straighter new leftists for which it had been intended. Down on Old Compton Street, the Two 'I's, hailed as the home of British rock, because Tommy Steele and Cliff Richard had once drifted through its doors, was old hat. Across in South Kensington the Troubadour had been an early target of *Private Eye*'s Andrew Osmond, due to its reputation as a 'CND stronghold'. The offspring of Beat poetry and folk music, Paul Simon and Bob Dylan, passed through London, picking up tunes and women from the CND folk scene. Spearheaded by Horovitz's *New Departures* were a cluster of small magazines, harking back to surrealism and Dada, but crucially covering what was new in the return of *modern* times.

In 1963 Miles and Haynes met for the first time, in Edinburgh. He dropped in at the still extant Paperback Shop. Within twenty minutes he found himself minding the store, while Haynes slipped out 'for a few minutes'. It was, he says, 'the casualest place you can imagine', an impression confirmed by his wife-to-be Sue's stock-taking of the stack of horrifying bills and invoices buried in the basement.

Haynes had moved on since *Lady Chatterley*. The Traverse Theatre had been born in the Grass Market in 1962 and that, together with his involvement in the Edinburgh Festival, had sucked him into a travelling show of poets, writers, actors, directors, and hype-merchants from across the western – and sometimes eastern – world. Through Haynes, Miles was introduced to Jack Henry Moore, labelled by Haynes later as 'one of the incredible characters of our time'. Moore, rare for those days, a declared homosexual, had, after a period running a Dublin detective agency, begun directing for the Traverse.

The theatre and the bookshop had sustained their influence on Edinburgh students. Open all hours, blending left literature, the Beats, the new absurdists, it attracted a clientele whose Scottish consciousness might repel them from London, the 'imperial capital', but attract them towards Paris, and New York, free of the effeteness of English culture.

Amongst the Traverse and Paperback Shop's habitués was the sometime editor of the university paper, *Student*, and future editor of the underground's *Ink*, and later *Time Out* and the *New Statesman*, John Lloyd. For Lloyd, from an east coast Scottish village background, the American appeared a charismatic character, exuding self-confidence, surrounded by women students, like some alternative Hugh Hefner. 'He was a really powerful figure for people like me', says Lloyd, 'who were looking for something new, and we weren't sure what.'

In 1964 Miles, via Cheltenham, Oxford, and Stroud finally made it to London, and by January 1965 to a job behind the counter at Better Books. The shop had been going since before the Second World War. In 1946 the premises at 94 Charing Cross road had been taken over by Tony Godwin, and under his ownership the place had become to radical culture what Collets, further down the same road, was to radical politics. Apart from selling books, the locale also provided a meeting place for such gatherings as 'Better Books writers nights', and in February/March 1965 housed 'the sTigma environmental exhibition', which included amongst its contributors Jeff Nuttall, and amongst its inspirations Alex Trocchi's *Sigma, a Tactical Blueprint* – drawing for *its* inspiration on the International Situationists. The impact of the exhibition – and increasingly the smell – was such that its March closure was widely welcome.

Miles began ordering books, stacks of City Lights' publications, and as many from Grove Press as he could get. Since the mid 1950s Grove had published much of the west coast American – and some of the international – avant-garde, including some of Kerouac, Burroughs, Trocchi's *Cain's Book*, Theodor Reich, and excursions into Zen Buddhism. It also published the *Evergreen Review*. The new material sold well, and Henry Miller's *Sexus*, *Plexus* and *Nexus* leapt off the shelves – under the counter – at ten shillings a copy. To help cover the import bills Miles would take half the orders around the corner into Soho where at a higher price the proprietor of a dirty book shop would retail them to less artistically minded purchasers.

Soon Godwin was to sell the shop to Collins – and trigger its slow decline – but before he quit for a job as chief editor with Penguin Books he decided to open a paperback section in Old Compton Street. Part of its inspiration was indeed Haynes's outlet in Edinburgh, and Miles was the man left minding the store.

While Britain got used to Wilson, the Americans didn't come to terms with the post-Kennedy era. *Peace News* reported on the revolt against the 'multiversity' at the symbol of liberal corporate America, the Berkeley campus within the University of California; it reported on the growing movement that had sprung out of the deep south civil rights campaign. Even in the early 1960s there had only been a few brave individuals. By August 1963 – three months before the President's assassination – 200,000 had marched on Washington. A year later in September 1964 the 'Free Speech' movement had erupted at Berkeley, and by Christmas 800 students had been arrested there. In March 1965 a civil rights march from Selma to Montgomery, Alabama, had been broken up by police. And alongside the internal battles partially catalysed by the hopes Kennedy's Presidency had aroused came the beginnings of opposition to the war his 'pay any price' foreign policy had finally ignited, Vietnam. Twenty days before Kennedy's assassination his South Vietnamese satrap, President Diem had suffered a similar fate, with the collusion of the US authorities. In August 1964 President Johnson claimed, falsely, that the *USS Maddox* had been attacked by North Vietnamese gunboats. The US had been sending combat troops into South Vietnam since 1961. This was the pretext for escalation: Hanoi, the North Vietnamese capital, was bombed. In November 1964 Johnson won the Presidential election by a landslide, and promised that the 'Great Society' would wage war on domestic poverty, on the racism that had triggered both the civil rights movement and the riots in Harlem that summer, and, if necessary, on the National Liberation Front of South Vietnam and the North Vietnamese government as well.

There were other straws in the wind. The hit of the summer of 1964 in the London theatre had been the Royal Shakespeare Company's *Marat-Sade*, theatre as revolution, and the dialogue between mind and politics. 'Marat we're poor and the poor stay poor', the chorus had chanted. 'Marat don't make us wait anymore, we want our rights and we don't care how, we want our revolution *now*.' The following month an 18-year-old Scottish anarchist, Stuart Christie, was held in Spain on bombing charges. By September the Franco courts had given him a twenty-year prison sentence. In January 1965, three days before the death of Churchill, that symbol of the past, Malcolm X, that symbol of the 1960s present, was shot by black separatists.

But for Miles, Haynes, and others a perhaps more significant event had taken place in April 1964 at the Renaissance Pleasure Faire on the outskirts of Los Angeles. John Bryan had already produced a paper called *Open City* in San Francisco, but Art Kunkin, a former Trotskyist, decided to put together a semi-spoof, semi-newspaper, the *Faire Free Press*, which he hawked at the Faire. Partly inspired by the *Village Voice*, across the continent, he developed the one-off. By the summer it had become the *Los Angeles Free Press*. It was in the right place at the right time, and the underground press, in the United States, was born.

One day in spring 1965, while Miles was behind the counter at Better Books, Allen Ginsberg walked in. He had been invited by Miles's predecessor at the shop. He had nowhere to stay, and ended up at Miles's place. He also gave a packed-out reading at Better Books in May. 'This could well turn out to have been a very significant moment in the history of England', wrote Tom McGrath in *Peace News*. Covering his tracks a little he added, 'or at least in the history of English poetry'. McGrath, the first editor of *International Times*, was then features editor on the pacifist paper. Born near Glasgow in 1940 McGrath was already established as a poet in his own right, with work in *Ambit*, Jeff Nuttall's *My Own Mag*, *Tribune*, and many of the small magazines, north and south of the border.

Whichever way, Ginsberg's appearance proved to be significant in the history of the English underground. Through the American Miles made a lot of connections. There was his friend Barbara Rubin, Andy Warhol, but, most of all, once in touch with the poet himself, observes Miles, 'it was like plugging into the main switchboard – he knows everyone'. After Better Books Ginsberg read at the Architectural Association, and the Institute of Contemporary Arts in Dover Street. He also pointed out that Ferlinghetti was in Paris and Gregory Corso was in Italy. They could easily come over, why couldn't there be a big reading? Amongst the people around Better Books then were New Yorker Don Richter and his English wife Jill. They had been living in Athens, and bringing out a magazine, *Residue*. An English poet, Harry Fainlight, who had been living in New York dropped in. 'All these Americans were sitting round saying what's the biggest place in town?' Miles recalls. 'So I said the Albert Hall.'

It cost £400 to book for a night. And, to the management, poets sounded like a good thing, a respectable thing. And Jill Richter's mother had money, quite enough to front the £400. The hall was booked, 7 p.m., Friday, 11 June 1965, for *Poets of the World/Poets of Our Time*.

The cast list expanded rapidly. As well as the Americans, Adrian Mitchell, Alex Trocchi, Harry Fainlight, and Michael Horovitz were to be there from Britain. Anselm Hollo from Finland, Andrei Voznesensky from the Soviet Union, Ernst Jandl, the sound poet, from Austria. Contacts with the Cuban embassy were good at that time, with the revolution just six years old. 'It was a really hip place to go', says Miles. 'They'd tell us stories about the Cuban Revolution and we'd sit round getting drunk and nostalgic about something we had never been in.' Consequently Pablo Fernandez, the Cuban cultural attaché, and a poet as well, was booked in.

On Wednesday 9 June an invitation went out to Fleet Street. It didn't emphasize the internationalism, it homed in on what it – correctly – saw as a Fleet Street preoccupation. 'The Beat poets invite you to a press conference at noon, at the Albert Memorial; if raining, inside the Memorial.' The *Observer* had already been excited about it in its preview the weekend before. 'It can hardly fail to be the biggest and liveliest feast of modern poetry we'll get in years.' Yet it devoted more space to a rival attraction at the London School of Economics that same evening, Britain's first teach-in; the subject, the Vietnam War. The two key preoccupations of the coming years came together.

In those days Covent Garden still had a flower market. The night before the reading John Hopkins organized friends to collect the lost flowers of Floral Street. But would anyone come? They did, and were greeted, as they forked out their ten shillings and five shillings, with the residue of Covent Garden, presented to them by women, their faces painted. Another aspect of the times had made its debut.

Once the more than 7,000-strong audience had packed the Albert Hall, and the smell of pot had begun to drift across its Victorian arches, it became clear that not all had gone according to plan. Pablo Neruda, the unofficial Poet Laureate of Chile, and holder of the Stalin Prize, had pulled out, and departed for Cambridge a day earlier. Pablo Fernandez was suddenly stricken by a bout of flu. Still, Voznesensky was there, but would he read?

With Trocchi in the chair, the evening began with Simon Vinkenoog from Holland. He didn't like the microphone and had to be cajoled into using it, he stalked up and down the front of the hall quoting from cuttings on the Vietnam War, and was heard by few. He was followed by Horovitz and Pete Brown, who were better received, but it wasn't easy for poets used to small back rooms to fill a hall of 7,000. Then came Ferlinghetti, whose call for 'an international fucking exchange' was well received.

During the interval the absent Burroughs was pumped over the PA system, via a tape supplied by Somerville. Nuttall and John Latham prepared their happening. 'One had a sense of constituency that was never there before', remembers Miles. 'All these people recognized each other and they all realized they were part of the same scene.'

'I have never seen so active an audience', wrote Tom McGrath in the following week's *Peace News*. It brought out Marxists, the lost armies of CND, Michael X, continuing his transition from Rachmanism, dress designers, artists, priests. 'Even if the poetry reading had turned out to be a giant bore, the audience itself would have been an event', McGrath added.

Not all went well as the second half began. Nuttall's happening didn't go as expected, when he became jammed in the bath in which he had placed himself, and Latham fainted while trying to drag him out. More seriously, Voznesensky had ruled that he would not read. The biggest ovation was reserved for Mitchell, reading his 'Tell us Lies about Vietnam'. In that vast space Jandl's sound poetry proved effective, but a nervous Fainlight read 'The Spider' about a bad mescaline trip, and flipped under unwelcome support from Vinkenoog. 'But', reported McGrath, 'the "great" lost temper of the night was Ginsberg's.' Horovitz disagrees, 'he communicated brilliantly'.

Ginsberg was infuriated by Voznesenky's refusal to appear on stage. As Ginsberg read out one of the Russian's works, the writer himself stalked out of the hall. It wasn't the 'gentle, angelic Allen of earlier readings in London', wrote McGrath, and 'some of the audience responded as if they were at a bear baiting'. But Ginsberg survived, and won the audience over. The evening ended with Davy Graham, a fixture in the folk scene and the basements of London, playing his guitar. The 6,000–7,000 people melted away into London, into Notting Hill, Chalk Farm, Covent Garden, Ladbroke Grove. Many of them were to meet again.

Chapter 3

Their very own and golden city

Once assembled, the contingent dispersed. In the wake of the Albert Hall Michael Horovitz had renewed enthusiasm to take *New Departures* on the road. Ginsberg remained for his fortieth birthday party. John Lennon dropped in on it, and got embarrassed when the poet, naked except for a pair of underpants draped round his head, kissed him on the cheek.

In July 1965 Adlai Stevenson, who had carried American liberalism's torch through the 1950s and into defeat by Eisenhower in the 1952 and 1956 Presidential elections dropped dead on a London street. As Kennedy's United Nations ambassador, he had defended the involvement in Vietnam which, by the end of the month, had put 125,000 US troops in that country. In Oxford Tariq Ali and Stephen Lukes had organized a second teach-in on the war. British Foreign Secretary Michael Stewart had given uneasy backing to the American representative, Henry Cabot Lodge, and his defence of US action.

Teach-ins had sprung from the American example. Week by week *Peace News* reported from Berkeley where the battle for the Free Speech Movement had, by May, led to the formation of the Vietnam Day Committee, pledged to stop conscription, and the war itself. By August that political movement found itself a paper in the *Berkeley Barb*. Up the Californian coast in San Francisco the LSD freak end of the underground was growing and pushing more people, and more pressure, on to Haight-Ashbury. The first wave of British bands was being supplanted by the new Californian sound. In San Francisco the *Oracle*, with its blend of acid graphics and peace and love exhortation, was to prove an irresistible lure to many in the 1967 Summer of Love.

Back in London the poets had dispersed, except for Gregory Corso. And Miles didn't want to stay with Better Books if Collins was to take over. He had discussed the prospect of setting up City Lights London with Ferlinghetti, but the San Francisco bookshop was tightly stretched as it was, and had no dollars to spare. The contact with Corso proved more fruitful. Through him he secured an introduction to John Dunbar, then the fiancé of 16-year old Marianne Faithful, whose virginal looks and upper middle-class style had put her into the charts as a complement to the art student

R&B bands. Dunbar in turn was a friend of Peter Asher, also in the charts as one half of Peter and Gordon, Westminster School's contribution to the mid 1960s. And Asher, the brother of actress Jane Asher, was in touch with Paul McCartney. Indeed the new millionaire of the Beatles was living in a small room in the Asher family's Wimpole Street home, next to Peter's Norwegian-wooded apartment.

The contacts paid off. Miles, Asher, and Dunbar became MAD Ltd, with the task of setting up a new bookshop. Peter Asher put in £700, and lent Dunbar and Miles £700 each. Dunbar was to run the art gallery attached to the shop, Miles would take care of the books. The next problem was premises. The Scotch of St James, off Piccadilly, was the club that pulled in the new pop generation. Next door to it, in Mason's Yard, was an empty shop, which MAD leased. 'Indica seemed a good name for an art gallery', says Miles, 'and it was the first name in Latin for marijuana. It was a supposed joke.'

Even in its construction the shop intertwined the strands of the counter-culture and the music scene. McCartney helped paint, and put up shelves alongside Pete Brown, poet, CND member and future lyricist for Cream. Ian Somerville did the electrical system. He was qualified. 'He wrote the technical parts of Burroughs's books like *The Ticket That Exploded*', explains Miles. In January 1966 Indica opened its doors.

Ever since 1959, and *Bomb*, Miles had been experimenting with small magazines and one-offs. In 1960 there had been *Tree*. In 1964–5, with John Hopkins, he set up Love Books, specifically to publish experimental writing and poetry. For company secretary they settled on a 34-year-old chartered accountant called Michael Henshaw. After twelve years with the Inland Revenue he had quit to work for Arnold Wesker's ill-fated Centre 42 project at Chalk Farm's Roundhouse. Wesker's dream had been a cultural palace for the workers; in the years ahead, through the Henshaw connection it was to become something else. And Henshaw was to become the first money man of the underground. In 1965 Miles and Hopkins produced *Long Hair* magazine, a collection of writings and poems that sold modestly. But it was a first run, and there were plenty of other inspirations.

In New York John Wilcock's relationship with the *Village Voice* was moving towards its conclusion. In between travel trips Wilcock ran into a woman at a party who lived with an artist manqué, Walter Bowart. Returning from Japan Wilcock got in touch, and Bowart told Wilcock of his plans, together with Allen Katzman, to produce a new paper for the 'east village'.

Ten years on the *Village Voice* was selling 80,000, getting respectable, and, thought Wilcock, staid. Everything that the east village – the downmarket part of the *Voice*'s patch – wasn't. Since it was to be the Village's other paper the name was simple, the *East Village Other*. 'Great', said Wilcock, 'send me a copy and I'll plug it in my *Voice* column.'

On 1 October 1965 Bowart and Katzman duly obliged, as the first 2,500 copies of *EVO* rolled off the presses – the same number as the *Voice*'s first issue ten years before. So impressed was Wilcock that he offered to provide a column free for the new paper. Less enthusiastic were Fancher and Dan Wolf, the *Voice*'s owners.

'The *Voice* was getting square', says Wilcock. 'The woman in the classified department would complain about how her advertisers didn't like my column. They didn't like the stuff I was writing about Vietnam and Fancher and Wolf had always sort of *suffered* me. They suffered me to the extent that I did my column for 530 weeks in a row but over the years there was more and more of a crackdown on giving me facilities in the office. Eventually I had to get my mail elsewhere. I think Fancher thought I'd have dope sent to the *Voice*. They didn't like the *EVO* column one bit and finally they made me choose between them and it.'

EVO won. The first column he wrote was about art and forgery, and he titled it 'Art and other scenes'. Bowart liked it, but thought it a trifle long. They agreed to shorten it to 'Other Scenes'. It was to be a title with a long and cosmopolitan history.

Another early contributor was Ed Sanders, whose *Fuck You – A Magazine of the Arts* had begun from a 'secret location' in New York's lower east side in 1962. Through Better Books Miles had been in contact with Sanders. Indeed he was appointed London correspondent for *EVO* when it was launched, a fact that initially escaped Miles, since he was unaware it existed until the third issue. But *EVO* went into Indica with the *Voice* and the *Los Angeles Free Press*.

So did a lot of people – many the worse for drink and other things – from the Scotch of St James. The bookshop was on the ground floor, and the gallery in the basement. The first account customer was McCartney, who, having heard a play on the BBC Third Programe, had picked up on Alfred Jarry and *Ubu Roi*. He was not alone, Ronnie Davis's San Francisco Mime Troupe had produced the play in December 1963, and Jim Haynes, in Edinburgh earlier that same year. Dunbar progressed meanwhile with his art exhibitions. In November 1966 he featured a Japanese artist, Yoko Ono. An invitation went out to – and was accepted by – John Lennon.

In Edinburgh Haynes's time was running out, and his attention shifting elsewhere. His relationship with the Traverse, rarely tranquil, was breaking down, with Haynes's suggestion that the theatre open a London base meeting with strong opposition. The bookshop was still open, and now, in addition to the paperbacks, the little magazines, and the *Village Voice*, the new wave of American papers was beginning to appear on the shelves.

The American papers were an inspiration to people like John Lloyd, as they were to the group gathering 400 miles down the A1. With two of his friends, Alan Hamilton and Alan Jackson, Lloyd would visit Jim Haynes in his flat above the Traverse. There they discussed Haynes's idea of a new paper. 'It was based on the *Voice*', says Lloyd. 'Here was this tremendously exciting anti-establishment paper. Hamilton and I did dummies of what an alternative paper might look like – we were then working on *Student*, and had access to design material. We conceived it much more narrowly than Jim did. We thought of it, I guess, as a left-wing paper. He was much more into the arts in general.'

But nothing came of it, then. In 1965 Lloyd went back to being *Student*'s editor, and Jim Haynes headed south to set up the London Traverse Company at the Jeanetta Cochrane Theatre in Holborn.

In 1966 Vietnam was becoming an irritant to the Labour government, but not a major one. At the end of March Harold Wilson had increased his majority from 4 to 94 in the General Election, but significantly in July there were arrests outside the US embassy of protesters against the bombing of Hanoi and Haiphong. CND was still marching, and although the numbers were dwindling it remained a focus of opposition. Indica had been open since February, and that month, too, the Marquee in Wardour Street had featured the 'Spontaneous Underground'.

Across in west London John Hopkins had been running, with others including Michael X, his London Free School. Love Books was continuing, Indica was open – although the premises rapidly became cramped – and there was *Long Hair* to look back on. But what there wasn't was a magazine, a newspaper of the emerging movement.

But there were Miles and Hopkins. And the CND march of Easter 1966 was where a new paper was given a test outing. It was called the 'Exploding Galactic Moon Edition' of the *Longhair Times*. It had a competition sponsored by McCartney to find a script for a movie, a declaration by Harry Fainlight about the (still legal) pleasures of LSD, it had letters, and, specifically, it had a long epistle from John Wilcock in New York, defining what was supposed to be going on. It was produced offset. 'Instead of setting it in type we got the original manuscript and made zinc plates', recalls Miles. 'It was great, the letters were just as they were when we received them.' It was also rather different from *Sanity*, the *Newsletter*, the *Daily Worker*, *Labour Worker*, and the other papers bombarding the marchers. Five hundred copies were produced, and

Miles believes they sold out within an hour. The paper had taken a day to produce.

Meanwhile Indica needed more space. At 102 Southampton Row was Jackson's booksellers. Just south of it was the Jeanetta Cochrane theatre, where Haynes was working with, amongst others, Charles Marovitz, another exiled American, but, in his case, from New York's lower east side rather than Louisiana. Marovitz, theatre director and critic, had quit New York in 1958, but had retained a writing relationship with the *Voice*, which led him, early in 1966, to cover the new-born Indica for the paper.

Across Southampton Row, a dull boulevard then, as now, of cheap Italian restaurants and tourist hotels were the little streets around the British Museum, and London University. Nearby on the Row was the Central School of Art and Design. The street might be boring, the neighbourhood wasn't.

Jackson's was. Its speciality, according to Miles, was the supply of improving texts to convents, which was supervised by a man called Chris Hill. Having met him, Miles made him an offer, a directorship of the company, and Indica to move in. Hill accepted the deal, and in September 1966 the new Indica was open.

Compared with Mason's Yard it was huge, with a main shop 90 feet long, plus a basement as large, and other rooms in a sub-basement. Marovitz and the Jeanetta Cochrane were early tenants down in the lower depths. So was Alex Trocchi's Project Sigma, the Situationist-inspired intergalactic switchboard of information, a project for 'invisible insurrection'. Fourteen years later McGrath told the *Guardian* that 'Trocchi used to say "Where Trotsky said seize the viaducts and bridges, we must seize the means of communication" '. As far as Miles could see the project did little. The storage and dispensing of such material was to prove one of the more baffling, wearisome, and occasionally lucrative obsessions of the underground in the years ahead, but by the end of 1966 Sigma was petering out.

It could, on dark days in Bloomsbury, be a dreary place, but Indica was a place to go to, to exchange ideas, make initial contacts with another London. Above its dull Edwardian frontage was the name, in stark white letters.

There was a growing movement: there were the *Los Angeles Free Presses* and the *Barbs* and the *Oracles* and the *Village Voices* and there was the example of that Easter's CND success. There were the people coming in to shuffle through the little magazines, Zen Buddhism, Burroughs, Ginsberg, Nuttall, *New Departures*, *Circuit*, four letter words, and Indian music. Above ground the modest experiment of the Labour government was degenerating into shadow boxing with Rhodesia's Ian Smith, compromises with the Americans' Vietnam policy, and economic crises. Yet what could never be achieved via Parliament could be experimented with in more exciting forms in Southampton Row and the network around it.

By that summer Miles had started taking his unasked-for post with *EVO* seriously. Having made contact with a group of students at the nearby Architectural Association he went to see them play at the Goings On Club in Archer Street, a tiny place largely frequented by poets. They were called the Abdabs, specialized in *serious* experimentation in sound and light, wore white coats, and would discuss their work, post-performance, with the equally serious audience. The week Miles reviewed them for *EVO* they changed their name to the Pink Floyd. The name went well with the acid, which from early 1966 had begun to arrive in London from the United States. In 1964 the Conservative Government had legislated against purple hearts, but in 1966 good and bad trips from lysergic acid diethylamide were still legal.

EVO, partly in reaction to the *Voice*, partly the result of its staff's predilections, had rapidly settled into the acid freak end of the underground, and away from the politicos of the American new left. 'The style that *EVO* had was the one I particularly picked up on', says Miles. 'It was the unedited, extended transcribed interview, no one had ever done it in Britain or America. It was an invention of the underground press.' Later too, via Wilcock, it was to provide Andy Warhol with his path into magazines. Another crucial feature of *EVO* was its printing: offset litho, cheap, and produced in Chinatown, below the Village.

Offset was exciting. Offset was freedom. At Better Books Miles had taken in the mimeographed magazines. At Indica they appeared from offset litho presses. New on the market were IBM electric golfball typewriters. Once typed on to special paper, the copy could be pasted on to the boards and, with no need for hot metal, or skilled printers, was camera-ready. 'Or', says Miles, 'what we regarded as camera-ready.'

And the bookshop had made the connections: Marovitz and the Cochrane theatre people; Haynes and Jack Henry Moore, with plenty of contacts in Scotland, in Europe; Burroughs and Ginsberg and Corso and Ferlinghetti; Simon Vinkenoog in Amsterdam; and through the art gallery Indica had access to the British avant-garde. A paper seemed the logical progression, a paper for the 6,000 at the Albert Hall, a paper for the people living in cheap rooms in Notting Hill Gate, Covent Garden, Ladbroke Grove, Chalk Farm, the Gate, the Garden, the Grove, and the Farm.

But there were problems. 'We didn't want to be press barons', observes Miles. And neither Hopkins, who had plenty of journalistic work, or Miles, who was running a bookshop, or Haynes, who was trying to run a theatre company, wanted to edit it, and probably couldn't anyway. Nor did they want a vast editorial board. It settled down to Moore, Haynes, Miles, and Hopkins, and Michael Henshaw, changing hats from Love Books, was made a director.

They also needed a name. This came from Bobo Legrendre, like Haynes a native of Louisiana. 'She was', suggests Miles, 'the last of the va-va-voom types.' She was big, well-off, theatrical, and lived above a butcher's shop in Shepherds Market, Mayfair. They met to discuss the project. 'Bobo marched across the room, floorboards squeaking', says Miles, 'and said "why don't we call it *It*?" '

It could be anything. *Intergalactic Times* – like *Longhair*'s child – *Interracial Times, Intravenous Times, Interminable Times. . . .* 'Other people called it *International Times* or even "eye tee" ', says Miles. 'We always called it *It*. To the people on the staff it was always *It*.'

It didn't have an editor. But Miles and Hopkins had the contacts with *Peace News*, and with Tom McGrath. And it had been while McGrath had been features editor that *Peace News* had carried the spread extolling Ginsberg's London readings, and the big page feature on the Albert Hall gathering. McGrath accepted the offer, and his assistant was David Mairowitz from New York. Hopkins took charge of production – it was seen as a part-time post, leaving him free for other work – but where was the cash to come from?

The literati and the US army hadn't been the only imports into Europe from across the Atlantic. With the American-funded boom sweeping Europe a new generation of American tycoons was arriving too. One was a former radical socialist, Bernie Cornfeld, whose IOS venture was to make him very rich, and many of those rash enough to invest in it extremely poor. At the beginning of IOS one of Cornfeld's associates had been Victor Herbert, who had quit early. From his Paris home Herbert was a funder of various cultural causes – including the Living Theatre – and he had met Haynes. The man from Louisiana felt it was time to renew the acquaintance. Would Herbert invest in the paper? No he wouldn't. It would probably never work out anyway. What he would do was lend Haynes £500, on a very short-term basis. He wrote out the cheque. 'I rushed off and called Hoppy, Miles, and Jack and said "roll the presses" ', wrote Haynes.

It wasn't quite that simple. There were seven offset litho printers in the country. All were approached, and all turned down the privilege of printing Britain's first underground magazine. So the paper's first seven issues were produced on old, hot metal. When should the paper come out? Since it was to be a fortnightly, the best thing was to alternate with the other half of what passed for London's alternative press, *Private Eye*. As for the starting date, that was simple: 'when we were ready', says Miles.

By luck rather than judgement they chose what, in publishing terms, was a good, if late, launch date, 14 October 1966. The colleges were back at the end of September, holidays had ended, the metropolis was beginning to settle down for the winter. Challenging the dullness of London was a key aim of *It*. A city where the buses stopped at eleven thirty, the pubs ushered their surprised foreign tourists on to the streets at five to eleven, and a meal after that meant Indian or Chinese. A city where the fringe theatre meant Jim Haynes, Charles Marovitz, and a few other expatriates from across the Atlantic, and avant-garde cinema a night out at the 35-year-old Academy in Oxford Street. There were clubs, true, upmarket places for the rock aristocracy, and places like the Marquee, the Flamingo, the 100 Club and Tiles – home of late-period mod pill-popper on Oxford Street. But these remained isolated in a sea where information was the preserve of the music press, the two London evening papers, and the 30-year-old *What's On* magazine, with its catalogue of hostess bars staffed by girls who had left home with men from the motor trade. It was a long way from New York, let alone the West Coast, Beatles, Stones, and all. The staff of the new paper decided to launch *It* with a party. The venue was the Roundhouse, still unused at the top end of Chalk Farm road. 'Centre 42 had the place for years and had done fuck-all with it', observes Miles. 'Through Michael Henshaw we got permission to have a party there. Later on Arnold Wesker severely regretted this.'

The Roundhouse was to flourish, in its darkness, with its cold and terrible facilities, as a key underground venue well into the 1970s. That night in October was to be its first successful trial. Once it had been a railway shed, indeed the tracks were still in it, later, in a period when Gilbey's Gin had used the building as a warehouse, a balcony had been added, which was only wide enough to take one person. There was a narrow staircase leading in, two lavatories, and laughable electrics. It should have been a deathtrap, but it wasn't.

'We always figured we couldn't afford ads, but we could make a lot of noise', says Miles. The result, hopefully, would be publicity, free, and the admission fees – five shillings in advance, ten shillings at the door – would do something to pay off Mr Herbert, waiting in Paris. The posters went up, in a scattered fashion, around the autumnal city: 'All Night Rave' they proclaimed. Back in 1961 at the Beaulieu Jazz Festival, a modest event sponsored by the motoring Earl of Montague, some mild disorder had occurred amongst teenagers inflamed by the wild sounds of terrible trad bands. The *Daily Mail* had proclaimed that a new and ugly word had entered the English language, 'raver'. That Saturday, 15 October, five years later, the ravers had come home to roost, this time accompanied by Strip Trip, Soft Machine, a steel band, and Pink Floyd.

The evening, largely organized by Hopkins and David Mairowitz did something to further that perpetually lost *It* cause – London as a twenty-four hour city. It didn't even start until 11 p.m. How the ravers were to find their way out of Chalk Farm and into their bedsits would also be a challenge worthy of the do-it-yourself times into which the metropolitans were moving.

It didn't deter the 3,000-odd who fought their way in. Down from Chalk Farm tube, shivering, stumbling up from Camden Town, past a then-deserted lock, to be confronted by the soon-to-be-familiar queue. An hour could be passed, meeting people last seen at the Albert Hall, on the marches of the last ten years, at rock concerts, in pubs, the London School of Economics bar, the London Free School, the Marquee, the Young Socialists.

The proto-underground drew out the proto-glitterati. Monica Vitti, whose film with Antonioni, *The Red Desert*, an enigmatic portrayal of capitalist alienation, had left most of its audience little wiser but feeling they were into something good, fought her way up the stairs with Antonioni, then working on *Blow Up*. She was in town to film *Modesty Blaise* for Joseph Losey. McCartney, true to Indica, appeared dressed as an Arab. Peter Brook, *Marat-Sade*'s director came. So, from America, did Kenneth Rexroth, friend of Ferlinghetti. He wrote the event up for the straights of the *San Francisco Chronicle*. Alex Trocchi tried to get in free, through the padlocked back door. When the queuers finally made their way to the head of the stairs they were greeted by a strange figure holding a tray of sugar cubes, sure sign that acid was on offer. Some said all the cubes were laced, others one in ten. In reality none apparently were, but inside the revellers could try drink – if they had brought any – and dope and speed, were they in possession of such substances, or if anyone else was prepared to offer them around.

In addition to the sugar cubes a large jelly had been made for the occasion, indicative of 1950s kids on a spree. Someone rode a bicycle through it, and the jelly and the bicycle disappeared. According to Miles some had succeeded in having trips on the expectations induced by Tate and Lyle.

Soft Machine produced a motorcycle – a considerable feat in view of the human congestion – which was driven amidst the quaking pillars and balconies before being wired for sound, and revved up as additional accompaniment. Indica's contacts with modern art had yielded, through the Robert Fraser Gallery a large American car which had been painted in fashionable stripes by New York's Binder, Edwards and Vaughan, interior decorators. Before that evening the Pink Floyd's gigs had been small affairs – such as the ICA, and for the London Free School at St Luke's Hall in Notting Hill – but their rudimentary light show meant they were paid rather better than Soft Machine.

'They were a bit nervous, but it was a big break for them,' remembers Miles. 'Rexroth's review said that as the band hadn't shown up a pick-up band was assembled from members of the audience, who just banged pots and pans and made odd noises. That was his interpretation of what the Floyd did.' The band also succeeded in blowing the fragile electrical circuit during their performance.

The London Film Co-Op had just started too, and for those too tired, smashed out, or bored for the music or perhaps with an interest in America in grainy black and white there were movies like Kenneth Anger's *Scorpio Rising*, and *Towers Open Fire*. The conditions were difficult, conceded *It* in its report of the night, 'yet the films went on. It may though, have been just the right setting for those particular films. Burroughs' inner space disappearance in *Towers Open Fire* somehow had more impact because of the vibrations from the "party".'

The vibrations may, on occasions, have been shivers. It was bitterly cold. It also rapidly became very wet, as the two lavatories gave way under the torrent from the streets. 'We had to put duckboards down to get to them,' says Miles. 'The girls would take their dresses off to tiptoe through that awful mire and then, coming back put them on again. There was nothing remotely erotic about these naked people wandering around the lake surrounding the bog.'

The police arrived outside. There was little anyone could do. The promoters could hardly get out and the police, in at the dawn of the new experience, couldn't really get in. It was just as well. Inside the building Tom McGrath contemplated the oil heaters with their exposed flames, the quaking balcony stuffed with people, and, in between exhilaration, feared disaster. Five years later, in *Watch Out Kids* the future *It* staffer Mick Farren noted that what he had seen there, that night, was more than a new rock 'n' roll show, it was 'the germ of a new way of life'. *It* observed the following week that the police had been very co-operative.

Others, semi-sightseers, put in an appearance. Amongst them was Michelene Wandor, later a *Time Out* poetry editor, feminist, poet and playwright. Then she was a Cambridge graduate mother of two, married to a successful young American publisher she had met at Cambridge, the future co-founder of *Ink*, Ed Victor. Marriage had effectively put paid to her career as an actress, and between household tasks she busied herself penning articles protesting at the pressures on people like her to cook beautiful meals *and* write novels like Margaret Drabble. She was relieved, later, that they weren't published. Through Ed, who, she thought had the right contacts because he was a man, they went to the Roundhouse that night. She contemplated the nubile, still just teenage teenagers, with their post jail-bait image. She had long hair, and a short-skirt, but she didn't fit in, she was a mum.

Across the globe, in San Francisco that weekend the Artists' Liberation Front, in rather better weather organized a weekend of free fairs in the ghetto parks. Tension was rising in that city; so was the militancy. The Front's formation the previous spring had been backed by Ferlinghetti, Rexroth, Bill Graham – whose role as a rock promoter around the Filmore ballroom was just emerging – and Ralph J. Gleason, then a little known *San Francisco Chronicle* columnist, later one of the main inspirations, and writers on Jann Wenner's *Rolling Stone*, just a year away from its first edition.

Back in Chalk Farm the crowds stumbled out into the dawn, past the shuttered Greek restaurants, the nearest thing to a chic London ice cream parlour, Marine Ices, the junk shops and cafes. 'The Pop Art Costume Masque Drag Ball Et Al' was over. But the community – that much abused word for the next two decades – existed and *It* was launched. There was, thought Miles then, and now, an incredible exhilaration.

Chapter 4

The disturbing world of the flower children

'*It*' hit the eye first, on the cover of that launch issue. Reversed out alongside the gaze of a 1920s movie heroine staring impassively out into the 1960s. She should have been the original 'It' girl, Clara Bow, but the staff, not for the last time, got it wrong, and put the more vampish Theda Bara on the cover instead. Bara, with her hint of eastern promise by way of Hollywood, was more appropriate for a time fixated on oriental and Asian culture, mysticism, dope and war.

Above it: '*The* International Times, October 14–27/1s.' A definite article ensured that it was the definitive paper, on this side of the Atlantic at least – except for *The Times*, which promptly began legal moves to get 'Times' dropped from the title. Since that was the year that the Thunderer had finally decided to put news, rather than ads on the front page, it would be embarrassing – if bizarre – should unwary purchasers confuse the two products.

The layout was rudimentary. It didn't have the inspired anarchic design of some later papers, nor the clean, sanserif appearance of editor Tom McGrath's previous paper, *Peace News*. Photo reproduction was bad, headlines eccentric, and little of the paper was taken up with London. But, significantly, half a page at the back featured the 'What's Happening' listings of events, printed in tiny type – one of the paper's key selling points for the future and, eventually, one of the sources of its downfall.

Soon after the departure of Roszak from *Peace News* McGrath had quit that paper, nursing an unhealthy obsession with drugs. Anxious to quit London, he had accepted an offer from the poet Adrian Mitchell of the loan of a cottage in north Wales. While there he received one of the fateful telegrams that were to dot the history of the underground: 'Phone Hoppy' it said. Hopkins had told McGrath of the plans for *It* and for the Scot to edit it. Taken up with the rather generous terms that he imagined – as it turned out – accompanied the post, he accepted. Talking to Gavin Selerie in 1983 McGrath detailed some of the influences that came to work on him at that time. Through Roszak's influence he had read Thomas Merton and Kenneth Rexroth, the anarchists Paul Goodman and Alex Comfort, and had absorbed the new literature of the civil rights movement, *Liberation* magazine.

'That was coming in from one side into *It*, but it was too moral for me – and it still is. Although peace and love is one aspect of me, I thought I'd like to go with the sinners: people like Laing and Trocchi.' The catholicism of McGrath's tastes, coupled with the contacts of Miles and his wife Sue Miles, and the input of Trocchi, Moore – whom McGrath had introduced to Haynes – and Hopkins were the core of *It*'s initial success.

'The first ten issues', recalls Miles, 'were deeply serious. You can't be frivolous in hot metal.' No, but even if the paper had been offset, its personnel would probably have prevented much frivolity. 'The argument dwindles into a kind of romantic liberalism', wrote Charles Marovitz on the front page. He was castigating the new Royal Shakespeare production, Peter Brooke's *US*, on the war in Vietnam, but he could almost have been talking about the magazine. 'The role of the theatre in times like today is to elucidate and give a positive lead.'

And the role of *It*? 'London is a comparatively free and happy city', mused the inaugural editorial. 'But it isn't quite as switched on as our ad men make out.' It continued by denouncing artists' tangos with the Arts Council, and pointing out that 'Change begins with you'.

Quite, but who was 'you'? They didn't want to be press barons, says Miles, they wanted a community paper, and it hadn't even been easy to find an editor amongst the founding group, preoccupied as they were with art galleries and bookshops, theatre companies and poetry, and preoccupied also with that sense of freedom, and the breaking down of national barriers which had accompanied the explosion of travel in the 1960s.

From the beginning the group had said it wanted the paper to be international, and *It* was. It was the internationalism of the 1965 poetry reading, cultural, post-Beat, off-beat, and art-oriented. Simon Vinkenoog, the founder of *Sigma Nederland* provided a piece from Amsterdam for the first issue on the then prominent Provos, the proto-Green anarchists who had just won seats on that city's council. From Paris, Jean-Jacques Lebel wrote an obituary for the surrealist André Breton, beginning a relationship between the French semi-Situationist and the British underground press that was to persist into the following decade. A giant inflatable woman-as-art-object was the contribution from Stockholm. Dope featured prominently. Yoko Ono's one-woman show at the Indica Gallery received a plug. And there was what Miles describes as 'our attempt at politics': an analysis of China's cultural revolution – then moving towards its climax – by Alex Gross. The writer assessed press reports, criticized the lack of western coverage, and likened the Red Guards to the children's crusades of medieval Europe. It wasn't the unthinking Maoism of which the underground was later – and usually inaccurately accused – quite the reverse. Culture was under attack, Gross suggested; it had to be defended. So did the London Free School, the creation of John Hopkins, with Michael Abdul Malik, and the victim, it was claimed, of neglect by Kensington and Chelsea council and harassment by the Special Branch.

Similar preoccupations dominated the issues that took *It* into the spring of 1967. Ono was still around in issue two; growing fast was an interest in censorship and pornography, to join dope, flying saucers, ley-lines, and rock as obsessions of the nascent underground.

It was in attitudes to sex – and specifically male attitudes to women – that *It* began to argue with the outside world, and itself, almost from the beginning. The 1940s and 1950s Beats had created a vision of lone men, and buddies out on the highway, fucking where and when they wanted to, an image that Kerouac *et al.* had carried to farcical, and imaginative, extremes. The Situationists, too, in their demolition job on the 'spectacle' of capitalism had used pornography for what they regarded as subversive purposes. Those attitudes fed into *It* and continued to inform – or divert – the underground press up to, and beyond, the inception of the women's movement. That autumn, in the *New Left Review*, Juliet Mitchell was writing her 'Women, the longest revolution' article, whose impact, eventually, on the new British feminism was to be enormous, but while the Marxist journal was on sale in Indica its message didn't penetrate *It* – or many other places – in those days. Thus was sexual liberation defined by an almost exclusively male heterosexual group, drawing on old subversions – Dada, Surrealism, Beat, Situationism – diffused through the mass-market expansion into commercial sex that *Playboy* had pioneered back in the 1950s. *It*'s staff would probably have decried any such connection with the upmarket skin magazine's Hugh Hefner, but it was there none the less. David Mairowitz's Censorship column covered the controversies around obscenity cases like *Last exit to Brooklyn* but also struck attitudes which others saw, even in those days, more suspiciously.

Mairowitz was, McGrath pointed out in an 'open letter' published in *It*, responsible for 'the pretty chicks' who appeared in the paper. The editor added that a girl had remarked to him that 'she thought that many of the supposed erotic pictures in *It* degraded the female'. He had, he added diplomatically, a sense of this himself.

'I would much rather define my intentions as pornographic than erotic', responded Mairowitz. 'I have no love for the very common attitude which places certain literature and pictorial matter in the realm of art to justify it to the establishment. . . . My intention is not to shock anybody. Nor is it to degrade the female (far be it from me to do so). I merely want to open all the doors as far as they will go at the moment.'

For the next six years doors opened and slammed. Meanwhile *It* girls continued to 'show their pretty faces' in the paper, and brandish candles, bananas, and transparent dresses 'designed by two local tripped-out chicks' and suggested as purchases for 'your psychedelic mistress'. Old-style male sexuality had, in the pages of *It* at least, reached, eight years on, Macmillan's dictum for the consumer society – complete with features on rubber fetishism and consumer guides to Soho strip clubs.

Issue two covered the birth of the London Film Makers' Co-op and its chairman, Harvey Matusow. The third issue provided four pages on London's underground film festival. A three-page interview with Paul McCartney in the sixth issue, says Miles, probably boosted sales from the 5,000 to 10,000 mark towards, optimistically, 15,000. Soon after Pete Townshend was questioned by Miles. Allen Ginsberg's pronouncements on war and peace rated double-page spreads, and radical black comedian Dick Gregory got a page. In between was the common currency of the underground, pieces on dope, and, at the back of the paper, the 'What's happening' section, which by issue nine was covering almost two pages.

And the ubiquitous Wilcock and his 'Other Seens' – as it was spelt – column had shown up too. Wilcock had written about Haynes and his Edinburgh bookshop in the *Village Voice* soon after it had opened, and had popped up in the one-off *Longhair Times* too. The Englishman's news from New York emphasized again the paper's tilt towards the United States; it might cover Italy, India, Denmark, but it was the America of LBJ, poetry, the Vietnam movement, and Golden Gate love-ins that exerted the magnetic attraction. Wilcock, the expatriate in Manhattan, also echoed in his concern with cultural anarchy rather than political action the preoccupations of the American expatriates in London. Within it were the strong echoes of the disgust with politics that McCarthyism had induced, and the early excitement of the Beats and their progeny in Greenwich Village. It was a leitmotif of the early *It*.

The background of the American pioneers was varied. David Mairowitz had been active in Berkeley's Free Speech Movement; the one-time editor of the *Insect Trust Gazette* Bill Levy's interest was Ezra Pound. He had produced the *Gazette*, it was suggested by one reader, as a 'post-Beat, post-*Howl* product of nihilist despair'. In the second issue of *It* the front page, and most of the second, had been dominated by excerpts from Pound's war-time broadcasts from fascist Italy to the allies. Edited by Levy, the speeches reeked of Pound's obsessions and anti-semitism. *It* was publishing the material because it existed, McGrath explained, and, while neither the paper nor staff were anti-semitic, 'Considering Ezra Pound's achievements as a writer, making work of his generally available would seem to need no excuse. . . . We can never know what folly and what wisdom is in the speeches until we have had a chance to read them.' The chance was short-lived. McGrath promised a further extract for the following issue, but by then Pound's publishers had stepped in, claiming breach of copyright.

Jim Haynes, meanwhile, tended to gravitate through London oblivious of politics, taking as much pleasure it seemed from a London night out with President Johnson's daughter, or a meeting with the US ambassador's wife – 'I don't see how anyone can meet her and not fall in love with her' – as from radical arts.

And for Jack Henry Moore, who had made his own commitment to sexual politics by coming out years before, the subject was now part of his past. At the end of the decade, when the Gay Liberation Front emerged in London, he was unimpressed. 'It was done man', he told a young associate on *It*, 'We've done all that.' Orthodox politics, too, including those of the left were also uninteresting to him.

Harvey Matusow, too, who featured in *It* and other, later underground papers, also disclaimed interest in straight politics. Apart from chairing the new London film co-op he had a small article in the first *It* detailing his efforts to phone the CIA at the American embassy. He didn't get anywhere, which in view of his past was ironic. Matusow was one of those lucky, and curious, souls who surfaced out of a curious past – like Michael X/Malik/de Freitas – in those fragmented times. Mainly regarded as a *victim* of McCarthyism amongst his London associates, he had, in reality, spent much of the early 1950s as a nark for the House UnAmerican Activities Committee. While on the Justice Department's payroll he had named 216 'Communists'; in 1950–1 he had been employed by the FBI – at $70 a month – to inform on the US Communist Party; and one of his early (1952) journalistic outings had been to write 'Reds in khaki' for the *American Legion Magazine*. By the time he had got to suggesting that 126 card-carrying Communists were on the staff of the *New York Times* Sunday supplement, Matusow's credibility was fraying, and, in 1956, after a series of volte-faces he found himself on the wrong end of a five-year sentence for perjury. By the late 1960s he also found time to set up 'Harvey Matusow's Jew's Harp Band'.

The Englishman, Hopkins, like Mairowitz, had embraced different politics. After Cambridge he had worked at Harwell Atomic Research Station, begun working as a photographer for the *Observer*, and been active in CND and Centre 42. But his work with the London Free School and around the early days of the UFO club, indicated the change in his priorities since Centre 42 and CND. For Miles those priorities had never really existed. orthodox politics in those days meant copies of the *New Left Review* and the other papers stacked on Indica's shelves. He met the new left, was sometimes intrigued by it, but it was a different, and largely incomprehensible, world. 'There was no contact with the straight left', he says, 'they hated us.'

And to some the left didn't seem relevant to the underground eruption taking place around *It*. Admittedly *It*'s hopes of a twenty-four-hour city remained dashed; in the paper's listings a motley collection of late movies, plumbing services, and such late-night eateries as the London airport restaurant were featured, but the Roundhouse launch gathering was rapidly imitated, and replicated. Just before Christmas 1966 was 'Night Tripper'; just before the New Year UFO, the club of the early underground, opened its doors.

UFO breathed life into the Tottenham Court Road of furniture showrooms and Quality Inns. Near Goodge Street tube station was the Shamrock Club, a venue for the Irish in the centre of London. The club had fallen on hard times, and the arrival of a travelling circus of the long hairs, trainee freaks and happening performers seemed like a good idea. Through the winter and into the spring the dedicated, the day trippers, and the voyeurs plodded their paths down the stairs of the club – complete with its incongruous Hibernian motifs – into an atmosphere of joss sticks, dope, new music, and occasional bad trips. When, in June 1967, the Beatles' 'Sergeant Pepper' was released, UFO, with its light shows, and globules of colour spewing down the old Irish walls, seemed the natural place to go and listen to it.

At the end of January 1967 Miles took stock in his *It* column of the 'London Underground Generation'. There were two main groups, he suggested: under-20s brought up on TV and 1950s rock 'n' roll; and post-20s conditioned by 'illustrated volumes of *The Great War in Pictures*, Dad's war stories, rationing, and Frankie Laine'. The latter split between what were to become known as 'weekend hippies' taking time off from the straight world, and those in Miles words, 'still trying'. In between were the Americans 'who are responsible to a degree for the professionalism and hustling that goes on around town'. The link, he suggested, was the 'intuitive poster art, words to songs that are not quite understandable, superimpositions in films that don't quite focus into a subject', all of which, he contended optimistically, 'move us towards the new era'.

But there were others too, some drawn from that old left milieu regarded with suspicion by Miles. One was David Robins, then a student at nearby University College, from a leftist Jewish London background. Later in the 1960s it would be great to be a student, but not then, not for Robins. Near his Chalk Farm flat was an entrée to another social scene, the world of the small magazines, of Pete Brown, Mal Dean – who had done design for the first *It* –

and Robins was drawn towards it. He worked for *Circuit*, another magazine following the path of Horovitz's *New Departures*, and at Indica he met Miles. To Robins Miles was a sophisticate, in touch, linked to Ginsberg and to *It*, and to Tom McGrath and the Americans abroad, Haynes, Moore, Mairowitz, and Levy. The Americans had, he thought, the edge on everybody else, they had been *doing* it, they had confidence, credentials, and they could write. The lure of *It* proved irresistible.

But at another college nearby – Central School of Art further down Southampton Row – another student, Pearce Marchbank, was less impressed. Marchbank, the designer later of *Friends* and *Time Out*, and one-time *Oz* editor, was also later to become a great friend of Miles, but the early *It* left him unimpressed. He was planning his own paper, the *Wall Street Journal*, which was to include posters by various artists, including Pink Floyd's Nick Mason and a story by Terry Jones, later of *Monty Python's Flying Circus*. But the format, almost more than the content, interested him: each front cover on each copy was to be different, and the magazine was contained, loose-leafed, in a bag, inspired, he thought, by Andy Warhol, and it was what he felt an *underground* magazine should be. *It* meanwhile was still being printed letterpress and seemed more an arts magazine than a product of any new movement, and put together by amateurs with leather arm-patches on their tweed jackets. Offers from the new paper that Central students help with *It* left Marchbank unmoved.

But outside London the paper began to sell, as in cities like Birmingham, Manchester, and Edinburgh attempts were made to match the expanding underground scene. By the summer of 1967 Birmingham had the beginnings of an arts laboratory, partly masterminded by the future *It* music editor, Mark Williams, who was street-selling the paper to supplement a meagre income as a trainee advertising account executive in Solihull. And in Edinburgh the appearance of *It* at the still-functioning Paperback Shop renewed the link with Haynes for people like Lloyd, who could regard themselves as the Americans' ambassadors in the north. And Lloyd found, in a milieu still heavily influenced by the Communist Party, that he had little difficulty in outselling the *Morning Star* when he took it on the streets.

And if the vagaries of distribution made it difficult to get *It* there were others on hand more than willing to give the new paper, Indica, and the new culture a boost. 'Pop stars and drugs', blazed the *News of the World* on 29 January 1967, the week following Miles's analysis of the new underground, 'Facts that will shock you.' The headline accompanied the story of the unfortunate Suzanne Lloyd who recounted her 'acid times' with the new pop/folk singer Donovan, which had included a visit to Jean Luc Godard's *Pierrot le*

Fou which she labelled as one of 'the "acid" films that are in vogue now'. The paper's initial foray suffered from a certain paucity of research and culminated in an attack on the impeccably orthodox BBC disc-jockey David Jacobs whose prime status was wilting under the impact of the new pirate radio stations. Jacob's folly had been to play 'Can't Happen Here' 'by a group of American male singers calling themselves the Mothers of Invention' on BBC TV's *Juke Box Jury*, adding that the record had been made on a 'trip'. Even worse, the paper suggested, two of the four-strong jury had voted the record – wrongly as it transpired – a hit.

By 12 February the paper had done some digging, which had taken it, bashfully, to Southampton Row and Indica, and had summoned up many of the spectres upsetting the generation still in thrall to Dad's war stories. 'Like so many sophisticated evils, the LSD craze began in America', it noted. 'Amongst the most active British groups advocating LSD are some members of the London Free School which comprises about 200 people and has many supporters.'

Having dealt with Hopkins's venture, the *News of the World*'s reporter thumbed through *It*, where he found advertisements for *Psychedelic Review* and 'editorial matter praising drugs and drug-takers'. The hapless Jeff Nuttall – whose cartoon strip had been running since the first issue – also felt the lash. 'The strip showed huge distorted bodies with monster heads and twisted limbs sprouting with such things as: "Vera, your beauty is unsurpassed in the undeniable excess of its obscenity and still you mouth me nothing but zero." ' By the following week Nuttall, whose attitude to LSD was far from enthusiastic within the underground, had been forced to issue a denial of drug taking, as had the Pink Floyd, another target. But it was Indica which seemed to most disturb the paper. Its 'investigator' reported that: 'Browsing through the shelves was like a glimpse of a madhouse. Books with poetry scribbled across erotic pictures lined the shelves. . . . One book called *The Four Letter Word* contains page after page of white space with four letter words all over it. There were rows and rows of cheaply printed books of weird poetry about erotic fantasies all of which had close links with LSD. . . . Posters on the walls invited customers to "All night trips", and Indian music is played gently in the background. The Indian music is significant, since it is a generally accepted part of many organized LSD experiences.'

The *News of the World*'s vision should stand with the many other bizarre sightings of that year, blending as it did fear of modernity – evil American sophistication – the threat of revamped Limehouse opium dens, courtesy of Indica's Indian music, and the throwback to holiday camp drilling thanks to 'organized' LSD experiences. The paper was to return to the theme throughout the year, but its early outrage began to be accompanied by a tone verging on envy. By June it was quoting Paul McCartney from *Life* magazine admitting to LSD experiences. By July it was observing the 'Disturbing world of the flower children' and a week later it featured 'Weekends with the flower children' complete with notes on make-up followed by 'Flower children at home' comprising pictures of radicals doing very little in a house off the Balls Pond Road.

While the campaign doubtless sent many young people off to London in search of trips, eroticism, and communal life it also energized the police. One result was a raid on the Rolling Stones, which, by June, had left Mick Jagger facing three months in jail, Keith Richards a year, and their – and Miles's – acquaintance, art gallery proprietor Robert Frazer, six months in jail. A July editorial by William Rees-Mogg 'Breaking a butterfly on a wheel' was to help free Jagger and Richards, not so Frazer, or John Hopkins, who was sentenced to nine months for marijuana offences on 1 June.

It, meanwhile, as a primary source of debate for many people having good, bad, and catastrophic times with drugs in that year, was doing its best to agonize over the issue. In between interviews with 'Men of grass' and 'Interpot reports' were editorials denouncing addiction, suggesting, as Tom McGrath had in November 1966, that 'if we ever get round to doing full serious research into drugs – as we must do soon – we might find that no one will want to use them again'; opposing moves to a US-style approach to addiction; and advising on ways to help junkies.

Such deliberation, while the youth of Britain were liable to go up in smoke, outraged many. When Jim Haynes had been planning his shift from the Edinburgh Traverse to London in 1965, the suggestion for the Jeanetta Cochrane venue had come from Harold Wilson's all-purpose wheeler-dealer Lord, then Arnold Goodman, the Chairman of the Arts Council. For Goodman, Haynes would have been just the kind of dynamic figure beloved of the Labour Government during its expansive tea-with-the-Beatles phase. Goodman's honeymoon with Haynes terminated with the launch of *It* and the American's plan to pull out of the theatre and set up his Arts Lab in Covent Garden. Haynes may have been apolitical, but his very naïveté, and openness to the cultural currents of the time, underlined the difference between the Labour Government's radicalism and the new popular movements. The Jeanetta Cochrane could be an alternative 'centre of excellence', a derelict warehouse in Drury Lane clearly couldn't. And *It*, with its drug connections, was the last straw for Goodman. The *It* connection also disturbed Haynes's fellow directors at the Jeanetta Cochrane, who considered it bad for the theatre's image.

Goodman didn't stop with Haynes. Miles too had been invited to join the Arts Council's literature panel, an offer which was promptly rescinded after Goodman got to hear of it, and which prompted a poem for page two of *It* on 27 February 1967, from Adrian Mitchell, suggesting that such an appointment would 'disrupt the council's true intent which is to fill the entire interior of the Royal Opera House with tins of chunkydogmeat and the rest of England with custard of the kind which thickens and grows a skin on top'.

The same issue featured Bradley Martin – as Hopkins tended to byline himself when writing on drugs – noting the *News of the World*'s 'sensational splurge on drugs and the pop world', the harmful effect the attack had had on Nuttall's work as a teacher, and Miles's self-proclaimed lack of enthusiasm for LSD.

The Sunday paper's attack fed into an older battle, that between radical theatre, cinema, publishing, and the state which had been smouldering ever since *Lady Chatterley* six years before. The publication of *It* had opened a new front and brought in new troops, and different ones, to the Hoggarts who had testified for Lawrence's novel. Around *Oz*, *The Little Red Schoolbook*, *Last Exit To Brooklyn*, the 'experts' would again be summoned to testify for liberalism and freedom of expression, but the cases would become inextricably blurred with others, about drugs, and, by 1972, about political challenges to the state.

Such concerns were unlikely to have interrupted the deliberations of the police when, spurred on by the *New of the World*, they raided *It*'s offices at Indica in Southampton Row. Subscription lists were taken, the premises were turned over, and the paper found itself with its first crisis.

New printers had to be found, which ended *It*'s uneasy relationship with hot metal. But by the end of April there was a new crisis. McGrath quit, taking the office's only typewriter with him. The return to London had not, despite the paper's success, been a particularly happy time for the Scot. Discussions about drugs' harmful effects were one thing, but McGrath was sick with heroin. Back across the border he began the painful process that was to make him, by the 1970s, one of Scotland's leading playwrights at, amongst other places, Haynes's old stamping ground, the Traverse.

Chapter 5

Dreams and dialectics

Hippy and student activist continue to recognize each other as allies. Certainly there is a common enemy against whom they both combine forces; but there is also a positive similarity of sensibility.

(Theodore Roszak, *The Making of a Counter Culture*, 1970)

The fact that hippies were so violently apolitical inspired a lot of my polemics for a long time on *Oz*.

(David Widgery, student activist and *Oz* contributor, 1986)

In 1965 Louise Ferrier decided she was sick of Australia and Sydney, which was, she remembers, a very small town in those days. Her mother waved the 20-year old off, and she set sail for England. In London she settled in Highgate and ventured out from there on the variation of the Grand Tour that beckoned for the young in Europe in the mid 1960s: Paris, Rome, Turkey, Lebanon, Jordan, Tunisia, and across north Africa.

Amongst those saying goodbye to Ferrier in Sydney had been Richard Neville. Involved in a relationship with her since his university days he missed her, and he too began to think of making the trip. He had stayed up three nights researching south-east Asia for a speech planned for a big demonstration against the Vietnam War. He had been through college, and yet, he reflected, he was still ignorant of the continent to the north. Then Martin Sharp rang up: let's go to London, he suggested. OK, said Neville, but if they were going to make the trip it should be through Asia. They flew to Singapore, traded in their suitcases for back-packs, and hit the pot trail. 'I loved every minute of it', remembers Neville. They went to Laos, Cambodia, but by the time they had arrived in Katmandu Sharp had decided to head on to London.

'By that stage', says Neville, 'I think Martin was tired of sitting round and vomiting.' But for both men it had been a spectacular and formative trip. Out on a train in Cambodia they had even talked lightly of setting up *Oz* again in London, even as Neville filed stories back to Richard Walsh and *Oz* in Sydney. But it was a vague idea, little more, Neville remembers, than an inchoate impulse. Yet the magazine's fame – or notoriety – was spreading: in Katmandu he was even shown a copy of the London *Observer Magazine* that featured Sharp, Walsh, and Neville and the story of the Sydney *Oz* trial. He put it out of his mind, and headed towards London. Having left Sydney in April, he finally hit London in September, and moved into a flat in his sister's house in Clarendon Road off Holland Park. Jill Neville was, and is, a novelist, whose arrival in Britain had been part of an earlier 1960s Australian wave, more tied to bohemianism than to the music and the scene that sucked in Australians in the mid 1960s.

Clarendon Road was a good place to be. His sister's connections in the publishing world meant that he quickly made contacts. A renewed one was with Louise Ferrier. To many within the underground, and in the media's eyes, in the years ahead Ferrier and Neville were to be the archetypal underground beautiful couple. Her cool beauty was to be the stuff of *Oz* covers and underground posters. The irony and cool eye she brought to the circus was sometimes lost in the *Sturm und Drang* generated by her partner's effortless flair for publicity.

Publicity quickly came. Others had noticed the *Observer* piece, and that Sharp and Neville had arrived in London, including the *Evening Standard*'s 'Londoners' Diary'. A young reporter, Mary Kenny, was despatched by the diary editor to go down to Clarendon Road, complete with a photographer, and get a story. Neville, fresh in from points east, had just been down to Carnaby Street and looked the very model of the new generation. 'They took a very nice photo which mostly showed my legs', says Ferrier. 'My legs looked very good. I was posing as his secretary, of course.'

'The photograph captured something alright', remembers Neville, 'it was almost better than the original, in terms of getting the mood, and Louise looked spectacular.' What, asked the reporter, was Neville going to do? Was he going to produce a London version of *Oz*? Yes, he was, said the Australian, not for the first or last time thinking on his feet. Duly, in December, the piece appeared. Neville, wrote the reporter, was the editor of the controversial Sydney paper *Oz*. Few had heard of it, but no matter. He was going to set up in London. 'The telephones began buzzing with eager contributors', he wrote three years later in his book *Playpower*, 'and what was once my merely exhibitionist impulse to impress a friendly gossip columnist soon gathered its own momentum.'

Indeed it did. Neville, to a London media sated with the word, if not the reality, was classless. Australians were still the butt of English condescension but he clearly came from a different mould from his fellow Australian Barry Humphries' *Private Eye* creation, Barry McKenzie. Jaggeresque in appearance he began to sail through the submarine defences of the class system, rather as the English in India had transcended the caste structure. He wasn't a bore or a boor, he couldn't be typecast or even neatly slotted within the underground, from which he always maintained an apparently effortless sense of distance.

Contributors were clearly not going to be a problem, nor were staff – Australia could take care of that. Paul Lawson from Melbourne had worked with *Oz* in Sydney and he automatically came round, and was appointed deputy editor. Andrew Fisher had been another contemporary from Sydney and an ability to write, a law degree, and a background in student papers and films made him a choice to handle much of the business side. Martin Sharp's ability as an illustrator and former *Oz* co-editor, made him the art director. He was joined by a young Londoner, Jonathan Goodchild, who rapidly moved from being Sharp's assistant to art director in his own right, leaving Sharp a clear run as perhaps the underground's most innovative illustrator. And Ferrier was always around, answering letters and the phone, shipping out the new magazine, rolling joints, making the coffee, doing, she says, the dogsbody things.

But just what was to be in *Oz*? And what was *Oz* to be? The ground rules had been set in Australia, but the ground had changed, and *It* had come into existence. Neville was interested, and sympathetic, towards the paper, but not deeply impressed. At Indica he had met Miles and had struck up a friendship with the ever-cordial Jim Haynes, and the early contributors pushed the new magazine beyond an Australian mafia, he emphasizes. Amongst the people who came visiting was a young Maidenhead medical student. David Widgery was deeply immersed in student politics, and deeply suspicious of *It*. On one hand he disliked its American disdain for Marxism, on the other what he identified as an English druggy self-indulgence. *Oz*, he thought, might be *Private Eye* all over again only this time without the smart-alec Shrewsbury and Oxford public school boys putting down grammar school boys with ideas above their station. It would be no-nonsense Australians without class hang-ups.

Neville had been to see *Private Eye*, and its staff had been courteous, but faintly aloof. There was to be no real rapport – with Peter Cook allegedly burning the first *Oz* in a Soho pub – until the *Oz* trial five years later. 'Richard Ingrams seemed to think we must be "pooves" because our hair touched our collars. He was quite extraordinarily obsessive about homosexuals and how marijuana would be the ruination of western civilization', says Neville. Thus the meeting between the Berkshire grammar school boy and the Australian was a meeting of minds, and style. 'I still remember David coming round', he adds, 'and thinking this man is a great writer, I was absolutely captivated by his prose style.'

Neville suggested he might write something on the *Eye*, to take on the ageing young men of Greek Street. Widgery acquiesced, aiming to do it from a position in keeping with the times, and from his revolutionary socialist stance.

Widgery's radical politics made limited headway within his medical school, where even the sprinkling of Labour Party careerists within David Robins's University College might have appeared perilously left-wing. But down in the Aldwych was the London School of Economics, where there were the first stirrings of student revolt, English-style, and to which the medical student often made his way. There, the Student Union, under the presidency of a left-wing socialist David Adelstein, and the Graduate Students' Association, under the presidency of the future founder of the underground's Liberation News Service Marshall Bloom, were in the early stages of a battle about the appointment of a new director. The LSE authorities' choice was the head of the University College of Rhodesia, Walter Adams, and the students weren't happy with it.

Like Miles, Widgery had taken the CND road from Aldermaston. Thereafter their paths diverged towards the two camps within the underground. While still at school Widgery had written for a short-lived national schools magazine, which rapidly collapsed. Through it Widgery became involved with another student venture, *U Magazine*, and managed to become its editor without even being a student, having been expelled from school for producing an irreverent magazine. Again like Miles, his path had crossed with Ginsberg's during the poet's 1965 visit. He interviewed him for *U* and they passed the day together. Speeding home to Maidenhead on his Lambretta he brooded on the exciting and slightly scary world of West Coast direct action, radicalism, Beat and homosexuality. That summer of 1965, prior to medical school, he took the almost obligatory trip to the United States.

He arrived as the black district of Watts, Los Angeles was exploding. The battles went on for four days that August and at least thirty-four people were killed. The riots were the culmination of rising unemployment, rocketing population, bad housing, and police racism. The *Los Angeles Times* had asked the local police chief why the riots had occurred: 'One person threw a rock, and then, like monkeys in a zoo, others started throwing rocks.'

His belief in non-violence, and in tales that the United States was a classless society, wilted. There was, he decided, an extremely oppressed working class, black and white, and an extremely greedy philistine group of people running the system. 'You gotta understand about America', an old black man had told him in Washington DC, 'it's a fucking capitalist nightmare.' Yes, thought Widgery, it is.

Heading south he got beaten up by the Miami cops for having

long hair. In Bogaloosa he drove cars for the Student Non-Violent Co-ordinating Committee which was then organizing black voter registration. Queuing for a bus he met another English student and they decided to head for Mexico City. On the road to Laredo they talked student politics, how the US Central Intelligence Agency had financed sections of the National Union of Students. Once in Mexico, Cuba seemed a good idea. They presented themselves to the Cuban ambassador. Widgery's colleague, an NUS vice-president, conveniently ignored the other fifteen people sharing the post and announced that *he* was *the* vice-president. Widgery meanwhile brandished his privately-sponsored *U* card and announced that he represented British student journalists. Six days later they flew into Havana.

Back from Cuba, his belief in non-violence now a fading memory, he fell in with the dope-smoking radicals of the key young radical movement, Students for a Democratic Society. With those SDS contacts he journeyed on to the West Coast, where the Vietnam Day Committee had started that May. Back in the east he sat in a bar one night and watched one of his idols, and inheritors of Charlie Parker's mantle, Roland Kirk, playing jazz. As he did so a white man put a dollar on the table and said to the barman, 'shut that nigger up'. In New York it was acid art in knocked-together Lower-East-Side lofts, and a meeting with John Wilcock on the verge of quitting the *Voice* and moving to Walter Bowart's new *East Village Other*.

'That', says Widgery, 'was my education.' From the early 1960s onwards it was to be a trip that many young English radicals were to make. Some went wide-eyed, some went in search of music, the world of *On the Road*, some went looking for Ken Kesey's Merry Pranksters, others for the new politics. Many, loathing corporate American power, fell in love with the movements that had emerged to counter it. Others eventually, as in the case of Widgery, developed an affection and a distance from that seductive New World.

Thus was an *It* still smelling of an earlier American decade's cultural anarchy unattractive to him, and the new *Oz* appealing. Thus did his byline appear in the first issue. From Australia, via Cambridge, there were Germaine Greer and Clive James as occasional contributors. In the first issue that seminal writer of London and Notting Hill in the late 1950s, Colin Macinnes, wrote on that seminal figure of London and Notting Hill in the 1960s, Michael Abdul Malik. Alex Cockburn, later to work for *Black Dwarf* and *7 Days* before decamping to the States and a 1970s career on *Village Voice*, provided a somewhat withdrawn interview with the *New Statesman*'s then right-wing socialist editor Paul Johnson. Greer wrote 'In bed with the English' which began to hint at *Oz*'s future development in its uncomplimentary analysis of the experience. Widgery, meanwhile, attempted to get to grips with the Greek Street gang. The fortnightly was 'Andrew pretending to be Kleenex. Tampax pretending to be Durex.' What this meant wasn't certain, but it sounded good at the time.

The *Evening Standard*, commenting on *Oz*'s inaugural issue, found it a great disappointment. They weren't the only ones. It was a magazine about the media, about London, but it wasn't an underground paper that hit the streets in late January 1967 with, as Neville wrote, 'a resounding thud'.

'The early *Oz*s were an uncomfortable hybrid of satire, Sunday journalism, and pirated underground tit-bits', wrote Neville four years on in *Playpower*. 'The art work of Martin Sharp and the excellence of some of the early contributors saved the magazine from total calamity. . . . In London not only did satirical intention seem redundant – other people were doing it better – but as a critical reaction to society it seemed inadequate and ultimately reactionary.'

It also seemed peculiarly irrelevant. At the London School of Economics the students had occupied the premises in February 1967 as their struggle intensified. The storming of the college gates – locked by the authorities – had been accompanied by the death of a porter from a heart attack. Radicals from across London, Britain, and Europe began to pour into the college to observe, participate, or make unsuccessful attempts to take the struggle into the correct channels. The LSE's walls were plastered with slogans – a favourite being 'Beware the Pedagogic Gerontocracy' – and suddenly the Situationists moved from the world of small magazines, happenings, and Alex Trocchi to hand out their leaflets, and flypost their documents on 'Ten Days that Shook the University'. This detailed the student takeover at Strasbourg University, and its apparent success in challenging the 'spectacle' of capitalism. It had little impact on the LSE students who, if they were in anything at all were likely to be inclined towards the Trotskyism of the International Socialists and the varieties of new leftism rather than this unknown creed.

At Alexandra Palace in north London the other side of the burgeoning movement was celebrating the 'Technicolour Dream'. With UFO established, the Dream extended the mood and spread the wave that the Albert Hall had initiated eighteen months before. Only now the coherence and the poetry were being deluged by the reality, or hope, of psychedelic drugs. The West Coast had love-ins; now London in considerably less welcoming climes tried the same, complete with an obligatory visit by Andy Warhol, Pink Floyd, and celebrants shinning up organ pipes as the night wore on and boredom or chemically induced demons had to be exorcized. As the freak end of the underground had dropped in on the LSE, so the politicos, or would-be politicos, packed their bags for Alexandra Palace. Britain, it seemed, had been black and white. Suddenly they were wearing the colours of the rainbow. And these weren't even, it seemed, the bombed-out hippies of later days, they were dandies, male and female, they glittered, they had what the left had always lacked – style.

Tom McGrath, in his last days at *It* responded with a '14-Hour Technicolour Dream Read-in Issue', printed in day-glo colours. For *Oz* the tide floated the magazine off the mudbank of media obsessions and into new directions. Sharp's graphics became more lurid. Widgery's attacks on swinging London more fanciful and, in keeping with the phallic times, more vitriolic. 'You can't see the prick for the codpiece'.

Not everybody could keep up. A correspondent, Victor Coughtrecy, wrote in to demand that 'you really must climb down from your ivory tower and admit that you (and I) represent a tiny minority of intellectual misfits. . . . I wish you would have more consideration for your undersexed readers. Your female contributors make us half-men feel pretty useless.'

By the summer the paper that had been interviewing Paul Johnson continued its move into youth, with a dose of Australian cultural snobbery directed against the 'Alfs': 'This bizarre cult of grey, short-haired nine-to-fivers', who worked as 'account executives, journalists, bank managers, doctors, lawyers, salesmen, dentists, insurance clerks, civil servants. . . . Most people are Alfs nowadays. They are a threat to world peace . . . a social embarrassment.' Amongst Alf achievements were listed the Crucifixion and 'not buying any of Vincent Van Gogh's paintings during his lifetime'.

Across the Atlantic John Wilcock worked on with *East Village Other*. After about eight issues he picked up a copy and noticed that Bowart – using the same technique he had used to appoint Miles London correspondent – had appointed him, and William Randolph Hearst as editors. The paper, in 1966–7, was doing well, the music industry had noticed it, and sex ads helped pay the bills.

Wilcock had developed another interest too, one that had burgeoned on the *Voice*, a fascination with Andy Warhol's factory, then turning out movies at the Factory by the dozen, and sucking in voyeurs, drifters, hopers, and no-hopers. Contact with Warhol introduced him to the Velvet Underground. After six weeks or so, three days a week, with the Factory Wilcock received hints that an article might be a good idea. He obliged with 'How Andy Warhol makes movies'. 'That', says Wilcock, 'is how I learned a lot about life and a Sophoclean scene where people were *learning*.'

It was also a time when the American underground press was

expanding, rapidly. By late 1966 the *Los Angeles Free Press*, the *Berkeley Barb*, East Lansing, Michigan's *Paper*, *Rag* in Austin, Texas, and the *East Village Other* were all publishing. In London *It* had started. Why couldn't there be a system? thought Wilcock, Bowart, and others. Wilcock, with assistance, wrote the preamble. All the information they got should be pooled, the only condition was that each paper was sent to every other paper, and that all could pick up anything they wanted. It was the Underground Press Syndicate.

'When Richard and Martin Sharp were in London it was my natural tendency to get involved with them,' says Wilcock. So he did. And by the sixth London issue Sharp's graphics had exploded, the paper wasn't a poor *Private Eye* or *New Statesman* anymore.

A lot of it was to do with Neville's desire to develop – alongside the graphics – the magazine's prose style. *It* was no model, the *New Statesman*, which he thought then 'superbly written', was. And by the fourth issue of *Oz* the plaudits were beginning to outnumber the brickbats. From New York, meanwhile, Wilcock had begun to send over copies of *EVO*, which meant that the Australian had become more aware than most in London of the underground explosion across the Atlantic. Wilcock arrived in London, and for the first time the two men met. The sixth issue of *Oz*, they agreed, would be a joint issue with *Other Scenes*, with contributions from Widgery *et al.*, and editorship from Wilcock. The Yorkshire expatriate, thinks Neville, was not tough-minded with copy, but crucially, he was *open*. 'He'd say things like "who is this Michael X guy?" and I'd say I didn't know', says Neville. You had to *meet* these people, Wilcock would explain, and thus they went off on the 31 bus to meet the Trinidadian. 'He got me out', explains the Australian, 'and off the telephone.'

In *Playpower* Neville wrote that the sixth issue was when *Oz* finally went underground. Wilcock looks back on it as a 'very heavy issue'. 'It even included a piece by Anthony Burgess – not a figure usually associated with the alternative culture – on 'flower language'.

'During those years', says Wilcock, 'I felt closer to Richard, in his feelings about life, news, his sense of playfulness, his serious concern about issues which had to be *dealt* with but had to be entertaining.'

'We skip the light fandango, threw cartwheels across the floor. I was feeling kind of seasick, the crowd cried out for more', sung Gary Brooker of Procul Harum in 'A Whiter Shade of Pale', on Deram, that June. It was a song with everything: baroque references, long sombre organ solos, and words so opaque that they could mean all things to all people, unless they actually asked what they *meant* – which was, unless one was very stoned, nothing –

which was why, for eleven weeks, during that summer it was high in
the charts. It provided a vocabulary for the mass marketing of
hippies. It also brought cheer to the giant Decca record company,
which had set up Deram precisely to capture back from the new
independent companies some of the money pumping into what
there was of Britain's counter culture. Having established the tone,
Procul Harum duly yielded their place at the top of the charts to the
Beatles, who settled on the essence of that summer with 'All You
Need Is Love', to be followed by Scott McKenzie's 'San Francisco',
which was, millions of radios announced, the place to be to skip the
light fandango, and where all one needed was love.

'The adventure of poverty by young white people in love
ghettos across the country, like Haight-Ashbury and the Lower
East Side', wrote Emmett Grogan in *Ringolevio*, 'was pleasant
fakery for most of them. But in the same way that real poverty has
always given birth to real revolution, this feigned poverty of the
adventurous would breed a false-bottomed, jerry-built revolution in
which the adventurers would continue their make-believe and be
followed by the rock-concert lumpen, tired of their own voyeurism.'

Haight-Ashbury got violent that summer. But not as violent as
Newark, New Jersey. Between 14 and 16 July twenty-two people
were killed in the battles between blacks, the police, and the
National Guard. By 24 July 4,700 soldiers had been sent into
Detroit. Fourteen people were killed. The battles continued into
August.

It wasn't like that in London, Edinburgh, Birmingham, Leeds,
Leicester. A new race relations act had been introduced, supposedly to counter white racism. In August the first prosecution was
initiated. Michael Abdul Malik stood accused, and was convicted,
of using the phrase 'white monkeys'.

Michael X's friend, Jim Haynes, was doing better. For him that
summer – Newark, Haight-Ashbury, Detroit, or Vietnam aside –
London was the capital of the world, and in July the Arts Lab
opened. Haynes and Jack Henry Moore, who worked with him on
the project, planned to be, as *It* predicted in late April, 'as
experimental and as international as the Lord Chamberlain will
allow'.

Things were being allowed. That month homosexuality was
legalized. Dope wasn't, but the drug legal advice service 'Release'
which concerned itself with the increasing number of busts – and
junkies – began operating in West London. And the population of
London swelled, both with naïve readers of *Time*, and with young
people from across the country. In the absence of a ticket to San
Francisco they felt that London would have to be the next best
thing. And other Londoners – traditional dwellers – were moving
out. Rachmanism had gone – or at least Rachman was dead – and,

before the property boom of the 1970s, there was empty property in places like Chalk Farm, Ladbroke Grove, Covent Garden. They were areas with a shifting working-class population, and ideal for putting down bohemian roots. With the roots came dreams of the creation of liberated zones, embracing the generation briefly flirting with peace, the new libertarian-oriented politicos, and, crucially, people doing what the period was supposed to be about, having a good time.

It made the gathering at the Roundhouse that July, 'The Dialectics of Liberation', a symposium which in other years, might have attracted a handful of people, an often packed and vital event. Compared with the activism of the United States, or the war in South Vietnam, Britain remained a backwater. Compared with five years before it was a raging torrent. The Vietnam Solidarity Campaign was beginning to take off – with the Communist/ Christian British Council for Peace in Vietnam eclipsed by its growth. The London School of Economics had provided a trailer for what was to come, black activism within Britain was on the rise, and three years of Labour Government was decimating its support amongst students and the young intelligentsia. They were turning towards Marxism, often of a neo-Trotskyist variety, and almost never via the Labour or Communist parties. The other inspirations were the revolutions of the southern hemisphere – the Portuguese colonies in Africa, Vietnam, Latin America – the peripheral appeal to some of the more deluded souls of the Chinese Cultural Revolution, and for a few the writings of the *émigré* Frankfurt Marxist, Herbert Marcuse.

But crucially 'Dialectics' was not organized by any political group, as such, but by a group of psychiatrists including R.D. Laing and David Cooper. It aimed to 'demystify human violence in all its forms', and, unsurprisingly, it failed. But what it did do was provide a unique workshop of the ideas that had been bubbling up in the years since the cracking of the ice in 1956, and in a context which leapt over the boundaries of 'official' politics, whether mainstream, Marxist, anarchist, reformist, or Maoist. The currents were all there, and they interconnected. Paul Goodman, the American anarchist writer; Stokeley Carmichael, the 26-year-old Trinidadian-born New Yorker whose black nationalism had just triumphed within SNCC; Laing and Cooper; Ginsberg – whose contribution took the form of a mantra; American radical journalists John Gerassi on the Third World; Trotskyist theoretician Ernest Mandel; William Burroughs; Angela Davis, the Californian activist and academic; the Marxist historian and biographer of Trotsky, Isaac Deutscher; the San Francisco digger, Emmett Grogan, who popped up for a fringe meeting 'still loaded with the sleepiness of heroin'; and Herbert Marcuse.

Perhaps it was the name of Carmichael – the closest that London was to get to contact with the black revolt that year – and the name of Marcuse that pulled in the crowds that went to the Roundhouse for the fortnight. Third worldism, Laingian theories of schizophrenia blended with Marcuse, black power, and elements of Trotskyism that excluded only two groups, not insignificant ones – women and the working class. Carmichael's sexism – not that the word existed: 'the role of women in the struggle is prone' – and the obsession with struggle *elsewhere* and male intellectuals' struggles *here* with an uncomprehending world, threw down enough issues to sustain a variety of competing tendencies, articles, and books for the following five years.

'It all looks ludicrous now', observed David Widgery, 'but if you realize there had been twenty years of Cold War normalism this was a very exuberant reaction to the world of Pepsodent ads, and the father-mother-children-aren't-we-normal? kind of thing which was still the prevailing mentality. I was very impressed by Marcuse who started his talk by saying: "What we are doing is hearing a lot of talk about the flower power, but the flower only has the power because the human being is watering it." I thought, fucking right!'

Chapter 6

New explanations

The British Empire spent two hundred years unloading beads on the natives. In nine months we get them all back again.

(*Oz*, 1967)

It's finances were rocky, and stayed that way. But after eight issues, early in 1967, the paper had a stroke of good fortune. A young man came in and asked if he could help with distribution. He had a Rolls Royce and a fortune. His name was Nigel Samuel. The son of millionaire property developer, Howard Samuel, the new recruit was quickly billed as an editorial assistant, and, shortly after that, joined the editorial board.

Inheriting a fortune on the sudden death of his father, and to the acute distress of the family trustees, Samuel Junior devoted much of his money to sustaining *It* and funding the activities of Michael X. *It* moved, first to Fitzroy Square, then to Betterton Street in Covent Garden, and later, in 1968, to Endell Street in the same neighbourhood.

In transit from Southampton Row to Covent Garden the staff, and the paper's orientation, shifted. After McGrath's sudden departure Jack Henry Moore filled in, but with Moore's commitment to the new Arts Lab a new editor had to be found. The police had dropped any action, following their March 1967 raid, by June.

New staff arrived. Bill Levy took over as editor, and Mick Farren, whose relationship with *It* was to survive the history of the underground made his first appearance. While Miles was influenced by the American Beats, and by a literary culture, Farren's somewhat more street-based style was born of the rock culture, which took in everything from Brando and *The Wild One* from the mid 1950s through early Elvis to Dylan and the Rolling Stones. Out of rock came a stance of the rock concert rebel, where the crises and contradictions of the times could be played out as theatre. The problem was that adherents to the vision had nowhere to go, as time passed, but onwards to the next gig. But in 1967, as the high tide of commercial hippiedom flowed onwards, who cared?

The *New Musical Express*, stumbling after the new wave, advertised bells and full hippy regalia, from the people who had brought Beatle jackets to the young. The conviction of Rolling

Stones Mick Jagger and Keith Richard, together with art gallery proprietor Robert Fraser, on drugs charges, together with the Stones' brief imprisonment – Fraser was not so lucky – triggered demonstrations running into hundreds outside the offices of the *News of the World*. The paper indignantly rejected charges that it had set up the case which had, it seemed then, consigned Jagger and Richard to jail, but outrage at the sentences had touched liberal consciences, and galvanized youth inhabiting that grey area between music and social protest. The old, it appeared, were on the attack everywhere; why, even pirate radio was being driven out of the North Sea. A new New Left, drawing from Dialectics of Liberation, brushed aside the tentative offerings of the old New Left, gathered in its May Day Manifesto group and comprising such stalwarts of post-1956 as Raymond Williams, E.P. Thompson, and Stuart Hall. By the standards of 1961 – or, perhaps, today – it was radical stuff, by the style of 1967 it seemed passé.

In London *Oz* and *It* had the field almost to themselves. *Private Eye* was flourishing, and even advertising in *It* its discreet 'God Is Love', 'Karl Marx', and 'Marquis de Sade' T-shirts under the slogan 'Plug in turn on freak out with *Private Eye*', but this was little more than a wobble in that paper's progress – and a chance for a satirical quick buck. With Paul Foot on board the magazine was heading towards its investigative period, an area into which the underground press was consistently to fail to make inroads. But in those times *Oz* and *It* had a wave to ride, and they did their best to do so.

They were aided by the stabilization of their market. The Arts Lab was in its honeymoon with London. The Great and the Good, excluding Lord Goodman, rushed in their donations – Tom Stoppard, Doris Lessing, Peter Brook, Ken Tynan, David Frost, John Schlesinger – while *It* told readers that the project wanted them to join, and 'for those few affluent *It* readers, founder membership is £50'. 'We had German TV, Polish TV, Japanese TV, Spanish, Dutch, Swedish, French, Italian TV', wrote Jim Haynes in *Thanks for Coming*, 'and, of course, Granada and the BBC; it was amazing.'

The Garden, the Gate, the Grove, and the Farm. . . . Chalk Farm had UFO; *Oz*, the London Free School and countless others had Notting Hill and Ladbroke Grove. Dick Pountaine, then in his final year of a chemistry degree at Imperial College, after two years of South Kensington had realized that Notting Hill was the place to live, with £3-a-week bedsits, and plenty of places to score. 'By my third year people in the lab used to joke "Pountaine's in, it must be Tuesday" ', he remembers. 'I was quite lucky to get my degree, had I gone up a year later I probably wouldn't have done. Being around Notting Hill meant we got involved in the Free School gigs, big social events that went round by word of mouth.'

Pountaine had gone up to Imperial a Communist Party member, but Notting Hill and the underground proved a stronger pull. 'In a strict Party sense this was all bourgeois individualism and bohemianism, to me it was infinitely more attractive than anything going on in the Communist Party, particularly the student Communist Party, which was largely in-fighting and sectarian politics. By the end of that summer I moved into this house in Lonsdale Road, Notting Hill, which was quite a little centre. It was visited regularly by Hoppy and all those kind of people. That was when I got in contact with the "official" underground.' Later it was to lead him on to *Oz*, *Ink*, and *Friends*.

Hopkins, during the later months of 1967 was being visited, rather than visiting, after his marijuana conviction. But as *It* celebrated a year of publication it had grown from twelve to twenty pages, with the 'What's Happening' section now, significantly, filling two tightly set pages at the back, and the Arts Lab offering a 'Black Power Week' complete with Stokeley Carmichael – bundled out of the country post Dialectics of Liberation – on film, and 'Michael Abdul Malik and guests'. That issue's front page proclaimed 'The Second Coming' and flashed Aleister Crowley, John Peel, and Alex Trocchi amongst its attractions. Drugs might make people schizophrenic – or the system, as Laing was suggesting – whichever way *It* certainly reflected it. Bradley Martin devoted a page to extolling the virtues of cannabis and the need to fight back against legal restrictions and police interventions. 'We fall into a trap if we admit to the government's right to pass legislation in areas concerning our own chemistry. This right to use our bodies as laboratories is basic to changed expressions of thought and communications', he wrote. 'Without such transformation we will never change "this horrible society", Tom Driberg admits his generation has created. . . . Listen man, don't talk to me like I was smoking a bomb. It's only the resin from the flower and dried up leaves of a very beautiful plant.' On the facing page, however, under the headline 'Acid Burned a Hole in my Genes', Joe Meltz reported on American research – later discredited – suggesting that LSD caused chromosomal damage, and *It* followed that up with a two-page 'Acid Report'. The drugs coverage underlined that the paper was shifting rapidly – if erratically – from its earlier goal of being a London community paper, or maybe that the community to which it was addressing itself had changed rapidly in the year since its birth.

On 22 October that year a small but significant march by the Vietnam Solidarity Campaign took place in Grosvenor Square. The day before, 50,000 had marched on the Pentagon. But as the year closed, the 'New Age' promised in *It* was still more to do with ley-lines and 'the ecstatic return of everything blessed', as John Michel, the paper's fixture on UFOs, Britain's 'holy places', and the 'centres and lines of latent power in Britain', put it. But more people were coming on to the paper. Graham Plinston replaced Farren as news editor, John Hopkins – still inside – was billed as 'research', while, significantly, Dave Hall was in charge of 'Business'.

Hall was a significant recruit. A fellow staffer of the time joked that his methods were 'street corner based'. A former convenor at Ford, Dagenham, his financial manoeuvres – plus input from Samuel – and his ability to get the magazine out, provided a core to its progress.

So did Peter Stansill. Like Wilcock a Yorkshireman, he was the son of a Barnsley mining family, and, again like Wilcock, had provincial and national newspaper experience. Stansill was not one of the extroverts of the underground, but what he did bring was method, in an environment with hardly any, and a philosophical view about the alternative which the underground could offer. It wasn't just going to be papers, it could be health clinics, bookshops, making a network of people sharing lifestyles and indeed an economic base.

Women had been on the paper since the beginning – with Maureen McGrath as news editor – and it had been women who had been providing the typesetting, the listings, the ad selling. But, says Dave Robins, who became assistant editor early in 1968, *It* remained very male, in its content, and in its style. 'Women were just "chicks" ', he says. 'The attitude to women's rights, equality, to a bit of *space* was at best indifference. There was a lot of downright exploitation. Yet women like Jane Nicholson were doing the really important things.'

Amongst them was Sue Morris, 'Hamburger Sue'. She came to *It* via an employment agency, and, while others slept on the floor, worked, argued, or posed, she would work through the clerical, jobs, type, organize. 'She treated it', Robins reflects, 'like a normal place. Some people did.'

Sue Small didn't. In 1966 she was a 17-year-old school-leaver living in a furnished room in Blackheath. She had worked for a bent company running credit checks on people, had temped for an employment agency, a bank, and as a telephonist. She had been a mod, but, after her brother told her to buy Bob Dylan records, she did so, being, then, an impressionable person. It was a pleasant place, Blackheath, a shade too respectable for someone into the tablets of the time, and full of kids – unlike Small – waiting to go to university. There was only one pub to go to and, since that closed at eleven o'clock, the alternative was her house. Thus did dozens of local kids materialize in the early hours to listen all night to the Beatles, the Butterfield Blues Band, the Pink Floyd.

One night, in the pub, ranging out of north London an *It* seller turned up. She had never seen anything like it, and nor had anyone else in Blackheath. She joined him on his forays into Covent Garden to collect the paper. It was her first real experience of central London, she liked it, she even stuck around on those nights in Betterton Street helping pack the papers. 'I was very young', she says, and I was impressed by those people. I was pretty odd for Blackheath but not in comparison with the people who were hanging out at the *It* office. They were a lot weirder than I was.'

It needed people to work all night sending out subscription copies, getting them down to the all-night post office. There was no money, just hot chocolate. She didn't feel she could make a contribution, but she wanted to, so 'I just went in and made myself useful.' Through *It* she got to know Dave Hall and his wife. But she still remained on the outside.

Until 1968. She got, and hated, a job in a fruit pulpers in Covent Garden, and would drop in at lunchtimes, and one day, in the absence of anyone else competent to run the switchboard, she took it over for an hour. Hall offered her a job, and there she stayed for two years working sixty to seventy hours a week and still commuting back to Blackheath, except on press night, which would go on all night, once a fortnight. She was usually one of the first in. Others would work more unpredictable hours, but, in those days the paper still hit the schedules. And Small moved on, from the switchboard to the 'What's Happening' pages, which weren't regarded as too important. 'Otherwise', she says, 'they wouldn't have let me do it. I had no knowledge of the arts scene.' And she also, later, moved into the ads section.

Meeting *It*, Sue Small, Blackheath retired mod, got hooked on it. Others did too. A succession of printers led the paper by 1968 to a Carlisle outpost of the Baring Family where, once a fortnight, Robins and Levy would arrive and wait overnight for the paper to roll off the presses. From there it returned, via an accommodating lorry driver, to Tottenham, and out by mini-van across the city, and the country. One week, when Robins and Levy arrived in Tottenham the paper wasn't there. Frantic searches followed, and the run was eventually located – in Totteridge. They called Farren. 'He got all the heads, liggers, lunatics in Notting Hill out of their beds', remembers Robins. 'They appeared in a convoy and, led by Bill, went to where the van was. At three in the morning they unloaded the paper. Bill said: "These are the people who care about the paper." They were the people who did it for nothing.'

By the beginning of 1968 *Oz* had established itself. And Neville, through Widgery and the Italian journalist Angelo Quattrochi had realized that the time was apparently right to think about fighting in the streets. On 29 January 1968 the South Vietnamese National Liberation Front launched its attack on Saigon, and across the country. It was a sign of what the year was to offer, and a clear signal that the United States wasn't winning the war in Vietnam. It was also a sign that the days of love-ins were about to change radically. In 1967 the hippies and the radicals, in Britain at least, had coexisted. Yet, as David Widgery points out: 'It's important to remember that there was quite a lot of opposition within the underground against whatever flower power was. There was a struggle about politics, and it was usually polarized about Vietnam. The hippies used to say: "Wow man, you know we *love* Lyndon Johnson", and people like Roland Muldoon – who was setting up the Cast street theatre group – were in a much more combative mood. They were standing up at UFO and saying: "This is fucking rubbish, people are being killed in Vietnam", and *some* people would say "It's all in your head man". Throughout 1967 there was this polarization going on, and when 1968 came along there was this very rapid divergence. I remember during the Tet offensive going round with a transistor radio in my ear to hear the latest news.'

Before Tet, Vietnam could be a place where an unpleasant war was being fought, some might even know that 525,000 American troops were stationed in the country, that the United States was convulsed by the issue, but as the NLF penetrated the US embassy in Saigon, and as its troops had to be beaten out, one by one, millions of people, and hundreds of thousands of western radicals were taken by the idea that the emperor might be dangerous, was dangerous, but had no clothes. And if that was true of the US government, it was true of the French, German, Russian, and British governments.

It was an idea whose time was coming. Kennedy and Wilson had both aroused expectations, which had not been fulfilled. The campaign against the war in Vietnam had taken the orthodox routes of left-wing protest, in the left press, in *Peace News*, around the Campaign for Peace in Vietnam. But something new was developing, something that put as much – or more – of a gap between the 1968 generation and the liberals of 1956 as that generation had delineated between themselves and the spirits of 1945 and 1951.

In the United States Johnson's Presidency floundered as, in early March, Eugene McCarthy, the stop-the-war candidate took 42 per cent of the vote in the New Hampshire Democratic Party primary. But for many American radicals McCarthy was not enough. Liberalism was not enough. In Britain Wilson's Labour Government sustained a half-hearted support for the war, and economic policies that were enough to drive Labour's constituency amongst the young working-class socialists and student radicals out of the Party. Revolution was in the minds of some of those people, together with the nagging doubt, despite the talk of Trotsky and Guevara, Mao and Marcuse, that the supposed motor of revolutionary change in the west – or Eastern European bloc – the workers, would not be prepared to do anything about it.

While *It* floundered between ley-lines, Burroughs, and acid, the first 1968 issue of *Oz* indicated that the magazine was sensitive to the change taking place. Much of it was to do with the personality of the editor, Richard Neville.

'He was aware that *Oz* had to be diverse', observes David Widgery, 'and that there was an interesting debate going on between the hippies and the politicos. Neville never was a hippy, he used to hate taking LSD, he used to wear the clothes, but he was a bit too shrewd to fall for that. He was a classic liberal, and was interested in debate.'

The *Oz* editor agrees. 'I never used the word "hippy" about myself except in a jocular way. I was and still am a liberal. Sometimes then I was a bit embarrassed by it, because I thought I ought to be a little more revolutionary, but I've always completely loathed violence and bloodshed and everytime I dived into Marxism all I could think of was Lenin shooting the anarchists. I could never come to terms with the Big Idea. I come from libertarianism'.

That January issue was the 'Revolutionary *Oz*', complete with Quattrocchi on the Russian Revolution; Widgery on the Cuban revolutionary Che Guevara, who had been killed the previous October in the Bolivian jungle, and whose name Widgery and *Oz* spelt throughout as 'Geuvara'; and even John Wilcock, whose 'Other scenes' reappeared in that issue, put in a piece on Regis Debray. Debray, later a minister in France's socialist President Mitterand's Government, had spent time with Guevara in the jungle, and had been sentenced to thirty years by the Bolivians. He was then in the full flight of his revolutionary phase. It must be total, he admonished, 'not just a coming to terms with the enemy'.

Not that the readers were willing to take *Oz*'s revolutionary package with the seriousness that at least some of the contributors had intended. By March Ladbroke Grove's J. Russell Wimbush was writing in complaining about Widgery's classic period rhetoric that 'men like Guevara are too big and angry for our world of typewriters and soft hands'. 'You said it', slammed back Wimbush, 'and I bet he'd puke if he could see the hollow tribute you've paid him.'

And while revolution continued to feature in the magazine – the more parochial Diggers got an outing in the February issue – by that month the caravan had moved on, rather unsteadily to a 'Flying saucers issue', where, with some difficulty, Lenin was dragged in for his views.

If Pearce Marchbank had been dubious of *It* he wasn't about *Oz*. Stylistically, politically, socially he was out of sync with the fortnightly paper but *Oz* 'was clean, well printed, the complete antithesis of *It*, which looked like the *Wellington Echo* from New Zealand.'

In the April issue that year *Oz* broke new graphic territory with a cover comprising stickers, removable from the cover. The idea wasn't completely new, the sleeve for Andy Warhol's Velvet Underground album in the United States featured a removable, stick-on banana, but for magazines – and British magazines in particular – the cover was revolutionary, and got *Oz*, and designer Martin Sharp, noticed. The slogans weren't bad either. An LSE post-graduate, David Phillips, provided 'We are lepers, give us bells, not degrees', which further strengthened students' welcome sense of apartness.

Elsewhere in that issue, with the aid of *New Statesman* contributors like Alex Cockburn and Tom Nairn, *Oz* provided a parody of that magazine, as it stumbled to come to terms with 1968. The May Events in Paris enthused the still socialist editor, Paul Johnson, if from a somewhat uncomprehending standpoint, but the *NS* was very much out of its time. Neville's take on the time was more acute. He provided a letter from 'Richard Neville, Editor, *Hippy Review*, Turramurra North', to the *New Statesman*: 'Sir: There's a new generation with a new explanation, everybody should get VD, when you come to Notting Hill wear a big flower in your wig. Why do Alfs still care about politics, Hitler, and Oxfam? Groove with Laing. "Hung On You" has mindblowing gear. Cops and clocks are all wound up. Flying saucers are . . . (to be continued).'

That spring the slow march of the Situationists through the London of the decade surfaced on the cover of *It26*, with a Situationist poster. It was, said the paper, a 'found object', but by then David Robins had been in touch with the group, and was to share a house with one of their then leading London lights, Chris Grey. The poster had been pasted on the building that housed *It*. It was a significant moment. Once there had just been Trocchi drawing on the group's ideas, there had been the sTigma exhibition in Better Books in 1965, the obituary of André Breton – one of the group's intellectual roots – by Jean-Jacques Lebel in the first *It* fourteen months earlier. Now they were seeping into the consciousness of people within a milieu which, rejecting straight left politics, was searching for a route out of a hippy enclave at a time when the political temperature was rising.

The Situationists had been born in the wake of the 1956 upheavals; indeed Trocchi had briefly been a member of their 'executive' before being thrown out. Most of its British followers suffered a similar fate at the hands of its arbitrary organizers – or anti-organizers. The key document circulated at the time was Raoul Vaneigen's *Totality For Kids* which was hailed by its supporters as doing for the twentieth century what Marx had done for the nineteenth. Since, according to the group – 'the Sits' as they became labelled in Britain – the problems of production had been solved, the question was one of consumption. 'In exchange for their real sacrifice', said *Totality for Kids*, 'the workers receive the instruments of their liberation (comfort, gadgets) which, however, are purely fictitious liberation since power controls the ways in which all material equipment can be used.' All were 'poisoned by the spectacle', the problem was to break it. 'Our guiding element could be the Durutti's Brigade moving from village to village, liquidating the bourgeois elements and leaving the workers to see to their own organization.'

It was an appealing image, and an appealing movement for radicals hunting their red snark, and tired of waiting for Godot. It promised involvement, rationalized non-organization, it dramatized outcast status, and offered the possibility of action, and, as the next decade opened, provided it for a few. It also endorsed the hostility which many of those radicals felt for the orthodox left. It would be propaganda of the deed, if, for many, it remained words. It also provided another link between the radicals and the radicalized hippies. For the Farrens might locate their struggle within music, but the music was part of the spectacle, and maybe 'people's music' was part of the process of shattering it. 'Yes! Men it can be done' said the ads for 'Magnaphall', the underground's most consistent advertiser, which offered larger and more reliable erections for those male members of the underground wilting under the strain of the sexual competitiveness of the era. So, it seemed, could the political revolution.

Other things pushed students centre-stage. In West Germany the socialist students' organization, the SDS, had grown into the most successful and radical challenge to the status quo that the state had seen since 1945. Its *de facto* leader – or so identified by the right-wing Springer press empire – was Rudi Dutskche. In March he was shot and seriously injured by a right-wing extremist. The student left across Europe was outraged; it was also confirmed in the notion that it was being taken seriously.

But was it in England? The answer came on 17 March, in Grosvenor Square. By then the Vietnam Solidarity Campaign had grown, but by just how much was to take even the organizers of that day's protest to the United States Embassy by surprise. The revival of non-Stalinist Marxism had breathed new life into the Trotskyist groups. While the Communist Party continued its decline, the Socialist Labour League, in isolation, had moved to producing a twice weekly newspaper, *Newsletter*. Meanwhile the International Socialists, who had spent the quarter-century since their birth in the wilderness, were growing in numbers. Six or seven hundred members – many of them students outwardly scornful of the underground – proved to be quite sufficient to provide an organizational web around which the VSC could be built. While the most prominent member of the VSC, Tariq Ali, was soon to become a member of a smaller, and less durable, International Marxist Group, it was the IS which did much of the groundwork, and which over the next five years was to reap most of the recruits. On the day a march estimated at 100,000 people threaded through central London in spring sunshine to Grosvenor Square. Shunned by much of the old left, the new recruits had proved more than up to the task of filling the gaps. The German SDS marched in neat formation – provoking racist jokes mingled with admiration – and the crowd was so large that the police lines proved incapable of resisting it. It was the antithesis of the CND marches. For many of the committed, for many of the organizers, the issue wasn't peace, it was war: victorious war for Vietnam's National Liberation Front, and class war on the bourgeoisie – a word that had faded from much of the left in the long years of 'The British road to socialism'. It was also play-acting, with Guevara look-alikes, berets suitably arranged, posing alongside scarlet flags atop lamp-posts. There could be none of the early 1960s sit-downs, it was implicitly recognized, this was no passive Ghandhi-like protest, the state had to be confronted. The state, in the form of the police line, broke, both to their and the demonstrators surprise. Many of the marchers had never been on a CND march. Violence ensued. Abroad other leftists noticed that even the British were fighting their police.

Not all approached it with such seriousness. 'The impact on me', recalls Pearce Marchbank, 'was blowing away all that love and peace shit which I thought was bollocks and complete pretence. People were on the streets being senselessly violent to the police, which I thought was a good thing at the time. It was completely anarchic, they could have been fighting for anything, cheaper tea-bags for all they cared, half of them. There were a lot of people there who felt seriously about what they were fighting for but people went there for a good fight really, they hadn't been able to show any aggression for the last two years. So then I was able to put in drops of blood and nasty black and white pictures and get rid of the Paisley patterns and bindweed round the edge of pages everywhere.'

On 4 April Martin Luther King was shot in Memphis. Violent protest erupted across the United States. Five days later, as the hysteria about the arrival of Kenyan Asians peaked, Home Secretary James Callaghan published his race relations bill. Then, on 20 April, Enoch Powell, a member of Edward Heath's Conservative Shadow Cabinet, commented to a public meeting on the race war. Like the Roman of old, he observed: 'I seem to see the River Tiber foaming with much blood.'

Heath sacked Powell. Three days later 1,000 London dockers marched in support of the speech. Suddenly the confidence of the new radicals received a body blow. They had talked of spontaneous workers' movements, of activity from below, and suddenly there it was. A few old veterans of the Mosleyite British Union Movement were identified amongst the marchers, and conveniently blamed by some of the more deluded, or self-deluding, but there seemed little escape from the truth. While the radicals had toyed with revolution, and while the underground had played with toys, workers were on the move, and in the wrong direction.

Yet other messages were coming from elsewhere. In March Victor Herbert reported from Paris for *It* on 'L'Affaire Langlois' – the controversy about the sacking of Henri Langlois from his post as head of the Paris Cinématheque. The same issue of *It* reported – as hardly anyone else had – how 'La Groupe Première Mai' had opened fire on London's United States Embassy. By April the paper itself had changed. Abruptly it proclaimed itself a tribe, featured all twenty-three staff, tribe members on the cover, reported on the growth of the yippies, America's politicized hippies, and on plans by Sid Rawle's Hyde Park Diggers to move to the country. By the following issue Rudi Dutskche was being interviewed, and John Hopkins was writing a critical letter to Tariq Ali on the 17 March demonstration. Politics were flooding into *It* too. Curious reports from France, changing hippies, tribal undergrounds, assessment of demonstrations.

A palace revolution on *It* saw 'co-ordination' put in the hands of John Hopkins with 'words' the province of Peter Stansill, Dave Robins, and Madeleine Neeson. Miles was slipping back, and, in his *It* interventions, more into music. He interviewed Mick Jagger for the first issue of May. Things were weird, said Jagger. They were, and were about to become a lot weirder.

Chapter 7

Demand the impossible

Clive Goodwin had done well. He was what the 1960s were supposed to be about: rich, successful, well placed in the media, what the cant of the time regarded as classless. That meant that Goodwin was from the working class and had made it. He held expensive parties and knew London's radical chic: Kenneth and Katherine Tynan, Tony Garnett and Ken Loach the film-makers, Jim Haynes, Richard Neville, David Mercer the playwright.

Indeed the subject matter of many of Mercer's plays – which was often Mercer – could just as well have been Goodwin. Plays about the fractured consciousness of working-class kids who had fought their way through the old class system, emerged on top, and still felt dissatisfied, still realizing that nothing had changed back where they came from, or where they had arrived. Born the son of a Willesden waiter Goodwin had worked as an actor, produced magazines, and gravitated into television. Quitting after a fracas he had gone to work as a literary agent and had prospered. He didn't suffer fools gladly and was obsessively professional. Where he'd come from and where he was ensured one thing: like Garnett, Mercer, and Loach, Goodwin was a socialist.

By 1966 he shared the disillusionment with the Labour Government spreading through the intelligentsia. What was needed, he suspected, was a new paper. *Tribune* had tail-ended Harold Wilson into power, and was, to a new generation, an irrelevant joke. The paper had to be independent, appealing to the new radicals, and to the working class. There were the papers produced by the political groups, but they seemed fatally restricted to the obsessions of other times, and to backbiting amongst themselves.

Yet Goodwin, through his progress through the media and up the class structure of Britain, had remained, or become, cut off from any grassroots action. He involved himself in Raymond Williams's 'May Day Manifesto Committee' and he talked to others about what could be done. Amongst them was Tariq Ali, whose background could hardly have been further from his own. The son of an affluent Pakistani landowning family, he had graduated from Oxford in 1963, with radical political ideas, and few prospects. He made a living by journalism, in the 1960s version of Grub Street eventually landing the job of drama critic for *Town* magazine. *Town*

– owned by Michael Heseltine – was a monthly, oriented ineffic-
iently to the male equivalent of the readers of *Queen*, and stumbling
blindly towards the market to be opened up within two years by
Tony Elliott's *Time Out*.

Charles Marovitz in *It* had not been the only reviewer from the
left dissatisfied with the Royal Shakespeare Company's *US* on the
Vietnam war. In *Town* Ali, too, slammed the play for failing to take
sides. In his memoir of the 1960s Ali records how, following the
review, Goodwin rang him, they met for lunch, and the literary
agent explained that he wanted to start the new paper. After the
Dialectics of Liberation another meeting was called, more people
were drawn in, and the need to raise money was stressed. Adrian
Mitchell, the poet, who had supported *It*, was there, so was his
fellow poet Christopher Logue, Kenneth Tynan, and the television
producer Roger Smith. The plans began to take shape.

An editor was found, D.A.N. Jones, the *Listener*'s drama critic.
Another Oxford graduate, but from the lower middle class, Jones
had apparently the right socialist credentials, but his activism
centred on his local south-London Labour Party. As 1968 dawned
and events accelerated Jones's politics began to skew from those of
his co-founders.

Sheila Rowbotham had taken a different route after graduation
from Oxford in 1962. She was teaching, living in Hackney, and, as a
member of the Labour Party's Young Socialists, became involved in
the internecine battles between the Trotskyist groups then active
within the Party. She had also started working for Agitprop, a
loosely based collective operating off the Euston Road and
concerned with posters, street theatre, action. But she kept in touch
with Tariq Ali. Indeed, his position as *Town*'s theatre critic meant
that she was getting some evenings out free as well. Then, early in
1968, Tariq Ali rang her; the new paper was going to be produced.
Was she interested? At the beginning of May the revised May Day
Manifesto was launched at Camden Town Hall, on a sunny
Saturday afternoon which wasn't matched by the tempers or
harmony of the participants.

Ali introduced Rowbotham to Goodwin. That evening the three
of them went out to dinner, and they got on. Rowbotham the
middle-class woman from Leeds, involved in local politics, Vietnam
action, and drifting towards the International Socialists; Ali the
upper-class Pakistani Oxford graduate moving towards the International Marxist Group; Goodwin the working-class boy made
good.

Through Agitprop Rowbotham had extended out of Hackney.
Vietnam activism meant contact with the Stoppit Committee,
founded by Americans based in London. They were different. The
politics she had encountered had been trades councils and Young

Socialist meetings; the Americans wore beads, mumbled, talked about direct action. And Goodwin was different too, with his emphasis on professionalism, and his links with those other people, older than her, who had moved into the mainstream media. It was not a world she wanted, but it was interesting, different. Goodwin, with his contacts, was a bridge, and for him Rowbotham, with her concern with grassroots activity, was an entry into another world too.

Others came into the new paper. David Mercer joined the editorial board; so did Mo Teitlebaum, involved in TV, the poet Adrian Mitchell, looking for rather more than *It* could offer, and Robin Fior, a designer. Offices were found, the *Black Dwarf* was born, and based in the *New Left Review*'s premises in Carlisle Street, round the corner from the old Partisan coffee bar of the early 1960s. The title came from the nineteenth-century paper produced by the Chartists that had combined satire with working-class reportage. Perhaps it too, thought Rowbotham would be able to reach back and tap that radical tradition.

The Powell speech and the dockers' march triggered a response. Partly through Agitprop and partly through the *Black Dwarf* group a free-sheet was produced to be handed out on the dockers' march. Despite the hostility of the right-wing core of the march the sheet went well. And there were other things to cheer the leafleters: Paris, and the May Events.

The sacking of Henri Langlois from the Cinémathèque had, curiously, been a sign of things to come in Paris. Langlois's sacking didn't shake the state, but it created concern. So did events at Nanterre, a concrete campus of a university on the outskirts of Paris. Surrounded by the slums of Portugese and Arab immigrants, the campus drew its students from the middle classes, but did so under an authoritarian system of education that seemed hardly to have changed in 150 years. The underground – as it had developed in the United States and Britain – was unknown. But Vietnam wasn't, nor was overcrowding, nor petty restrictions. The shooting in Germany of Rudi Dutskche by a right-wing extremist triggered protest amongst Paris's student population. They gathered in the Latin Quarter in their thousands. In comparison with British students, the French were larger in number, and paid – if at all – badly.

In the wake of Dutskche's wounding in Berlin the Nanterre students descended on the Sorbonne, the ancient university of Paris. The 'Mouvement du 22 Mars' had begun to take on a momentum of its own, as April turned into May. Pitched battles took place between the students and the police in the narrow streets around the Sorbonne. Liberal opinion began to waver as the extent of the violence was revealed on newsreels, on television, in *Paris*

Match, across the globe. The students went out from the campuses into the factories, to be greeted, initially, by hostile Communist officials and puzzled workers, but the agitation continued, the slogans proliferated.

'Be a realist, demand the impossible.'

'I take my desire for reality, because I believe in the reality of my desires.'

'The general will against the will of the General.'

'To bargain is to capitulate.'

'Run forward comrade, the old world is behind you.'

'Freedom is the consciousness of our desires.'

'When the last capitalist will be hanged with the guts of the last reformist, humanity will be happy.'

And the agitation worked: workers became realists, initiated the general will, refused to bargain, and ran forward towards freedom. What had started as a movement of rich kids in a concrete jungle seized the imagination of urban workers in an efficient, technocratic state, being hailed, in a *Times* series that appeared the week the revolt became widespread, as the very model of a modern major power.

On 13 May the Communist Party shifted under the pressure of a general strike, on 17 May Renault was occupied. The day after, General de Gaulle cut short his visit to Rumania and returned to Paris; by then two million workers were on strike, 120 factories occupied; within three days 250 factories were occupied, and eight million on strike. De Gaulle visited his, hopefully, loyal troops in Germany; tanks were reported on the outskirts of Paris. The ruling Gaullists and the Communists alike were in danger of cracking under the strain of the May Events. The Communists put in for wage rises, holiday increases; a new cabinet was formed, Prime Minister Pompidou offered deals, new talks; the strikes continued, but dwindled in number.

Car workers, astronomers, TV producers, students, transport workers, strippers, began to reassess; demoralization crept across the strike zones. By 6 June the metro had started running again. A day later the Renault workers were evicted from their plant at Flins, as 2,000 riot police, the CRS, held back solidarity demonstrations. Slowly the tide turned. By 12 June the authorities felt confident enough to ban all demonstrations, yet only four days later the students, still fighting, battled with the police around the Sorbonne. Then, with the collapse of the revolt, new elections took place between 23 and 30 June. De Gaulle was swept back to power. The events were over, but their impact shook Europe that year and echoed down the decade that followed. The Emperor did indeed have no clothes, and, when challenged, would run.

Everybody within the radical/underground milieu had something to say, to learn, to argue about from the May Events. It wasn't a proper revolution, argued disgruntled, orthodox Communists, it had been a bunch of rich kids. 'Revolution is the festival of the oppressed', came the rejoinder from other Marxists, quoting Lenin. Eighteen years later Jean Genet commented that he could see the revolution couldn't work after a visit to the Odéon, occupied by students and workers. Speakers would take it in turn to speak, would be applauded, and would return to the auditorium to applaud more speakers, more poseurs. This wasn't serious, he suggested; serious revolutionaries would take the banks, the stock exchange, which was fired, the broadcasting stations. It had been theatre.

Maybe. But it was theatre which sucked in an eager audience across the channel. *Oz* produced a Martin Sharp-designed 'special' for distribution in Paris. *It32* appeared as a 'Special Rush Paris Alternative Society Now' edition, for 1/6d (7½p) in London, but in Paris it was free. Inside, Robert Tasher, Sue Haussmann, and Mike Lesser reported, in appropriately breathless terms, and in dayglo scarlet, on the situation, via an interview with Jacques Tarnero of the Mouvement du 22 Mars. 'We need money', Tarnero told *It*. 'We have no money to buy gas masks. We have no money to buy dressings for the wounded. We have no money to buy paper to print pamphlets.' It was a rush-job from *It*, complete with copy stripped on to the pages with uncorrected passages hastily crossed out – but it was immediate.

The May Events marked the chasm within the underground, and as the comrades – or would-be comrades – ran forward it became obvious that much of the old American guard on *It* had become part of the world left behind. They were a generation for whom Beats, jazz, art, and existentialism was what Paris was really about, not the hedonistic, free-spirited outburst of the revolution.

Not so for Dave Robins. Suddenly his status as a student was no longer something to be concealed, it was part of his consciousness. 'Socialism was back on the agenda', he points out. 'I went to Paris and I saw with my own eyes – either that or I was young and I dreamt it all – workers and students and young people together, fighting, helping each other – socialism was on the streets.'

On 5 June the opportunistic hope of American liberalism, Robert Kennedy, was assassinated in California. In London the Ronan Point tower block collapsed, taking with it the certainties of high-rise technocratic change of the early 1960s. Later in June Valerie Solanas, an *habitué* with Wilcock of the New York Factory, shot Andy Warhol. He was having too much influence on her life, she explained. Suddenly her 'Society for Cutting Up Men' *SCUM Manifesto* became popular reading, if regarded as eccentric, on women's oppression, but interesting none the less. In *Oz13* and *It33* a letter from a 'surrealist group' including jazz singer/writer George Melly was published giving twenty-one reasons why they needed 'Danny the Red' Cohn-Bendit, the media's nominee for 'leadership' of the May Events. The twenty-first reason was: 'We are very very frightened.'

Interestingly the traditional centres of student power in England yielded their place to two art colleges, at Hornsey and Guildford, which were occupied. 'In the six weeks of the Hornsey revolution', wrote a student the following Christmas in *Revelations* – the Hornsey students' paper – 'I had more education than I had ever previously experienced. A new sort of freedom emerged, a freedom to work, learn, and develop. A new surge of life.'

Other colleges erupted. Essex, one of the new universities born of the last years of Macmilan's rule, was occupied. In Hull a student, Tom Fawthrop, later a fixture on *It* and other underground papers, ripped up his finals papers.

It was a perfect time for the launch of *Black Dwarf*, but there too there were problems. The paper's first deadline had been 15 May 1968, but it became impossible to hit it, and there was, as the May Events washed around the staff, another problem. Jones's politics were more of an older and more traditional left, drawing on roots within the Communist and Labour Party traditions. He produced a *Black Dwarf*, 20,000 were printed, but it wasn't, thought the editorial board, what was wanted. In retrospect, wrote Ali in *Street Fighting Years*, 'it was not so bad as we thought', but it ended up in the incinerator, rather than on the streets. D.A.N. Jones quit, to be replaced by Tariq Ali.

On 1 June the first eight-page issue was finally published. Its page size was bigger than *The Times* and its front-page message summed up, with a tinge of pomposity, a degree of wishful thinking, the hope of the month, and indeed the year: 'We Shall Fight We Will Win Paris London Rome Berlin.'

Rowbotham, meanwhile, had been sucked into the paper, but not on to the editorial board. For her the idea of the working-class orientation was important, but in those months, as the student tide swept on, other priorities dominated. Before its publication Goodwin had sent her off to the British Museum to research the old *Black Dwarf*. She spent two weeks inside and returned with a vast stack of photocopied originals and a bill for the astronomical sum of £25. Goodwin was furious. What, he asked, were the staff supposed to *do* with the photocopies? Other women were drawn on to the paper, but as on *It* they were supposed to know their place. 'We were sent upstairs to address envelopes as "the girls" ', she recalls, 'while Clive got on with the serious business of deciding about the paper. This was a completely assumed division of labour. In the Hackney Young Socialists there was formal recognition that women should be allowed to be the chair, or vice-chair, but in Clive's world women were the secretaries, unless they were very sophisticated cool people.'

When not upstairs, in those early days, Rowbotham, in evangelical mood, was out selling. With the first issue she hitched north to York and on to Hull, where the students were occupying the campus in solidarity with the May Events at first, but rapidly in pursuit of 'One Man – One Vote' within the university. The paper touched a heady mood. She went on to Newcastle, where Goodwin was speaking on local TV about the *Dwarf*, and she was selling the paper at the local anarchist centre, giving it away along the roadside.

The wave swept everywhere. Having tried the Tribe, *It*, by issue 34 in late June, had changed its (official) owners and its designated organization. Out went the Lovebooks set up by Miles and John Hopkins; its new holding company was KNULLAR, which could be, the paper suggested in August, the 'Karmic Neo-Universal League for Liberty and Reality'; but to a Swede, *It* pointed out 'it could mean something entirely different' – 'fuck' to be precise. *It* was now also, in keeping with the times, to be a workers co-operative. Meanwhile Hornsey students moved into the paper to design two covers, and the paper covered the occupation with a two-page feature, next to Steve Abrams's 'Legalize Pot Rally'. Abrams, another American, was the director of the Society of Mental Awareness, SOMA. *It*, partly through Stansill's interest in the possibilities of an alternative economy, and largely through Hopkins's enthusiasm, had triggered the birth of BIT in late May, which aimed to be an information service for the 'community'. Somewhat ironically, by August BIT had got round to recommending the *Daily Telegraph*'s information service as a useful source. Significantly, in August too, *It* was promoting 'a new information publication on what to do and where to go in London, a comprehensive directory of events and places covering clothes, food, help, lectures, exhibitions, groups, jazz/folk clubs, films, theatre, cinema, music, swimming, fairs, puppets, and many other things, telling you how to get there, and what to expect when you arrive'. It cost a shilling (5p) and its name was *Time Out*.

The new magazine was just a folded poster-format sheet. It sold, but it was little-noticed. *Black Dwarf*, because of its size, if nothing else, was. Not that the early issues had learnt anything from the underground. Pictures were almost non-existent, long columns of grey, illegible type propped up its pages. The material in the early issues indicated a group high on advice, but low on the reportage for which at least some of its founders had hoped. Its fourth issue devoted a page to analysis and views of the smaller, 21 July Vietnam demonstration half a page to strike reports from Manchester and London, two pages to a suppressed BBC script on racism, and almost a page to Malcolm X and an excerpt from American black power advocate Julius Lester's *Look Out Whitey*. Huge pages underlined the scarceness of resources, and hot metal setting its distance from the offset litho of *It*, let alone the colour and verve of *Oz*. And while *Black Dwarf* staff might have protested their separateness from the two underground papers, readers in London, and students and hippies elsewhere, would not. All were part of the diffuse, confused, but radical mood of the summer and autumn. Why, even Richard Neville wrote for *Black Dwarf*.

Sheila Rowbotham continued with her belief in the paper as one with a working-class perspective. It wasn't a view that sat easily with the *Dwarf*'s student orientation as the autumn and the new student academic year approached. In July the paper's front page had proclaimed: 'Students: The New Revolutionary Vanguard.' Upon seeing it – some said a question mark had fallen off on its way to printing in North Wales – she sat down and wept. 'I didn't want the students to be', she recalls, 'I didn't really want *anybody* to be, and I certainly didn't think students had any right to be. It was completely against my dream of the *Dwarf* which was going to be this working-class paper.'

The debate continued into the autumn. By then the working class had made it back on to the front page, if only in a supporting role. 'Don't Demand, Occupy', it blazoned, addressing *its* demands to workers in factories and students in schools.

Elsewhere on the left the International Socialists had, that summer, revamped their fortnightly *Labour Worker* into, under Roger Protz, the sharper, more Fleet Street, tabloid-oriented *Socialist Worker*. There was the SLL's bi-weekly *Newsletter*, there were myriad other left papers, and there was the *Dwarf* coming out monthly, and severely underfinanced and understaffed. It did however have commitment and Goodwin's fund-raising abilities. It was his conception, his baby, and for it he would tolerate most things, including his suspicion of Trotskyism – whether of the IMG or IS variety – and of what he may have seen as Rowbotham's 'hippy sentimentality'. But it needed new blood.

One infusion came from Cambridge economist Bob Rowthorne, still nominally a member of the International Socialists, but moving, unfashionably for the time but a precursor of things to come, towards the Communist Party. Ali rang Rowthorne and invited him round, and an invitation to join the editorial board followed. 'This is ridiculous', Rowthorne replied, 'why don't you ask Sheila to join?'

'They probably hadn't seen me', observes Rowbotham, 'because I wasn't as tall as them.'

Thus Rowthorne and Rowbotham joined the editorial board, and thus also a change began on the *Dwarf* which was significantly to affect the development of the underground, and ultimately prove its nemesis.

How could the *Dwarf* expand? That was the question that faced a group gathered in the Carlisle Street offices one Saturday afternoon that autumn. *Socialist Worker* appeared to be soaking up the potential trade union readership, while the audience of students in revolt could dwindle – although with the formation of the Revolutionary Socialists Student Federation there were hopes that the 'new vanguard' might survive to detonate the proletarian uprising. One suggestion was drawn from the experience of the German socialist magazine *Konkret*, part-founded by the later member of the West German urban guerrilla group, the Red Army Faction. Why not, I think *I* suggested, put pin-ups into the paper? There was no point in being *stuffy*; it would attract new readers, show that the paper was iconoclastic, broadminded.

It was the time that the women machinists at Ford had gone on strike for equal pay, a struggle that was to continue, intermittently, for the next eighteen years. It was also the time that the National Joint Action Committee for Women's Equal Rights had been formed. The Ford strikers had been portrayed in the mainstream media as 'petticoat pickets'. Through the IMG Ali had noted that many Trotskyist women had gone into the National Joint Action Committee for Women's Equal Rights (NJACWER). It made Ali susceptible when Rowbotham exploded at the idea of pin-ups. Indeed it had been the combination of Rowthorne's suggestion and her fury over the pin-up issue which saw her on to the editorial board.

By then an issue on women's rights was already in the planning stage. In the United States the women's liberation movement was beginning to emerge. Not so in Britain. Back in 1966 Juliet Mitchell had opened the question with her article, 'Women: the longest revolution' in the *New Left Review*, but few had noticed, and its impact had been slight. Women, increasingly, were engaged in industrial struggle: at Ford in Hull with Lil Bilocca's fishermen's wives. The underground press survived on female labour, but it remained out of the limelight; the Sue Smalls, Caroline McKechnies, 'Hamburger Sues', Madeleine Neesons, Louise Ferriers, Marsha Rowes; and on the *Black Dwarf* Sheila Rowbotham and Anne Scott, who, at 17, was secretary, organizer, and dogsbody.

The mover behind the women's rights issue had been Fred Halliday, another cross-over from the *New Left Review*. Halliday had read the works of Wilhelm Reich, the German Freudian/

Marxist psychologist-cum-sexual revolutionary whose works were by then rivalling Laing's in the attention they were receiving across the revolutionary left and the underground. The difference being that Laing was alive and living in London and Inner Space, while Reich had killed himself fifteen years before in the United States. Halliday had not been greatly inspired by the prospect of the women's issue, and increasingly Rowbotham took over its organization. The future Labour MP Audrey Wise provided 'Equal Pay Is Not Enough'; through her contacts with the Institute of Workers Control's Tony Topham in Hull, material on Bilocca arrived. Anne Scott wrote her first piece – on contraception – and a woman whom Rowbotham had met wrote a description of what it was like being an unmarried mother. A description of what it was like being a female secretary in a male-dominated office received much attention, and much fury and hilarity when it was realized that the office being described was that of the *New Left Review*. And Rowbotham wrote a piece based on her feelings as the *annus mirabilis* of 1968 drew to a conclusion.

Her article was to go far. It was reproduced in the Boston underground paper, and the following year, when Jean Luc Godard came to England to film *British Sounds*, Rowbotham read it over the soundtrack. Godard's intention had been to accompany the reading with its author descending stairs, naked, in order to contront the viewer, it was assumed, with the contrast between argument, theory, and the sexual objectification of women. But she declined. She felt, vaguely, that it wasn't the right feminist thing to do, but also, she suspected, vanity came into it.

Robin Fior had left, and a new designer had arrived. Contacts between the revolutionary left and the rest of the underground continued, so who better than a designer who had worked for *Oz*? 'When I saw the design', remembers Rowbotham, 'I went bananas.' It graphically illustrated the arguments in a style which left little of the arguments, and a lot of dubious illustration. 'I suppose he thought it was boring stuff about equal pay and women', she says, 'I went berserk. Tariq, to his credit, said we should take out as many pictures as we could, and taking them out cost £70 which at that time was ever such a lot of money.'

The *Black Dwarf* had, via another route, made news outside its normal orbit. Working with Rowbotham on Agitprop had been John Hoyland. Coming from a Communist family background in the early 1960s, the pull of the underground – and a trip to South America – had sucked him away from politics. The war in Vietnam pulled him back, and into Agitprop's poster work. It was the year that the Beatles released 'Revolution', a record one American critic charged would be suitable for the Democratic Party's 1968 platform, with Lennon's put-downs of people who went talking of

Chairman Mao and weren't going to make it anyhow. From his eyrie in Euston Road, and through the *Black Dwarf*, Hoyland wrote an open letter to Lennon challenging his views, with all of 1968's radical fervour. The system poisoned people, said Hoyland, so it had to be destroyed. To Hoyland and the *Black Dwarf*'s gratification, Lennon wrote back. You knock down the system, retorted the grand Beatle, and we will build around it. It was an instant when the *Dwarf* found out what it was like to be one of the beautiful people. 'When I read it now', says Hoyland, 'I blush with shame, it was so patronizing. Basically it said "John Lennon, why are you such a hippy, why aren't you a revolutionary?" It got noticed.' It also got Hoyland an invitation, which he accepted, to join *Black Dwarf*.

The promise of 1968 had begun to fade before the year had ended. After the violent climax to the 17 March Vietnam demonstration, and the anticlimax of the July action, intense organization went into the march planned for 27 October. It was to be the largest march ever organized by the Vietnam Solidarity Campaign, with profuse pre-publicity, and an obliging media reaction – talking of 'revolutionary threats', and Home Secretary James Callaghan being quizzed on television as to whether the gathering should be banned. Callaghan presented his reasonable, unflappable, policeman-on-the-beat face to the nation, and said that it shouldn't. He was right. So successful were the organizers in *organizing* that the spontaneity of the demonstration quite drained away, and a vast crowd marched around central London and marched away again.

'How do we feel now', asked Peter Stansill in *It*, 'in these first strange cold days of our next winter, having just had our minds raped by rationality? . . . . No banner represented a frontal conceptual attack on established mediocrity and habitual thinking – with the exception of the International Situationist banner which read: "Storm the Reality Studios: Retake the Universe". Where were the cosmic slogans of the non-causes and non-movements? "Victory to Ecstasy!" "Liberate the Global Consciousness!" Where were the people demonstrating the embryonic reality of a cybernetic age, an Aquarian age?'

Cold winter maybe, but it had been a long summer that ended that afternoon, from Powell, through the May Events and, at the end of August, the Soviet invasion of Czechoslovakia, which had again pulled the demonstrators on to the streets, but on this occasion down to Notting Hill and Olympia, the homes of the Czech and Soviet embassies, and an ill-timed eastern bloc trade exhibition. Across the Atlantic the riots had continued, and, even as the Red Army moved into Prague, Mayor Daley's police force was in pitched battle with demonstrators outside the Democratic Party's convention. Eight men were to be charged the following March with conspiracy in Chicago, and it was to provide a *cause célèbre* by proxy for the British radical movements.

Unrealized at the time, 1968 was *It*'s highpoint. Behind it lay the Anglo-American fusion that had powered the paper in 1966 and through the first eighteen months. In the year of revolutionary upheaval *It* had seen some of its predictions fulfilled, and a movement created which, as it developed, had less and less to do with the first publication out of the underground. In the autumn *It* moved to offices in Endell Street, still in Covent Garden. Although the staff had not appreciated it, the listings of London events were quite crucial, and had given *It* a stranglehold on the London market, which was to be broken. While UFO had gone, Middle Earth continued in Covent Garden, and the Arts Lab continued, even if the beautiful people were getting shabbier, and the dossers beginning to arrive. In November a fracas developed between two factions within the Lab, but Haynes and Moore remained.

Colour had crept unsteadily on to *It*'s pages, and the paper reported in its second birthday issue that 'hopes of a permanent 24-page *It* have had to be tempered with reality otherwise we would find ourselves expanding into debt.' The paper had to wait, *It* announced, 'until our much talked about "profits" materialize in the form of hard cash.'

On the facing page Peter Stansill ruminated on the meaning of the second birthday: 'most of us are roaming through 1968 internally screaming and writhing in the wilderness of our various human relationships. Things are as sordid as ever.' It was an indication of *It* facing both ways, torn between a youth culture stumbling around politics and the embers of 1967. 'Overwhelming negativity marked this year off from the last', he observed, '. . . the real revolution is poetry, the revolution is in your mind.'

Up to a point. The swelling letters pages were occupied with responses to Michael Eaves, a correspondent who had suggested axing the 'What's Happening' section, record reviews, and ads from the paper – which would have neatly killed it some years before its time – led by a contribution from one of *It*'s founders, David Mairowitz, 'who broke his b***s [asterisks his] seeing that *It 1–10* got put together and printed.' 'Established cinemas, theatres etc. . . . exist in the police universe to repress the very things that *It* stands for. Michael's letter refers very nicely to "export-oriented consumed-productivity bullshit" and it's all there *It* . . . Live *It*. We need you. Everybody loves you, even me and Michael Eaves. But we don't need or love you as an organ gone sour that stinks in the wind. We need you to attack, to rape and plunder, shout and rage, dance and sing all over the graves of bad faith mongers. Look to it, *It*, on this your glorious second birthday. Be beautiful, but don't be too nice.'

Being confused was more *It*'s line, but not *Oz*'s eclectic blend, mediated through Neville's editing. *It* faced in fifty-seven directions at once, but kept from the old American contingent, and from the anarchic underground, dislike of any political organization, a terror of being bored, or boring, and a tendency, at times, to be both, and incomprehensible with it. What did remain in that paper, that year, was a hankering after what had survived from 1967, exemplified in the prose of John Peel. With the effective collapse of the offshore pirate radio stations in 1967 Peel had come ashore and been swallowed within the recesses of Broadcasting House, and its bastard infant, Radio One. From there he sallied forth to the underground, and by 1969 got profiled in the *Listener* as the aesthetic end of the underground, and the acceptable face of pop. Peel's sense of self-parody could sometimes get submerged in the column he contributed to *It*. 'I have just been given a flower – the second in two weeks', he told readers in the birthday issue column. 'I love you so much.'

But not so much as the readers and staff of *Gandalf's Garden*. While the first issue of *Black Dwarf* was being planned, across London its diametrical opposite was taking shape. Back in February 1967 John Michell, the ley-lines and saucers correspondent of *It*, wrote to the paper, explaining his concern with *It*'s 'interest in political forms of thought and protest. . . . We must reject political influences in every field. The great centre which Michael Abdul Malik will build will not be, or look like a political centre. It will be white with a god-like figure like those Tibetan Buddhist temples which reflect the old vision of the winged disc and prepare us for the new. It will be "religious" in that it will appeal directly to people's dreams and real desires, not to greed or the lust for irrelevant political power.'

When Michael Abdul Malik's centre – the 'Black House' in north London's forbidding Holloway Road – was established eighteen months later, the god-like figure was missing. So too, by then, was *Gandalf's Garden*. Founded by Muz Murray, who was featured on the first issue's cover breaking out of an egg, *Gandalf's Garden* distilled the essence of the time's peace, love, mysticism, and delusion. While *Black Dwarf* could trace its roots back, through Trotsky to Marx, or through radicalism to the Chartists, *Gandalf's Garden* took as its theoretical base – if theoretical is the right word – J.R.R. Tolkien's *Lord of the Rings*, and tended to see the unfortunate Peel as its prophet. It was to be a monthly, the first issue announced, while the second qualified the assertion into a 'monthlyish periodical published for people with love'. By issue four a fifth issue was promised 'when the weather is right'. The weather turned out to be right, for the last time, in November 1969, when, promoting the shop which accompanied the publication, it was announced that: 'The garden is not just a magazine and shoppe set-up, but a dedicated life-style.'

During its short life *Gandalf's Garden* evolved a style which made *It*, *Oz*, and the others that were to come later models of detachment and worldliness. Published at first from W8 the paper developed its shop-cum-'spiritual oasis' at World's End in Chelsea. The first issue interviewed Tyrannosaurus Rex, a band which, in their hippy phase, and before their reappearance as a chart group, T. Rex, had long been popular with Peel. 'Out of the land of legends comes the sound of the Tyrannosaurus Rex, awoken in the incredible voice of Marc Bolan (of Elfin descent) and hairy-toed Steve Peregrin Took', breathed the introduction. Bolan himself, setting the standards for pop's comments on the other world and philosophical observation for the underground, observed that 'Christ must have been a gas. I think he was a very turned-on guy and very much with God. God is the coolest thing of all. I think if I'm just a splinter out of his head, then he must have been a bit like me, not much though.'

Yet the times continued to breed strange bedfellows. Peter Fryer, the *Daily Worker*'s 1956 correspondent, wrote in, commending the paper; the jazz musician Cy Laurie contributed on the Maharishi; and Timothy Leary, fulfilling his papal role, announced that 'We have received your wonderful *Garden*. . . . It is sweet and good. . . . It will bloom, blossom and perfume the planet.'

It was *Gandalf's Garden*'s task to carry, assisted by divine and hobbit hands, the purest expression of the hippy philosophy across the city, and country. It did, on occasions, meet with approval, but, largely, within the underground with incredulity. But, as Muz Murray pointed out to Bristol's Occult Bookshop's Robert Gilbert who had been attacking other underground papers, it was wrong to be too hard on the others. 'They may seem Mordor-made', he explained in the letters column, 'because of rendering unto Caesar what is Caesar's – uncovering society's hypocritical filth and throwing it back in its teeth. But the real problem is that no matter how reactionary their articles seem to be the writers still tend to be enmeshed in the thought patterns of the Straightworld even when deriding it, which can only work like walking on a treadmill towards the new World. Even so they are still honestly doing their thing from the only angle they understand.'

But Straightworld proved closer than Murray thought, in 1969, and a tough place for hobbits, and others.

Chapter 8

The hell of it

Jann Wenner in 1967 was living in San Francisco, and enthusiastic about rock 'n' roll. It was the city of the summer of love, the San Francisco Mime Troupe, the *Oracle*'s bizarre psychedelic graphics and ultra-hippy prose, the Diggers, and Haight-Ashbury. In November it also became the birthplace of *Rolling Stone* magazine.

Rolling Stone was a serious paper about rock. So serious on many occasions that it subsided into ponderousness, pretentiousness, and treated the subject as life-style, liberation, and meaning of life. It also produced some of the best journalism *on* the underground – and the above ground – written in the 1960s. The *Fortune* magazine of the rock era, it made Wenner a fortune.

By 1968 it had begun to appear in Britain. Its format was unconventional: a folded-over tabloid with the cover printed A4 size on the fold. But its design, contrasted with underground papers, was conservative.

A stack of copies was piled up at the entrance to the Arts Lab. Some people even bought it, and often assumed, wrongly, that the paper was connected with the Rolling Stones. This annoyed Mick Jagger, who felt that, since the paper was called *Rolling Stone*, it should have a connection with him, if not the band. So it was in March 1969 that an English edition of the magazine hit the newsstands. Wenner's idea was simple. London, like San Francisco, Chicago, and New York, was a rock city. Thus London *Rolling Stone*'s product could be fed back to the West Coast parent. Autonomy for the London staff was not one of his priorities, but a connection with Jagger was, so the paper was, initially, based at the Rolling Stones' offices in Maddox Street, Mayfair. By early summer it had moved to still more opulent quarters in Hanover Square.

It appeared to have arrived at the right time. 1969 was the year that rock festivals took off in Britain, and exploded into celluloid myth – and real murder – in the United States. True since the early 1960s the British had gathered in wet fields to hear jazz, and rock and the movie *Jazz: On A Summer's Day* with its tantalizing performance by Chuck Berry helped break the hold of cool on popular music. And then there had been the Pennebaker film *Monterey Pop* of the 1967 festival in California, complete with Janis Joplin and Jimi Hendrix.

1968 had seen an outbreak of small festivals, with even a fair-sized event (12,000) on the Isle of Wight. But then in 1969, following the break-up of Cream, the three-man band for rock fans with artistic aspirations, came the formation of Blind Faith: Ginger Baker, Eric Clapton, Ric Grech, and Steve Winwood. Its short history provided one album, denounced for a dubious cover by the popular press, and a huge concert in Hyde Park in early June. The success of Blind Faith's concert encouraged the Rolling Stones to try the same trick, and, come 5 July, three days after the death of the band's Brian Jones, Jagger *et al.* filled the park with a crowd estimated at between 250,000 and 500,000. Then, at the end of August, came, in the United States, Woodstock, and in Britain, Bob Dylan on the Isle of Wight.

Both were huge, one, Woodstock, was filmed. While the Rolling Stones had sucked the counter-culture, hell's angels, hippies, street theatres, and rock fans into the park for a day, the Isle of Wight created an encampment that lasted a week, and peaked, for good and ill, for three days.

Alongside the festivals, the dalliance of the music business with the counter-culture pumped more money into the underground press than ever before. With the cash came a new direction for much of that press, *Rolling Stone* or – as quickly was to happen in London – no *Rolling Stone*.

For Mark Williams the appeal of fund raising for the Birmingham Arts Lab palled in 1968. He and the residue of the small group around the lab organized all night 'mixed media' events entitled, in keeping with the times, 'Strange Daze' to raise money. All the right bands came – Love Sculpture, the Nice, Family – and, he remembers, 'various acid-crazed hippies performed what might obliquely be termed experimental music'. But no funds were raised, money was often lost. The living was easy, and based in a squat, since Williams had abandoned his ad agency. The flak increased on the project as it lurched on, directed from the local authority and the local arts centre. And the pressure was getting to him. Meanwhile his sales of *It* continued as a profitable sideline. Life was too tame, while the world depicted by *Oz* and *It* was exciting. In 1968 he visited *It*. He had been sending in listings, even reports, on the gigs they had been running in Birmingham. To his surprise they offered him a job as music editor. He was out of Birmingham; not only that, he got himself space on the floor of a flat above the Two 'I's coffee bar in Old Compton Street. Things, he reflected, had worked out well.

There were problems. One was that Williams knew nothing about *being* a music editor. What was one supposed to do? How was one supposed to cut copy? To spell? Peter Stansill provided the bare essentials, and Williams, hurriedly schooled in the importance of deadlines, learnt on the job. And *It*, with the growing new rock culture as a new fixture within the magazine, appeared to be doing well.

'Where is *It* at now?' So asked the paper's business manager Dave Hall in February 1969. 'Rumours are going around about the bread *It* is making, the increase in circulation, the increase in ads, and yet that cat is still hustling for bread.'

It's circulation was peaking as it reached its fiftieth edition. Despite dire tales of distribution being ripped off outside the paper, figures of 50,000 sales were being quoted, and 40,000 was probably being touched. From a paper selling to dissident literati and the children of CND *It* was extending out to a new rock culture, and this accelerated the departure of the old American influences. New transatlantic currents were making themselves felt. In March the Californian Governor Ronald Reagan cordoned off dissident Berkeley, and the US remained convulsed by the war in Vietnam. But the aftermath of the European Events of May 1968 still made waves, and the politics of papers like the *Black Dwarf* meant that alongside *It*'s report of American Ed Berman's Inter Action and its development as a 'community arts centre' were stories of 'Communications for a Revolutionary Europe and World', and reports from Prague under Soviet occupation.

Another issue was creeping into the paper. In *It52* Lee Harris reported on a new play by Jane Arden at the Arts Lab. *Vagina Rex and the Gas Oven*, reported Harris, indicated that women were 'in a prison of their own making, they are the continual affirmation of man's potency.'

They were, and just as much within the underground as outside it. Apart from providing substantial contingents of foot soldiers for the papers they, as 'chicks', provided a *raison d'être* as madonna/whore/'old ladies' for men. 'There are times when beautiful women come like food to the starving', wrote Jeff Nuttall in *Bomb Culture*, first published in 1968. 'Not to hold or make love to or talk to, but just to be there with their lovely hair and breasts, with their peaceful flesh.' Having established a role for women – beautiful and otherwise – Nuttall went on to ask: 'Can we apply a quivering phallic strength to our civic organization and our economy?' Nuttall was no better – or worse – than the rest of the men within the underground milieu in his choice of language. It was just that the straight world's men, from Strategic Air Command to the invaders of Prague, seemed to think along similar lines, if leading to different ends. Which underlined the significance of Harris's note of Arden's play in February 1969. By October Arden was being interviewed. 'Meeting her', reported the interviewer to his male (presumably) compatriots 'shocked me into realizing how little we normally expect from women.'

Indeed. 'Women, learn to give of yourselves a bit more (with adequate contraception)', suggested Emmanuel Petrakis in *It50*. 'Even if you don't enjoy it at first, why not give pleasure to others? Given time, you might learn to enjoy the experience.' Petrakis went on to urge men to remember 'that a woman is a human being with feelings too, not just a cosy hole'.

This was too much even for men still undisturbed by the first stirrings of the women's movement. An angry reader, Ian Phipps, replied, displaying in his language that he too was having problems in moving from being part of *the* problem to the solution. *It* was 'nothing more than a clearing house for sexually disturbed cranks, the biggest of whom is Emmanuel Petrakis. . . . Young chicks who genuinely want to be part of, and help develop, the scene will swallow his rubbish (coming from the leading headpaper) and will soon be mentally and physically ruined and incapable of normal deep feelings.'

Young chicks were soon, within the underground, to have other possibilities. But, meanwhile, on *It* they still provided the back-up. For Sue Small this meant working on ads and compiling the 'What's Happening' listings section at the back of the paper. 'Editorial', she notes, 'didn't regard it as important, otherwise they wouldn't have let me do it.' And, she adds, she had no knowledge of the arts scene.

But listings, plus music, plus music ads were the backbone of *It*'s success in that period. Yet the staff hadn't realized it, and nor had some of the readers. 'Over the last four or five months we've become static and a little stale', said a March 1969 editorial under the headline 'What we want to hear from you'. What the staff got on 28 April was a second police raid. The move had been preceded by police visits to the printers of *It*, *Oz*, and *Rolling Stone*. 'The heat's now really on for *It*, *Oz* and possibly *Rolling Stone*', claimed the lead in *It56*. 'If you want revolution – sexual freedom, freedom of thought, freedom to discover who you really are – in short, if you want a new world and won't settle for less, then these journals are your only overt communications media.'

The raid was eventually followed by prosecution and, the following January, by court appearances for Dave Hall, Graham Keen, and Peter Stansill. And the police, disregarding the reds, heads, freaks, revolution, and rock at the front of the paper, made their target the gay contact personal ads at the back. The charge was that the trio had 'conspired with persons inserting ads and with other persons to induce readers to resort to the said advertisements for the purposes of homosexual practices and thinking to debauch and corrupt public morals contrary to common law.' A side order was a charge of 'conspiring to outrage public decency'.

'Don't compromise', urged CBS record ads in the *It*s of the time, 'because the music doesn't.' It might have been a suitable sales pitch for conglomerates shifting Blood Sweat & Tears albums; it produced some qualms amongst *It* staffers and others. At the newborn London *Rolling Stone*, editor (short-lived) Jane Nicholson was at pains to point out that the paper wasn't, in any way, 'underground'.

'Poor baby, it's awful to be so misunderstood', slammed Germaine Greer in *Oz22*. 'You just want to talk about music and fucking and dope and that's all. We know you have no intention of overthrowing the Vichy government. Nothing is clearer than that the English *Rolling Stone* presents no threat to any political institution of any kind.'

Greer's onslaught was rewarded with a reply from *Rolling Stone*'s Gene Mahon replete with the fashionable vocabulary of the times. 'Revolution is a happening thing', he admonished. 'I hope you won't be stuck in your bag of "defending" the underground; like the man said, let's make it for the hell of it.'

Over in Hanover Square, as Wenner began to pull the rug on his London venture the 'hell of it' was getting the upper hand. Back in Endell Street queasiness set in with the raid's aftermath yet it blended with a certain sense of excitement. 'There was a feeling', observes Small, 'that we must be doing something right.'

They weren't sure what it was. 'Everyone was very worried', recalls Mark Williams, 'but very shortly after that an attitude prevailed that: "Oh well this is the way the man acts and we are above all this, it's a joke." Whenever there was any adversity with the law there was this not quite convincing idea put about that this is the way that society works and we shouldn't take it too seriously. But I don't think anyone was *totally* convinced by that.'

Music should have sold *It*. Listings should have sold *It*. And they did, but there were problems, internal and external.

The centre of the paper, under Williams's editorship, had become the 'Plug and socket' section. He lacked the apparent knowledge, or confidence in the political verities displayed by what he saw as the heavyweight end of the editorial group, and friction occasionally surfaced. But it was the music that was bringing in the advertising, and maybe the extra readers. An uneasy balance was maintained. Outside readers could thumb through the paper and brood on the bread that was doubtless being baked and stashed away by the one-time cultural revolutionaries of *It*.

The conflict between commerce and commitment, music and movements, had resonances elsewhere. *It* got a lot of visitors, passing heads, the curious, the indigent, the bombed out, the Hell's Angels. In the early summer of 1968 a Keele University student and his friend passed through.

'Bill Levy had really originated the idea of the "25-hour city" ', says David Robins. That, later as 'What's Happening' under Sue Small and others, was *It*'s key product. 'We were stupid enough to think that people wanted long and boring articles about sex', he remembers, 'how wrong we were.'

Amongst Robins's acquaintances was Robert (Bob) Harris, whom Robins had got to know when he came down from Keele and worked with him on *Circuit*. Harris's companion had also visited *It* before. Tony Elliott had just finished his third year at Keele University and was preparing to spend a year in France as part of his four-year French and History degree course. But magazines had already begun to fascinate him. At Keele he had edited the student *Unit*, with the future *Time Out* and *City Limits* editor John Fordham as deputy editor. It aimed to be an arts magazine, and had, in the autumn of 1967, produced a special on the underground. And the arrival of the first *It*s had inspired him, as it had Williams in Birmingham and Lloyd in Edinburgh. He offered to sell it on the Keele campus. Selling fifty or sixty issues a time proved to be good business. 'And I was probably one of the few people who ever paid *It*', he suggests. Elliott's interest was avant-garde culture and *It* seemed, almost, ideal. It had rudimentary listings of events, it had previews, but it didn't really have *enough*.

The visit that afternoon was a vague affair. Being in London, and still with the idea of returning to Keele, Elliott wanted to sound out an idea. The information at the back of *It* wasn't really adequate. 'If they had turned round and said to me, "That's a good idea, why don't you do it for us here?" I would have done it', says Elliott. 'I had no definite idea that a new magazine could be something I could live off.'

But they didn't. 'We poo-pooed it', says Robins. 'Stansill said that a magazine would never last. We looked down our noses at this pair of student hicks. But Elliott was shrewd. He realized that listings were what people liked about *It*. That was *very* smart.'

And there were other factors. *It*, like the rest of the underground, encouraged new papers. Starting more was to be one of its responses to the April 1969 police raid. Around the country small groups were doing just that. Alternative information services were another obsession of the times, hence John Hopkins's Bit.

So Elliott and Harris went away with their idea. It was to be a modest little magazine devoted to telling London what was going on. The underground had indeed developed its own theatre, music, and politics. Perhaps alongside giants like *Oz* and *It* there was room for an A5-sized fold-out paper devoted exclusively to listings. And he got other encouragements. At a new universities festival in Bradford he had run into Richard Neville. That summer they renewed the acquaintanceship in a coffee bar in Kensington. 'If you get this into W.H. Smith's', observed the Australian, 'put your name down for a Rolls-Royce immediately.'

It didn't work out that way, that fast. They thought about distribution, and Harris went to see Brian Moore whose Moore-Harness operation had put *Private Eye* on the road to money. By then a title had been decided on, they had thought of *Where It's At*, right for the times, but wrong for any *other* time. Idly scanning an LP cover Elliott's eye was caught by two words, 'time out', and *Time Out* it became. At Moore-Harness Harris received an unequivocal reply. The pornography squad had just visited Brian Moore and warned him that if he took a new 'adult contact' magazine, *Way Out*, the law would move, fast. Hearing the word 'Out' Moore wasted no time, and without scanning the new publication flung the bemused future disc jockey into the street.

Thus in the initial stages Elliott and Harris were flung on their own resources. Around £100 was raised as start-up capital. The staff was small: Harris, Elliott's then girlfriend Stephanie Hughes, and Elliott himself. Potential sympathizers were rung for assistance. Activism was obviously important, so Sheila Rowbotham was contacted for help with the 'Meet the Fuzz' section. Over at Bit Jane de Mendelsohn was *in situ*. She and her husband Felix had been around the London underground since its birth, apart from a sojourn in the backwater of Munich. In London she had been one of the founding members of Bit. A regular caller was Richard Branson, working on an obscure student magazine. Another was Elliott who explained that he needed access to information, from 'A' to 'Z'. That was what Bit provided, and she did.

In August 1968 Elliott-Harris Publications, operating out of Elliott's flat, had produced the first edition. It was indeed insignificant: a single large sheet, folded into an A5 format, with an abstract cover design courtesy of 'Cybernetic Serendipity', a heavy reliance on Letraset and a primitive lay-out. The first *Time Out* covered 12 August to 2 September 1968.

Over at *Oz*, busy producing their Agit *Oz* issue, a little ad for Elliott's plucky little venture was included. Another feature was by Clive James. It denounced the purposelessness and anarchy of the underground. 'I *still* think', he observed, 'on present showing they have their own doom built in.'

The underground, still high on festivals, fuzz, and activism hadn't noticed. With the first issue of *Time Out* finished, Elliott went back to *It*. 'He came in with this folded mag', remembers Sue Small. 'I think I was quite patronizing. I said "jolly good luck, and if you need any help from me, don't hesitate to call".'

In the 23 August 1968 issue of *It* the plug was provided, next to news that Knullar had taken over the *It* workers' co-operative. '*Time Out* is a new information publication on what to do and where to go in London', *It* explained.

It was fat and 1/6d (7½p); *Time Out* was 1/- (5p) wafer-thin, devoid of features, but portable. By the third issue in late September it had become a little A5 booklet, to Elliott's distress. He had liked the fold-over format, but printers had disagreed. With the rebuff from Moore, he and Harris had been forced to split west and north London between them and do their own distribution. It had advantages. It meant that a cash flow – an almost unknown concept in the underground – was immediately instituted, and through street sales they gained an instant feedback, instant market research on the product. The results were encouraging. Elliott wrote to Keele and announced that his university career was over.

But there was still no real money. It wasn't until the beginning of 1969 that they realized the paper could provide them with a regular income. Yet by that third issue ads had begun to appear: 'Hung On You', Housmans, the Caledonian Road doyen of pacifist book-shops, the Flying Dragon Tea House, and even a page from Apple, meaning, for the time, big money. By the following issue record reviews had crept in. By the New Year comments were creeping into the film previews, the poetry section was expanding, and permanent offices had been found in Princedale Road, Notting Hill.

Such was the success that Elliott took on an ad manager, John Leaver, then contemplating a nebulous publishing project with another newcomer to London, Felix Dennis. Leaver, then camping out on *Oz* art director Jonathan Goodchild's floor, joined the staff. *Time Out* had effectively sealed *It*'s fate.

Chapter 9

Friends and enemies

In 1968, had the staff of *It* known it, or wanted such a fate, they had the possibility of becoming London's answer to the *Village Voice*. True, they lacked the pipe-smoking liberal American politics of Fancher and Wolf thirteen years before, but they had, briefly, the market, caught on the cusp between the old and the new wave of 1968, and they had the listings. By the summer of 1969 the game was slipping away. *It* was under attack from the law, its sexism was earning it brickbats from sections of the readership, and even the new rock reading section of the market was beginning to note the changes coming over the *NME*.

And then, briefly, in the autumn of 1969 some of the staff, and readers, of the paper took against *It*. An almost unquestioned belief in the street people had long been part of *It*'s rhetoric, with or without the romanticization of the drop-out, from Kerouac through to Emmett Grogan. People just dropped in, even though many had been less than welcome with some of *It*'s staff.

Michael X/Abdul Malik, for example, was respected and liked by some of *It*'s editorial board, such as Bill Levy and Jim Haynes. For Sue Small, on the other hand, he was an 'obnoxious bastard'; for Robins 'a small time Trinidadian criminal with a machete often in the back of his trousers'. But Malik was, supposedly, a man of the people, a black power activist – or the best that London could, in white media terms, offer in that line – and he was taken seriously.

Before the property boom took off in the 1970s there were still cheap flats around in London. But there were also new people arriving in London for whom even cheap property was out of their price range. And there were poor Londoners for whom squatting was the only option. From the mid-1960s the squatting movement had grown. Some squatters were incorporated within the local housing orbit, some weren't. Squatting became part of the rebel ideology, and was sympathetically covered in *It*. Squats were 'repeopling the ghostly empty English houses', noted *It51*. Early in 1969 they also repeopled a ghostly London hotel, the Bell, just up the road from the Arts Lab in Drury Lane. Renamed the 'Genesis Hall' the building was planned as an overspill for Haynes's venture, an arts centre and accommodation for artists. Divisions emerged. An opposing faction favoured a 'digger commune' and resisted plans for a £1 rent, and the presence of London's somewhat tame Hell's Angels as a 'security force'. Haynes and others strove to reach a compromise of sorts between the warring groups. It came to nothing, the police moved in, evicted the squatters, and the Bell/Genesis Hall was rendered uninhabitable. The popular press hailed this triumph of law over anarchic visions of order.

But *It* had problems over the issue too. In covering the story they had suggested that dope-smoking in squats might not be a good idea, and that Hell's Angels might be good people to discourage such provocative acts. In April Alex Trocchi, William Burroughs, Ken Kesey, Dan Richter, R.D. Laing, and stalwarts of the Anglo-American underground gathered to brood on the 'state of revolt'. During the meeting Trocchi criticized *It*'s coverage of the affair. Were orderly, dope-free communes and tolerating authority the right way to fight the system?

The issue was dropped, that evening. But throughout the summer the squats continued, and received their fair share of *It* coverage. And media attention focused on 144 Piccadilly where, on 3 September 1969 the 'London Arts Commune' moved in.

But then, on 12 October, *It* found itself the target of a takeover. Having ridden the contradictions, the paper suddenly found itself in the middle of them. Success – or apparent success – had gone to the heads of the dissident group, if not the people on the paper. *It* came out regularly, and an illusion grew that the process was almost automatic. Around *It* an elite had formed, dictatorial, pontificating, divorced from the streets which had supposedly given it succour, ran the argument.

Some twenty or thirty people staged their invasion that October evening. One full-timer and three part-timers led the move, with a former guest editor and the ever-present – they had little else to do – Hell's Angels.

Sue Small was sitting in the offices, sorting through files, working late. The invaders, and farce, intruded. Would she like to abandon the old guard, she was asked? She wouldn't. The paper was rocky, as circulation, distribution, legal fees, arguments were building up. For Small, getting out the magazine that had absorbed her for two years was the commitment, not this eccentric lurch into the unknown. 'I got very tearful', she recalls. 'The whole vision was crumbling around me. This wasn't the love and peace of 1967, this was something else. In a fit of madness I started tearing up all the ad records.'

It took her two weeks after the abortive occupation to stick them together again. Meanwhile she phoned Sue Miles (Miles's wife) Graham Keen, and Mark Williams. Over at Lord North Street in Miles's flat a council of war of the Old Guard met. It was suggested that they call the police, and they did.

Back at 27 Endell Street arguments and occupation continued. But with police assistance, out went the occupiers, off to set up the one and only edition of the *International Free Press* from a distributors' warehouse off Old Street. But now *It* had changed 'There were ideological arguments amongst the existing staff', Williams remembers, 'some argued that we should have allowed them to continue, to take over. It was the "right on man, it's the people taking power" argument. They wouldn't have known *how* to run the paper, but what did it matter? The atmosphere after that changed significantly. Some people did feel guilty about having called the police and having stopped the upsurge. Yet basically it was a team of people trying to wrest power, not a populist-based overthrow. They were people who thought *It* was important – and that it could make money. My leanings had always been towards the listings and music and entertainment side. By then Tony Elliott was rumbling along and previously *It* had been providing that function.'

It's long honeymoon with London was ending. Yet, says Small, plenty of people emerged to help the paper. 'There was still a lot of affection.'

It's upheavals were echoed elsewhere. That summer, in Berkeley, the *Barb*'s staff had risen in revolt against the founder/proprietor Max Scherr. 'The *Barb* was not socialist, anarchist, utopian movement, or radical', a staffer complained, 'basically the *Barb* was capitalist, and Scherr was the owner.'

'Around *It*', observes Williams, 'some people thought that someone was profiteering. I don't think that ever happened.'

'We precipitated the 13 October thing', stated the occupiers, 'because we dispute the fact that *It* belongs to, or is owned by, anyone, or any small group of people.'

From the Pacific coast to the Thames, movements which had started without financial backing, and without thinking about money, found that the possibility of cash could crash against fragile structures.

By the time *It* had gone through its trauma Jann Wenner and Mick Jagger had pulled the plug on the London *Rolling Stone*. Its move from Maddox Street to Hanover Square had not been a happy one. Large spacious offices dominated by a Chesterfield reputedly used by the Rolling Stones singer and Marianne Faithful for amorous interludes attracted the traditional crowd of hangers-on, plus the few who came into work.

Amongst them was Alan Marcuson. A South African, he had arrived in Britain in 1965 and commenced a never-to-be-completed degree in textile engineering at Leeds University. In London in 1969 he concluded that *Rolling Stone* would be an extremely fashionable thing to be involved in, and dropped in at the magazine's Maddox Street offices. To his amazement he got a job. It was selling ads, but it was a start, and things moved rapidly. The young South African concluded he was in the right place, and at the right time. It wasn't just bombed-out hippies who dropped in, but the likes of Jagger, Watts, and Brian Jones as well.

Marcuson was interested in magazines, in graphic design, in rock, and in the events convulsing Europe and the United States. And editor Jane Nicholson's involvement was fading rapidly. Marcuson found himself increasingly taking on the editorial running of the paper. Times were confusing. Wenner would fly in to issue instructions to an increasingly disconsolate staff and Jagger would pay the bills. Since the Stone and *Rolling Stone*'s founder rarely talked, no clear editorial line evolved from on high. For Jagger a London paper was probably what he wanted; for Wenner, a service to the San Francisco parent. Meanwhile the staff got on with producing the magazine. Mark Williams, freelancing out of *It*, did some work, and fresh out of Oxford, Jonathon Green was trying to get a job in Fleet Street. He failed, but did manage to sell 'a bloody awful piece on rock managers' to *Rolling Stone* London. Did Green want to be news editor? asked Marcuson, by now eased into the editor's chair. 'Absolutely', replied Green. 'What's it worth?' 'Twenty quid a week', replied the South African. In the days of rock bottom underground pay, £20 was not to be sneezed at. Marcuson, thought Green, was obviously in his element, and while his own job might be more lowly, there were compensations, like Hanover Square parties, with stoned guests graffitiing the immaculate Jagger-financed walls.

It was not to last. The Dylan Isle of Wight festival piece was commissioned and written, within the London office by a British freelance. But San Francisco was not pleased. Wenner ditched the piece for the American edition. 'Wenner', recalls Marcuson, 'was fuming at the bit. Most of the time he was really uptight, and to be honest, looking back, we weren't truly professional. I remember one article on Bob Dylan where, throughout, Dylan was spelt "Dillon", which was wonderful ammunition for Wenner to say what an incompetent bunch of shits we were. He got mad, *really* mad with us.'

With the first stirrings of Jagger's plans to out-Woodstock Woodstock at California's Altamont race track, the London magazine office was low on the singer's list of priorities. The simple answer was closure. Meanwhile, ultimatum followed ultimatum from Wenner.

With Nicholson on her way out, others considered their position. As Green sat in his Hanover Square office one morning, in came art director Gene Mahon. 'Right', said Mahon, 'you're the art director now. I'm going.'

Green knew his limitations. One of them was design. His old

friend from Bedford School was Pearce Marchbank. Even before his official graduation from Central School of Art and Design Marchbank had become art director on *Architectural Design*. 'It was', observes Marchbank, 'the Bucky Fuller version of *Architectural Review*:' Bizarrely, but appropriately for the times, the management wanted *AD* to look like *Oz* and Marchbank had gone some way to meet their specifications, but was not altogether happy in his work. 'The Architectural Association was in its phase of producing architects who couldn't design buildings. Central produced in me, in a way, an art director who couldn't design magazines. I had to pretend I knew how to mark up blocks.'

So Green rang Marchbank. Would he like to be Mahon's replacement? Contemplating his career on a prestigious but uncharismatic magazine, Marchbank made a rapid and fateful decision. He quit *AD* and moved to Hanover Square. As he arrived, amidst a collection of amplifiers mysteriously left behind by Crosby, Still, Nash & Young, a fateful meeting was taking place in California. Wenner and Jagger were finally deciding to kill the paper. 'He arrived', recalls Green, 'as *Rolling Stone*'s designer. By that evening the poor bastard was the designer of something called *"Friends of Rolling Stone"*.'

'I was art director of *Rolling Stone* for about two minutes', says Marchbank. 'Not long enough to get a pay-off cheque from Mick Jagger.' Yet advertising for the next issue had been booked. Indeed many advertisers, fearful of too close a relationship with *Oz* and *It*, dismissive – or completely ignorant – of *Time Out*, but wishing for a way into a market that the then flagging *Melody Maker* and *NME* were failing to tap, seemed optimistic about the prospects for a new alternative British music paper.

Thus the 18 October issue of London *Rolling Stone*, the last, hit the streets. 'The new life-style growing in this country feeds on everything and anything', proclaimed a brief editorial amidst a large white space on page three. 'Sure the music is important – very important – but a million and one other things have their own potential (and actual) importances. We want more feedback from you.'

Who didn't? New offices had to be found. The evicted and scorned *Friends of Rolling Stone* moved briefly into Hans Crescent, behind Harrods. It was a far cry from the squalor and grainy reality of *It*'s Covent Garden premises, or the cosmopolitan chic of *Oz* in Notting Hill. And it was just a bad place to produce any magazine. The magazine teetered from Hans Crescent to Redcliffe Square to Park Lane, with parts of it strewn over Pearce Marchbank's flat in Hampstead. Eventually, in the first days of the new decade, it was to find a more permanent home in the socially acceptable Portobello Road.

Meanwhile *Oz* expanded. In 1968 Felix Dennis had been recruited; in 1969 Jim Anderson joined the paper.

Thirty-two years old, Anderson had been born in Suffolk, but had spent his life in Australia and had graduated in law from Sydney University. Being gay had done nothing to further his legal career, and he had quit the country to take the hippy trail to London, and to *Oz*. His organizational talent, his ability to provide a framework within which the magazine and its designers and writers could operate, was to become central to the magazine.

Anderson tended towards introspection. Dennis didn't. Out of Surbiton, with an accent that veered between Sydney – which was where many people located him – and outer London, his initial work on the magazine had been selling it on the streets. A masthead designation as 'hustler' was apt, and he rapidly shifted over to become *Oz*'s advertising manager. The magazine, through his influence, became more regularized; readers noted that something perilously close to marketing had intruded into its anarchy. The grammar school boy didn't have Neville's sophistication, Greer's polemic talents, or Widgery's politics, but he had a grasp of the new generation picking up the paper, and, as he was conclusively to demonstrate in the 1970s, he had a great talent for making money, a loyalty to his friends – and talent for paying bills, eventually.

Police and straight media interest in the paper grew. Neville's genius was to subvert and turn round press attacks on *Oz*, but they could still cost dearly. In 1968 the then Labour MP Woodrow Wyatt had an interest in a Middlesbrough printing firm that produced *Oz*, the contract ceased after an exposé in the *News of the World*. And the raid which hit *It* in April 1969 had its effect on *Oz* too.

Both papers – and *Rolling Stone* – shared the same printers, and after a police visit 6,000 copies of *Oz* were destroyed. The printers demanded changes in the paper's 'visual content', and then threatened to ditch the printing contract.

The result, once again, was that *Oz* had to move on. It had been the pattern of *Oz*'s early production, and it remained so until the end.

With the magazine's success, Neville had begun to pull back. Wilcock had edited an issue back in 1967. By January 1969 Andrew Fisher was in charge for *Oz17*, while for *Oz18*, under Dennis, the magazine briefly adopted a *Rolling Stone* format, complete with an acknowledgement for 'the inspiration of San Francisco's great music paper'. The following issue found 'staff writer Germaine' talking to 'Dr G., a celebrated (and over-educated) international groupie'.

Greer's introspective interviewing gave way in the following issue, post-police raid, to a defence of a movement under attack. 'The underground . . . is where the life is, before the establishment forms a crust on top and changes vitality for money. . . . The people who belong to the underground all the time are very few, but almost everyone had spent a season there. The establishment has to draw nourishment from it, and plunders and is plundered by the underground.'

But being under attack could become boring, as the summer of festivals, Blind Faith, Stones, Dylan, wore on. And *Oz*'s response was to draw further out to explore new avenues. A key turning point was the issue, *Oz23*, produced to coincide with the Isle of Wight Festival that August.

'They look a bit, a bit *dossy*, don't they?' said a skinhead, surveying the beaded middle classes fighting their way on to the site. 'I like rock steady myself. I'll remember to bring my mallet next time.' Sometimes it rained, but mainly the sun shone on the army first summoned into existence, without the impact of commercial pop, back at the Albert Hall in 1965, and the Roundhouse in the cold October of 1966. 'I got up at four in the morning to wash', complained a Geordie. '*Four*, and there were ten people in the queue then.'

As in 1966, inflatables made their appearance, bigger and more erratic than ever. Joss-stick and Asian artefact merchants added to the atmosphere of the Indian countryside suddenly taken over by the children of the long boom. But there were key differences. Release's Caroline Coon wrote in *It* that 1969 was the year of the festivals. But it was also the year that the class structure of the underground, under pressure from a voracious music industry, ensured that a sizeable enclosure was partitioned off, in front of the stage, for the great and expensively attired of the new aristocracy. Not that the foot soldiers of the movement were completely excluded. A girl, overcome by enthusiasm for the occasion, took off her clothes and sprung forward through the crowds. Her nudity provided a *carte blanche* that hours of queuing at the press tent could never have done. The multitude parted, the enclosure opened its gates, the press photographers descended and engulfed her, shielding her from the view of all but the tabloids. By the autumn her image was to be used to sell records and *Oz* in ads. By the following year that innocence of 1969 had turned into the appearance of the first page three girls in the freshly Murdoch-bought *Sun*.

The festival was an ideal opportunity to shift papers: *It*, *Rolling Stone*, and, most of all, *Oz*. And, once again, the magazine pulled its trick of producing the right issue at the right time. In the spring Petrakis's survey of sexuality for *It* revealed, amidst a cluster of curious statements, that 'it is true to say that homosexuals are neurotic'. On 27 June 1969 homosexuals had done something about such designations. At the Stonewall Inn in Greenwich Village eight cops moved in for another raid on a gay bar. Only this time the subjects of their attention fought back. It was the birth of the American Gay Liberation movement.

Despite the recent legalization of homosexuality between consenting adults, in private, gay politics and gay life-style remained resolutely unnoticed even within the underground press – a silence only broken by the occasional tabloid exposé. True, gay sexuality had featured with the Beats, with Kerouac's ambivalent relationship with Ginsberg, his semi-love affair with Neal Cassidy; and the subject had been touched on by the early underground, but rather in the way that Ezra Pound's fascism had been treated, as an interesting eccentricity. *Oz*'s contribution was different, low on analysis, but high on shock content, complete with a naked black man and a naked white man embracing on the cover. The article inside was an import centring on Angelo d'Arcangelo's *Homosexual Handbook*, published in New York. It was about sex – not about sexual politics – but another show was about to go on the road, and *Oz* had got there first.

Neville was at the Isle of Wight festival, as *Oz* sold amidst the joss-sticks and damp grass. There were too many people, he thought, but on the other hand there were *so* many people. It looked as if the entire world was suddenly on the side of the underground, and they were buying *Oz*. Not that the gay *Oz* had been his idea, or even that he had provided much input, apart from advice on the telephone. Just then he had another preoccupation, and he left the compilation and editing of the issue to Sebastian and Tina Jorgensen, and to the new arrival from Australia, Jim Anderson.

That the core of the issue was hedonism was unsurprising, it was a key credo of the paper. *It* always had the problem that, no matter what it dealt with, the copy came out in the blacks and greys of its newspaper format. *Oz*, with its use of colour, could somehow, at the time, get away with an approach to sexuality which was condemned in retrospect – and occasionally then – but which somehow retained an innocence.

Across the Atlantic things were different. In mid July, at Ann Arbor, the 'revolutionary media' conference had come out against sexism in the underground press. The seriousness with which the good intentions were taken varied. The women's movement was, then, more deeply rooted in the United States, but within the left male contempt for the 'diversion' that the phenomenon represented was also entrenched. This was to change. In January 1970 in New York women staffers seized control of the city's leading radical underground paper, *Rat* – both a continuation of staff revolts – as on the *Barb* the previous summer – and a sign that the new movement was coming of age.

But in 1969 women and *Oz* effectively meant Germaine Greer.

And women's responses to *Oz*'s sexual attitudes were muted. By that time Sheila Rowbotham was beginning to come into peripheral contact with the magazine. And *Oz* pornography didn't outrage her, because it wasn't the old-style pornography, and because within the underground, she supposed – unlike on the different *Black Dwarf* – they did that sort of thing. 'It was giving a symbolic shape to sexual fantasies. They were male-defined, but they were beautifully drawn.'

For Michelene Wandor, the night-tripper to the *It* launch in 1966, her husband Ed's connections had brought her into contact with *Oz* too. The upheavals of 1968 had almost passed her by. She dabbled in the outer reaches of the publishing world from her position as a wife and mother: after the birth of *Time Out* she began to contribute to its nascent poetry section. But left politics and feminism for her remained unformed. She complained, she got fed up, but there were no ideologies. The first meetings with Ferrier and Neville had been soon after their arrival, via Jill Neville. By 1969 Victor had suggested that Neville wrote a book; it was to be *Playpower*, and the foursome went to stay in a Devon country house where the Australian worked on the manuscript. The couple were fascinating, she thought, very different. They had the edge, a way of living for the moment that she envied. It created, for that holiday, a family of innocents.

And for her *Oz* wasn't identified with sexism, not that the word existed. She felt uncomfortable with some of the material but she didn't know *why*. 'The life-style itself was so charismatic. There was something that seemed very easy for lots of these people, and I was looking at it as somebody who didn't feel quite so easy about what they were doing. "Sexual liberation", the appearance of pornography seemed, again, to have a freedom and an ease that I thought I didn't have. So I might have thought "well, why aren't I much younger and having this wonderful and exciting life?" '

But at another level she didn't want it. She and Ed were, after all, young marrieds. And perhaps lots of people were wondering why they weren't having this good time. 'Yes', she says, two decades on, 'maybe even Richard and Louise.'

'Maybe we did look like an ideal exciting couple', says Ferrier. 'But it wasn't really. A lot of things were happening, sometimes I was having a good time, sometimes it was ghastly, and I used to get totally paranoid smoking dope. Richard and I didn't have a fantastic relationship.'

Which would probably have cheered an angry *Oz* reader, who signed himself 'J.F.' in a letter to the magazine that year. 'Reading your magazine makes me feel very small', he wrote. 'There was the time I turned up at the Arts Lab (first and last time) to see the Dylan film and couldn't afford it. Fifteen bob for a fucking film! I was thrown out by some irate trendy who kept muttering something about royalties. I thought the idea of kids doing their own thing was that it would be cheap and for everybody, not a clique. I can't play the guitar, I can't write poetry, act, paint or sing and my understanding of politics and economics is very limited. So what happens to me in the great cultural revolution? In my nineteen years I've had three women, a nervous breakdown and some poor education. Can't you people in London realize that twenty miles north of *It*, *Oz*, Arts Labs, etc., *nothing has changed!* So what's all the fuss about? Do I hear smug laughter?'

In March of 1969, as *Vagina Rex* had opened, so the conference of the grandiosely titled Revolutionary Socialist Students Federation had taken place. 'The eventual aim', wrote Alexander Cockburn in *Student Power* 'is the cementing of a revolutionary bloc with working-class forces; but the immediate power of the student lies in his university, his college, where he works as a student.'

While the masses went to the Isle of Wight, the inheritors of 1968 contemplated the declining value of their capital. For Cockburn, by then a 27-year-old journalist, student days were behind him. The same was true of much of the core of *Black Dwarf*. The RSSF, of which much was trumpeted, yielded little. Members of political groups went on brief raids into its ranks, and returned with little except contempt for its prospects. Factionalism was rife, and the British Situationists – what there were of them – did their best to recruit amongst the underground-oriented malcontents despairing of the prospects of that movement.

Yet Tom Fawthrop could write in *It52* that the RSSF represented a move away from 'the sectarian left' and 'the move into a deeper, more imaginative level of politics . . . we will be the first generation in history to consciously plan and map-out its own future, and create a society of its own.'

Which map? For Dick Pountaine, fresh out of his Imperial College science degree, and moving within Notting Hill's underground milieu, a visit to the RSSF's inauguration had been a gloomy experience. The proceedings were enlivened by an intervention from the producers of *King Mob Echo*, which would have been Britain's Situationist paper had not the local branch – if branch is the right word – been excluded by its international secretariat from membership. John Gravelle, one of *KME*'s luminaries, culminated his intervention by pointing at the RSSF's freshly produced banner, in Richard III style: 'As for this', charged Gravelle, 'dogshit by any other name would smell as foul.'

The rhetoric might not have been original, the problems were genuine. The more traditionalist Marxist elements within the student movement rubbed shoulders uneasily with those who claimed to be – or occasionally were – of the streets. Around the latter group were many who had tried the traditional Marxist left and found it wanting. For some the Situationists were to be appealing. For the *Black Dwarf*, that June, celebrating a year of publication, it had been a rocky time, financially and politically.

A division was appearing between those on the paper linking their politics to Ernest Mandel's branch of the Trotskyist Fourth International, and those – like Clive Goodwin – anxious to keep its independence, and relationships within the paper had begun subtly to shift. 'A revolutionary socialist newspaper should exist for a specific purpose; it should have a clearly defined perspective', wrote Tariq Ali ominously in the anniversary editorial. 'For a revolutionary journal. . . . We would obviously like to see ourselves as the organ of a revolutionary party, however embryonic it may be.'

No such party existed, he added, but the tension between those who backed Ali's International Marxist Group and the rest grew as the year advanced. And the tensions coincided with a downturn in sales that indicated both the ebbing of the 1968 wave, and the growth of other revolutionary papers which did have links to particular groups.

Something was draining out of the movement as 1969 ended. Hippies believed in love and peace, they had said back in 1967. On 8 August 1969 Sharon Tate and four others were found slaughtered at her home in Beverley Hills. On 9 December the long-haired devotee of the Beatles' 'White Album', Charles Manson, and five of his followers were indicted for their murder. The day before, in the same city, Los Angeles, a four-hour battle between 300 police and 12 members of the Black Panthers ended with the Panthers' surrender. Twenty-one-year-old Fred Hampton was shot dead. The Panthers, were beginning to crack. The trial of the Chicago Seven dragged on, and received heavy British underground coverage. In *Oz* David Widgery took time off from musing on the revolution to provide an obituary for Jack Kerouac, one of the people with whom the entire movement had started. At *It* Hall, Keen, and Stansill were contemplating their freshly arrived charges. Michael X moved into his Holloway Road 'Black House'.

Others were moving on too. The Drury Lane squat and the police evictions were a sign of the times for the Arts Lab. By spring 1969 the Lab was deep in debt; sponsorship from the Arts Council an impossibility; the wealthy of 1967 had vanished; and Camden Council was pursuing Jim Haynes for an accumulating rate bill. The end had come in October. The Lab closed, and Haynes moved on. 'The end of the sixties came as a kind of incredible collapse', wrote Haynes, 'a collapse of hope, and of the innocence and the naïveté of the decade when everyone felt we were changing the world.'

1 *Memorial meeting: the press conference at the Albert Memorial, June 1965, before 'Poets of the World'. Clockwise from top left: Anselm Hollo, Marcus Field, Michael Horovitz, Ernst Jandl, David Richter, John Esam, Allen Ginsberg, Alex Trocchi (© Michael Horovitz)*

2 *When* It *was new: Jim Haynes in London, March 1967, note the Lenny Bruce poster (© BBC Hulton Picture Library)*

3   *The picture that captured something: Louise Ferrier and Richard Neville,*
post-Australia, pre-Oz, autumn 1966 (© BBC Hulton Picture Library)

The Black Dwarf

Est. 1817   Vol. 13 Number 6   13 October 1968   Fortnightly 2s

"They say that in Mexico we have the most cultured army of all Latin America because it is continually in the universities"...... Page 5

WORKERS AND STUDENTS

DON'T

DEMAND

OCCUPY

YOUR SCHOOLS   **YOUR FACTORIES**

reports from: Leicester/Columbia/Hull/Birmingham/Japan/Frankfurt

Also: Peter Sedgwick on Herbert Marcuse/Rudi Dutschke on Capitalism
Fred Halliday in praise of Max Beloff/Alberto Moravia on the Cultural Revolution

ALL POWER TO THE CAMPUS SOVIETS!

4   *The workers make a guest appearance,* Black Dwarf, *October 1968*

5 *Despite the fracas it was an anti-climax. The October Vietnam demonstration 1968 (© BBC Hulton Picture Library)*

TIME OUT
London
Aug 12-Sept 2

1s

6   *From small beginnings: the first edition of* Time Out, *August 1968*

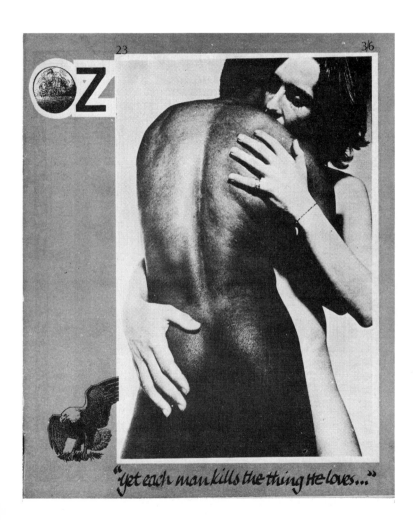

7   Oz *steps out, August 1969*

GERASSI ON AMERICA
CAMBODIA: THE BACKGROUND
TONY CLIFF: INTERVIEW
ELECTION POSTER

NO 6 · LONDON · JUNE 1970 · MONTHLY · 2/6

En France, 2·50Fr

8 *A quiet death off Old Street,* Idiot International, *June 1970*

9   *They hadn't noticed the women's movement,* It, *March 1970*

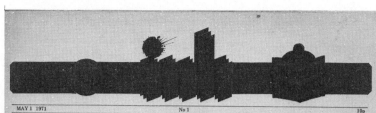

THE GREAT URANIUM ROBBERY

by ALEX MITCHELL

FIVE BARS of uranium, almost enough to make an atomic bomb, have been stolen from a nuclear power station in Wales. This is the biggest nuclear fuel theft in history.

The thieves made off with five bars each 42 inches long and weighing

about 40 lb from the Wylfa power plant on Anglesey Island. One of them carries the serial number:

JAB 006038
VIC UX 26 509 06821
A 6850 J A

The theft has been ignored by the national Press because of its explosive political and security implications.

Mr Philip Holbrook, the Wylfa station superintendent, confirmed this week that the robbery had taken place and said, 'I'll be very relieved to get them back.' A spokesman for the Central Electricity Generating Board this week described the theft as 'unfortunate', and added that the stolen uranium is 'harmless and worthless'.

This is not true.

The Nuclear Installations Inspectorate of the Department of Trade and Industry lays down stringent regulations for the handling of uranium bars to protect workers. And far from being 'worthless', natural uranium is priceless.

The Nuclear Installations Act 1965 empowers the Minister of Trade and Industry, Mr John Davis, to 'at any time direct an inspector to make a special report' on such things as thefts; and also 'where he thinks it expedient so to do, direct an inquiry to be held'. The inquiry, says the Act, shall be public except where 'interests of national security direct otherwise'.

But although the theft took place in July last year, Mr Davis has done nothing.

Wylfa power station, built at a cost of £100 million, commenced operations in January this year. In mid-1970 120,000 uranium bars were transported to Anglesey to be fed into the two giant reactors when they went into production. A total of 48,000 rods were placed by hand into each reactor.

Last October an audit was conducted and the five bars were discovered missing. But the Central Electricity Generating Board and the UK Atomic Energy Authority did not report the theft. It was hushed up.

Five weeks ago the police received an underworld tip-off that the uranium was floating around London. The thieves, it seems, were having great difficulty in selling their nuclear loot – despite discreet contacts with foreign embassies.

In their authoritative book, *Perils of the Peaceful Atom*, the authors Richard Curtis and Elizabeth Hogan wrote: 'With the increased movement of radioactive material along world traffic lanes, a new and incomparably frightening hazard poses itself: piracy...these shipments could attract criminal organizations that might divert the enriched uranium or plutonium.

'...the possibility that some countries could build - if they have not already built - secret installations for the purpose of producing atomic weapons from "diverted" material has been raised by reliable observers.'

If the missing rods do get into foreign hands, what is the chance of them being converted into weapons? As Theodore Taylor, the nuclear physicist who headed the US Defense Department's atomic bomb design and testing programme for seven years, said, 'I've been worried about how easy it is to build bombs ever since I built my first one.'

And in the five rods of natural uranium (which weighs 100 lb), there is approximately 1 lb of radioactive isotopes - and you only need a minimum of 4 lb to construct an A-bomb.

There are three alarming aspects to the robbery:

1. Why did it take so long for the authorities to discover the uranium was missing? Is the security at the plant so haphazard that someone could have stolen five bars or uranium without anybody knowing?
2. Why didn't the authorities make a public appeal for the return of the five bars as soon as they were discovered missing? What are they doing now to persuade the thieves to return the loot in the interests of public safety?
3. The whole incident is being treated with *ancient casualness* by the authorities. Is it the intention of the powerful nuclear lobby in Britain to speed up the process of nuclear contamination by letting the stuff slip over the fence every time the nightwatchman goes for a piss?

A last quote from Curtis and Hogan: '...it may well turn out that the atomic weapon that triggers the next and final world war will be fashioned from fissionable material "diverted" from a power plant dedicated to the innocent purpose of producing electricity.'

INK

1

10 *The scoop that wasn't, for the launch that sunk the ship: the first* Ink, *May 1971*

11   *Felix Dennis, Jim Anderson, and Richard Neville outside the Old Bailey during the Oz trial, November 1971 (© BBC Hulton Picture Library)*

3 March no 22   15p

Frendz

UNION OF
NATIONAL · MINEWORKERS
· YORKSHIRE AREA ·

" NOT THYSELF, BUT THE CAUSE "
BRODSWORTH BRANCH

12   Frendz *finds the workers, March 1972*

13 *The future was feminist: Marsha Rowe (left) and Rosie Boycott of* Spare Rib, June 1972 (© BBC Hulton Picture Library)

Chapter 10

The women's room

Chilly in winter, dark and stuffy in summer, the offices of *Idiot International*, which we used to call in moments of moral seriousness (or what we used to think of as sardonic wit) 'the non-sectarian paper of the revolutionary left', were located in a side turning off Old Street. That limbo land between the City, Islington, and Hoxton was unprepossessing at the best of times. The best of times, for those of us on the rapidly changing staff, were hard to find.

The monthly's first edition appeared in January 1970, edited, largely in absentia, by a woman who soon disappeared, to be replaced by an affable and witty anthropologist and future film-maker, Hugh Brody. His speciality was to become the Eskimo people of northern Canada. After his subsequent departure for what I, in my insularity, took to be the frozen tundra of the north, I idly speculated that this might be Brody's equivalent of escaping to join the Foreign Legion. But forgetting would be difficult, and the staff of *Idiot* and the native people of the northern American wastes shared certain things in common. Both were starved of resources amidst plenty, left out in the cold, at the mercy of economic forces beyond their control, and both were driven to drink.

I joined the paper while Brody was still on it, in company with Neil Lyndon, a graduate of Cambridge and co-founder of that city's alternative magazine, the *Shilling Paper*. Soon afterwards Brody departed, leaving Lyndon, myself, and the two founders of the magazine, Douglas Gill and Vidya Anand, to preside over its collapse that autumn.

Some people joined the underground and alternative media to propagate causes, some to make an entry into journalism. On *Idiot* we increasingly found ourselves less guardians of the truth, or the flame of revolution, more guardians of a printing press. Machinery, as Karl Marx had pointed out, should make us free, instead through the play of market forces it enslaves us. And the gap between what we do, and what we wish to do, can be covered by that convenient word, alienation. There was plenty of that abroad on *Idiot*.

During its ill-starred history *Idiot* developed an insatiable appetite for money. With its associated ventures it consumed around £50,000. And, for the times, this was *big* money. The kind that *Ink* and *7 Days* during 1971 tried and failed to raise. Yet *Idiot*'s money didn't line the pockets of its producers. Most of it found its way speedily back into the cash-tills of the very multinationals the paper was dedicated to help topple.

Idiot's luck was the receipt of that £50,000. Its ill-fortune was the inexpert way it was used. The ground from which the monthly sprang was the increasingly rutted soil of *Black Dwarf*. By the autumn of 1969 the *Dwarf*'s early success had passed. 'In 1968 revolution seemed to be in the *air*', says John Hoyland, 'and *Black Dwarf* was a key part of it. In retrospect the period was full of absurdity, but it was also full of tremendous energy and drama. But the post-1968 situation needed more thought.'

It didn't always get it. The Revolutionary Socialist Students Federation had been tried and found wanting. But students were still in revolt. The February 1970 occupation of Warwick University was in many ways the most significant, in terms of what was uncovered, of any of the upheavals of the time. The student action sucked in many sympathetic Warwick academics, including Edward Thompson, the 1956 dissident Communist then teaching at Warwick. It revealed both the over-close links between the university and the local Coventry (and, through the car industry, the national) business community, and evidence (as the private files of the authorities were unveiled) of surveillance on the students. It was shocking but it was also faintly gratifying; student militancy was being taken seriously.

The link between Warwick and business was also another reminder of the souring of the Wilsonite dreams of 1964. A new alliance between business, brains, and technology had been one of the catchwords of those days. By 1970, at Warwick, the corporate reality of a university which, charged critics, had tailored the pursuit of knowledge to the demands of motor manufacturers seemed yet another example of the shoddiness of the original vision. Fleetingly, in the summer of 1970, it seemed that Labour's electoral prospects had revived, but there was precious little sign of it as 1969 gave way to 1970. 'There was something in the air', Thunderclap Newman had sung in July 1969; what it might have been was the last of the dust settling as the last of a generation of young activists walked out of the Labour Party towards the then flourishing far left groups, community activism, or the lure of the counter-culture. And early in 1970 the marchers gathered for the last great Vietnam demonstration, in the darkness of the Embankment by the Thames, to march candle-lit against the US invasion of Cambodia. It was to be a short-surgical operation, claimed President Nixon. It was to be the death of Cambodia. At home Wilson continued with his brand of social-democratic conservatism, but badly dented with the failure of the 'In Place of Strife' package of union legislation introduced by his Employment Minister, Barbara Castle.

Yet the far left was in disarray, torn between the golden memories of 1968 and the sneaking suspicion that they were just that, and that a meaner, nastier decade was opening up. 'Forward to the Red Seventies!' the veteran Marxist Isaac Deutscher had told LSE students. It was an appealing slogan, but was it to be the reality?

In the *New Left Review*, barometer of the older, Marxist ante left, an article appeared extolling the 'red bases' that needed to be established in universities as the hoped-for detonator for more widespread revolt. Many on the left, student activists amongst them, regarded such notions with a scepticism bordering on hilarity.

And when the activists had marched for Tet, marched for Paris, Berlin, Phnom Penh, where did they go?

One place was Ireland. The 1969 disturbances across the province had sucked in the British Army. In April 1969 Bernadette Devlin had won a Westminster seat as a Republican and a revolutionary socialist. Solidarity action developed in Britain, and the impact of the Irish conflict rippled outside the left into the underground, to such supposedly unlikely characters as Alan Marcuson, the editor of *Friends*. Meanwhile brisk sectarian debates took place among the British Marxist groups on the right line to be taken on the issue. Was it to be support for the IRA? Support for a socialist Ireland? Critical support for the IRA? And *which* IRA?

Black Dwarf had addressed the issue, but getting the paper out and locating cash to keep going were pressing problems. So was the tacit division which had opened up on the paper between supporters of the International Marxist Group and those who wished to remain non-aligned, or less aligned. For Clive Goodwin the paper was the priority, finding money for it, holding it together, almost conducting a love affair with it. One source of money was a newcomer to the paper whose private wealth helped sustain the *Dwarf*'s erratic bank balance. But, introduced to the paper via Tariq Ali, his allegiance to the International Marxist Group was to spell problems when, in February 1970, the paper split.

Tariq Ali, whose charm and wit had often stilled political squalls, had relinquished the editorship of *Black Dwarf* for periods during 1969. In his absence Douglas Gill had been one of the people who had taken over. Another product of the British upper middle classes – this time with a military background – Gill was regarded with a mixture of affection and exasperation by many around the paper.

Gill's tenure on the *Dwarf* was short-lived. Ali might, on occasions, have been sloppy on details, his IMG membership unwelcome to some, but his generally more open style of editing meant that Gill's attempts to impose a more orthodox method could create problems.

While at the paper Gill had heard encouraging news from

abroad. Jean Claude Hallier, a French political journalist, was mooting the publication of a paper to reflect the internationalism that the new European left spent so much time talking about. Initially it was to be produced in British, French, and Italian editions, swapping copy, contacts, and information. At last socialists would match the internationalization of capital! And there was money. Via an obliging French heiress some £50,000 was available to set up the British end of the operation. In September 1969 Gill, having collected the cash from Paris, set vigorously to work. By the winter of 1969 the first French edition rolled off the presses. And, in Britain, gone would be the familiar underground unpleasantness with printers. *Idiot* would do its own printing, thanks to a spanking new Heidelberg offset litho press. Not only would the press produce *Idiot* but, perhaps, other papers too, such as the *Black Dwarf*.

Others took up on the idea. The new press, stumbling into operation early in 1970, took on the job of printing *Friends* until the cheque for payment failed to materialize. Some out-of-London papers made approaches. A delegation from *Socialist Worker* dropped in, surveyed the new technology, and departed, contemplating the wealth that erring members of the capitalist classes were willing to shell out to the bourgeois sections of the far left.

But for Gill and Anand – and for those others sucked into the operation – the dream rapidly became a nightmare. The Heidelberg was a magnificent press, but was it really suitable? Surely it was more a poster press, ideal for whipping off appeals for mass action, should barricades begin to be flung up, but not really appropriate for revolutionary magazines or for the other, more bizarre material that began to issue from its gleaming machinery. And presses mean printers, and *that* meant a member of the National Graphical Association, poised, pipe in mouth, by the customarily silent equipment.

Problems didn't end with the printing equipment. A bright young Australian, Pat Masters, arrived to work on the typesetting equipment. No more was it the old IBM golfball typewriter, the Kalashnikov of the guerrilla journalist. In its place came the latest in computer typesetting, programmed to spill out copy in inscrutable computer tape, ready to feed into immaculate processing equipment.

One day it would happen. But not then, not on *Idiot International*. Pat Masters wrestled with the equipment, experts were brought in, tape spewed out, and from the processor came forth strange concrete poetry of a style popularized in avant-garde circles in the early years of the previous decade. Unknown typefaces and characters communicated with distant computer terminals in the heart of the corporate state.

With substantial overheads on the office, and idle equipment, work was sought outside. The flowering of the new wave of

literature had been cultivated in Paris ten years before around
Maurice Girodias's Olympia Press. But its publication in Britain
had been frowned on by the authorities. Thus Larcular Press –
Idiot's parent company – stepped into the breach. Into the machine
was fed avant-garde pornography, out came indecipherable script.

Thus were Lyndon and myself interrupted as we brooded over
our copy by a worried Douglas Gill. 'Has anyone seen', he inquired,
' "Sea of Thighs"?' Our laughter followed him down the corridor.

Not that in the early stages the journalistic side was any better.
'The internationalism of the new left lies not in mustering support
for other peoples' struggles', proclaimed the first editorial grandly.
'During the May uprising in France, the English, the Germans, the
Italians, felt called upon to send no protest letters to De Gaulle;
they came out, instead, against their separate national institutions.
They took issue with the government and state. Similarly the new
left press. . . . How different this from the empty stridency which
marked an earlier Western European left.' Different indeed. 'It will
be written by militants, for militants, about the problems most
immediately at hand', the editorial continued briskly.

But where were the writers, militant or otherwise? The layout
artists? The designers? If *Black Dwarf* was debating the virtues of
commitment and non-alignment, *Idiot* encountered considerable
difficulties in finding anyone to align with at all. Gradually, as first
Brody, and later Lyndon and myself attempted to fashion – on
rather limited experience – a paper out of random contributions,
Idiot began to take a shape of sorts. Since *Rolling Stone* had done
well, perhaps a revolutionary rock section was a good idea. Thus a
young graduate, socialist, and rock writer, Dave Laing, was brought
in to edit the 'Rolling Idiot' section. This, on Lyndon's suggestion,
featured a logo centred around the dead Rolling Stone, Brian
Jones. Thus we simultaneously exposed the shabby façade behind
the drugs and corruption that was the music business while, we
hoped, draining from it a seepage of ad money. It proved a forlorn
hope.

If the nucleus of a journalistic team had been formed, other areas
had been neglected. A photographer, George Snow, fresh out of
college, began to help with pictures and layout. But distribution, in
the hands of an elusive American off the City Road, proved to be
more complex. No matter, thought the editors and Gill and Anand,
it was probably satisfactory. And every month there was the *frisson*
of watching the Heidelberg – deftly if laconically operated by the
NGA man – at last earning or contributing to its keep, pumping
copies of *Idiot International* out for militants. Wherever they were.

Some 'militants' did turn up on the magazine's doorstep. True we
were down at the bottom of a list of possible outlets, behind *Black
Dwarf*, *Friends*, *Oz*, and *It*. But if *Idiot*'s minuscule staff had few

friends, it also lacked enemies, apart perhaps from *Friends*, which in January 1970 was wondering where its money was coming from. '*Idiot* is about as revolutionary as any other fickle trendy wank', it commented uncharitably. 'The only hope for the English edition is that it will undergo an internal revolution.'

Revolutions entail the seizure of power. Since power was eagerly shed on *Idiot* by whoever possessed it, we were more in the position of hapless minders of a sick infant than keepers of the flame of revolt. Yet despite the obstacles the paper developed. Rather than being a paper written by and for militants it attempted a lofty tone, apart from the battle, observing the fancies and nostrums of the left with what its staff hoped was a cool detachment. Attempts were made at news reportage. Noam Chomsky – that American savant of the New Left – was interviewed. Sheila Rowbotham and a young Beatrix Campell wrote on women's liberation from conflicting standpoints. Rowbotham the committed feminist and socialist, Campbell the committed Communist Party member arguing that when middle-class women's liberation 'has stopped pouring out its sorrows and wiped its eyes, it may see that it must eventually formulate an in-depth programme if it wants to enhance women's lives both inside the bedroom and kitchen and outside.' Hans Magnus Enzerburger was interviewed; Malcolm Caldwell wrote on the Far Eastern crisis. Later, Caldwell, a sincere and dedicated academic Maoist – itself a rarity – was to die mysteriously in Phnom Penh at the hands of one of the two groups he had extolled, the Khmer Rouge or the North Vietnamese.

By late summer a visit to the distributor in nearby City Road revealed the final, awful truth. For every copy of *Idiot* that had made it to the militants poised by the news-stands ten had languished in the warehouse. They were surrounded by towering ranges of unsold American editions of *Rolling Stone* – further proof for its proprietor, Jann Wenner, of the lack of get-up-and-go in Britain. By the autumn it was over for Lyndon and myself. He went off to a more promising radical venture, *Time Out*, and subsequently to the *Sunday Times*. The unfortunate Gill, confronted with a mountain of debts, swam into 'Sea of Thighs' offshoots and the printing of the sporadic organ of a crazed Maoist sect.

At least on the *Dwarf* there were more staff to argue with, and a tangential connection with a real movement. But even as Gill had been collecting his £50,000 that previous autumn, heated argument broke out on the paper over a piece denouncing the African National Congress, and accusing its leaders of corruption. Was it genuine, or a plant from the South African security services? Rowbotham instigated an extraordinary editorial meeting to discuss the feature. Opposing the publication, she lost, and the article was published that November. But the debate underlined the divisions within the paper, and the lack of any coherent structure to make decisions. It was a problem that bedevilled the entire counter-culture.

Within the *Dwarf* Rowbotham felt isolated, and she was also poverty-stricken. She derived more income, and probably more pleasure, from her job on a Dalston market cake stall. From being a chore, going to editorial meetings was becoming a nightmare. Faction fights were not her forte, and one night before Christmas 1969 her enthusiasm evaporated. Already a *Dwarf* denunciation of the International Socialists' behaviour at a farcical memorial meeting to the recently deceased Ho Chi Minh, to which her signature had been appended, earned her suspension from member-ship of that group. As faction followed faction the pull of the nascent women's movement which had occupied much of her interest on the paper became irresistible. Effectively she was the only woman on the paper. True, there was Anne Scott, who did most of the secretarial work, but at 17 her contribution was unlikely to be absorbed within the main debates. Finally she had to attend an editorial meeting, and, as she set off, her feet became heavier and heavier. In a dentist's waiting room she wrote her letter of resignation. Imagine, she suggested to her comrades, 'you are black, not white, imagine you have cunts, and not cocks. . .'

Amidst discussions on Ireland, the Fourth International, Venezuela, the war in Vietnam, these were not questions which were likely to have been asked by most of the *Dwarf*'s editorial board. True, skin pigmentation found both Ali and Vinay Chand on the other side of the colour line. It was Ali whom Rowbotham asked to read the statement. It culminated with her request that the board did their imaginings in silence, for five minutes.

The meeting did so. 'There was', remembers John Hoyland, 'a marvellous, shocked, silence. Everyone looked so embarrassed, waiting to see who would actually break the silence – and how. Nobody knew *quite* what to say.'

Eventually a male staffer cracked. 'I think', he exclaimed, 'that's absolutely preposterous!'

Preposterous or not, Rowbotham was gone. And, whatever the impact on the *Dwarf*, she was in the first flush of enthusiasm for the women's movement. They were not particularly encouraging times for the men of the counter-culture. For the more orthodox there were the relative security and certainty of the left groups; for the radicals within the underground inherited from the mid 1960s there was a move towards what passed for community politics; a few embraced Situationism; a very tiny group moved towards the politics of what was to become the Angry Brigade. None of it could compare with the heady excitement that the women's liberation movement was beginning to generate.

In the United States, after the publication of Betty Friedan's *The Feminine Mystique* in 1963, the author and others had, by 1966, set up the National Organization of Women, NOW. By 1967 a radical women's movement had begun to germinate. The process was slower in Britain, but a catalyst was the publication in 1966 of Juliet Mitchell's 'Women: the longest revolution' in the *New Left Review*. After its publication members of the 'Nottingham Group' – precursors of the International Marxist Group – met with the *NLR*. It was to prove a fruitful encounter.

In 1967 had come the Dialectics of Liberation. And its very origin in a psycho-cultural initiative meant that some of the old verities of the left were leapfrogged.. New groups were coming into contact with politics, and politics in that pre-1968 atmosphere was going through a fundamental shift of priorities. The personal was beginning to become political.

In January 1968 two Hull trawlers were lost in storms. It led Lil Bilocca and other fishermen's wives into a fierce campaign to improve safety standards. Media and employers' criticism of Bilocca intensified. Middle-class women in the town began to take an interest, and out of the process came an Equal Rights Group. Rather than the 'red base' model of students triggering workers' revolt, the reverse had happened.

And it happened again in Dagenham. What was to be almost two decades of struggle began around the issue of equal pay for women employed at Ford. In January 1969 Ford, Hull, and other issues came together in *Black Dwarf*'s venture into the 'women question'. The Ford dispute also triggered the National Joint Action Committee for Women's Equal Rights. Dominated by old Labour and Communist orthodoxies NJACWER made limited headway, but active in its inception were supporters of *Socialist Women*. This was a paper instigated, but not entirely run by, the IMG. The rival International Socialists had made recruits from the Vietnam Solidarity Campaign; the hold of the Communist Party on industrial militants was still strong; thus it was on the apparently peripheral issue of women, aided perhaps by that early meeting with the *NLR*, that the group was able to progress. Sustaining its momentum proved more difficult.

In 1965 and 1966 it had been the spark ignited between the children of CND, the Nuttalls, and the Horovitzes and the expatriate Americans that ignited the counter-culture. In the winter, spring, and summer of 1969 scattered working-class disputes, radical middle-class women, encountered another American influx that led to the birth of the women's liberation movement. There was the new American literature of feminism, and there were Americans living in London.

Nottingham and London had *Socialist Women* groups. In

Peckham another group had begun meeting by early 1969. North of the Thames in Tufnell Park another group was formed. The majority of its members were American. Its politics still echoed to the reverberations of the US New Left of the early 1960s, the era of the civil rights campaigns, the Students for a Democratic Society, before the factions and splits that were to wreck it later in the decade. Some of them had been active in the Stoppit Committee against the Vietnam War set up in London by Americans. There were other influences too on the Americans in Tufnell Park. 'We admired and discussed Helke Sander's statement to the German SDS conference. That piece also influenced our attempts to organize something for our own children and we met a number of times as adults and as adults with children with the German SDS people in Golders Green', a member wrote later to Sheila Rowbotham.

The SDS then had a presence that had not ended with the phalanx through Grosvenor Square in March 1968. The influence of its thought was to continue to pervade sections of the left and underground as the new decade began, for good and ill.

By 1969 Michelene Wandor had begun to write for *Time Out*, and her marriage was beginning to go through strains. Her children and those of Audrey Battersby, recently moved into Belsize Park, began playing together. Battersby, a member of the Socialist Labour League, and Wandor, a member of nothing, became friends. Battersby had contacts with the Peckham women's group. The group in Tufnell Park with its, as Wandor saw them, 'right-on American women' had already started. Someone suggested a local group. The friendship with Battersby, their role as mothers of kids, her discontent led her to join.

And focuses were developing for the groups as they emerged across Britain. In the spring of 1969 a 'revolutionary festival' at Essex University included a meeting on women's liberation. It was open, as all meetings were in those days, to men and women. It led to another meeting, predominantly attended by women. And that led to another gathering, and it was women only.

Few men then could understand the reasoning behind women-only meetings. The New Left was committed to revolution, argued the men. The emancipation of women would be part of this, in time. Why the need for the separation?

If for no other reason it was so that development would be possible without men there to present the correct line. But, as so often, what began as a tactic, an attempt to find space, became more, a tradition. Yet long after those Essex gatherings the idea of women-only meetings – outside the local groups, and sometimes not even there – was not common. Not until 1971 and an organized gathering of the women's National Co-ordinating Committee was the change finally made. Bitter experience mingled with farce to institutionalize the arrangement.

In May 1969 the first *Women's Newsletter* came out. The second issue was called *Harpies Bizarre*. Issue three was produced as *Shrew*. The name remained, and the collective editorship was passed from group to group.

Another child of 1968 had been the History Workshop, oriented to the history of the common people. In its inspiration it dates back to the events of 1956 and the tradition of Communist Party historians – Christopher Hill, Edward Thompson – who had broken with the Party in those days. It also drew on the talents of a younger labour historian, Raphael Samuel at Ruskin College, who had been one of the organizers of the Partisan Coffee House in the London of the early 1960s. An autumn 1969 meeting of the Workshop led to the suggestion for a meeting on women's history. Somebody else said, why history, why not women's liberation? Thus planning began for February 1970, at Ruskin, Oxford's trade union education college.

In New York the women of *Rat* had stuck around for the flowering and pending degeneration of the American movement. The arrival of a 'sex and porn' issue of the paper, at a time when other sections of the underground were lurching blinding or deliberately out of politics and into pornography, outraged New York feminists. Some demanded the right to produce their own issue. And they did.

The British women's liberation movement in its early stages played largely, but not exclusively on indigenous preoccupations of socialist politics and class. It drew on de Beauvoir's *The Second Sex*, the Marxist-oriented work coming out of West Germany, and the new American material. The US movement, in its anger, in its partial location amongst the enraged of the counter-culture, and without the ballast – or dead weight – of the Labour Party, took a more direct route.

'*Rat* must be taken over permanently by women', wrote Robin Morgan, radical feminist playwright and poet, in the first women's *Rat* 'or it must be destroyed. We have met the enemy, and he's our friend.'

It was a far cry from *Socialist Women*, February 1969: 'We are not anti-male, a charge often thrown at those concerned with the woman question. We are opposed to private property, the aliena- tion of labour under capitalism, the exploitation of the entire working class, we are opposed to men who do the "gaffer's" job and assist him to do the dirty on women workers – whether in the home or in industry.'

The first issue of the women's liberation *Rat* marked the end of men on the paper. Later it was to become *Women's Liberation*. An attempt to restore the *ancien régime* was thwarted immediately after the first women's issue. The last straw in triggering their move, the women said, via the Liberation News Service, had been the 26 January 1970 issue of *Rat*. The cover featured a woman hitchhiker lifting her skirt to get a ride. The blurb trumpeted the enticements to be found inside: Masturbation (female) page 7; Pornography page 11; 'No woman staff members had been consulted – of course not, for they would have objected. The uprising began when the women on *Rat*, one of the best and most notorious American underground papers insisted that the 6–23 February issue be drawn, written, photographed, edited and laid out entirely by women. After the issue appeared, another meeting was held. At that meeting, attended by both men and women, the women demanded, and got total editorial control of *Rat*. Men were invited to relate to the paper, but decisions will be made by closed meetings of the women's collective.'

It was a different world. As *Rat* was taken over, Nixon was invading Cambodia, US soldiers were still dying across Indo-China, the Black Panthers, torn by internal rifts, were being shot down and imprisoned across the United States, and the Chicago Seven trial, complete with institutionalized clashes between Judge Julius Hoffman and the defendants – who labelled him 'Mr Magoo' – continued. In Britain the upsurge that had floated disparate groupings towards each other was ebbing. As it did so people found themselves in different rock pools, creating new movements, new ripples, new waves. There was not the bitterness, the violence of the US anti-war, radical, and black movements in their decline, nor the anger of the new American women's movement. Yet here too 1970 was a turning point.

While some people prepared for the Oxford conference *Oz* ended 1969 with an image of Louise Ferrier, looking every inch the beautiful woman of the male hippy dream. It began the new year with its own contribution to women's liberation. The timing, as ever, was perfect; the content indicated that *Oz* encountered difficulty in reading the graffiti on the wall. The cover featured a woman gleefully brandishing an axe next to a suitably bandaged and pissed-off looking man. The catchline was 'Pussy Power', and on this occasion *Oz*'s iconoclasm left it not just on the outside but in the cold. Inside Germaine Greer waxed sceptical on lesbians. It was left to David Widgery reviewing Richard Neville's new book *Playpower*, on the age of the underground, to herald changing times. The reviewer, drawing lightly on his International Socialism and more substantially on the feminism of his friend Sheila Rowbotham, noted that the Australian wrote with 'extreme intelligence and wit', but remained a 'raving reactionary' about women. He continued, in a vein that was soon to be exhaustively mined by every right-on man from Southampton to Stornaway, that 'women are doubly enslaved, both as people under capitalism and women by men. The hippy chick has always been one of the most unfree of women; assigned to be ethereal and knowing about Tarot and the moon's phases but busy at cooking, answering the phone and rolling her master's joints.'

The hippy chick was still very much around. The Chicago conspiracy trial provided a last issue for the radical end of London's underground to provide activism by proxy. From then on they were to have their own domestic causes. But on a Saturday in January 1970 a Chicago benefit was held, thus keeping the Roundhouse in business and rallying the bewildered battalions. 'These were English freaks and not American Yippies', noted *Friends*. 'The distinct non-hit was a very sad little scene. Sam Cutler, organizer of the Stones' Altamont free concert, was elected, or maybe grabbed the post, to auction some polythene-swathed chick for the funds. She, poor thing, was either too smashed or too resigned to take much part in the proceedings.'

At the end of February in Oxford 560 people appeared for the women's liberation conference. They weren't all women, sixty men and forty children were amongst the crowd that were forced – because of the size of the gathering – out of Ruskin College and into the Students Union. Most were young, middle-class, but not all, the old and the working class were there. The days of women's 'welcoming flesh', and another kind of sexual liberation, were numbered. The welcomes were going elsewhere.

Papers were presented: on politics and the family, women's work, crime, history. The size of the meeting made the gathering inchoate but, to many, exhilarating. 'I'd never seen so many women looking confident in my life before', wrote Rowbotham in *The Body Politic*.

There was, reported *Idiot*, a 'near absence of the usual "female" rivalry, self display, subterranean murder, surrealist fetishism of sexual fear or rage – all these features which a male-dominated society has cultivated in us with millennial art.'

Not everybody agreed. It had been, reported three women from *It* under the headline 'A Conference of Women in Drag', 'one of the most frustrating experiences in quite a long time'. The size of the gathering had been intimidating, they reported, and there had been no attitude expressed towards 'new life-styles' and communes. 'The most vital thing we can do is sit down with each other in small groups, and start talking.' Which, as the months went by, was what happened.

The following month, in *Oz*, Wandor was in print on the conference. In 'Women on the Moon' she challenged Greer's criticism in *Oz* the month before, and her absence from Ruskin. 'Where was Germaine?' she queried.

Greer was completing the book that was to set the stamp on the British media's understanding of the women's movement in the 1970s, and to influence profoundly that decade's generation of women as they moved towards feminism, *The Female Eunuch*. Yet Greer, together with Eva Figes whose *Patriarchal Attitudes* was also a key influence, remained resolutely detached from the upsurge. For many women the sense of belonging, of sharing the experience of consciousness-raising, was crucial.

From Ruskin on the women's movement existed. During 1970 it mushroomed across Britain.

For *Black Dwarf* the weekend of the Ruskin conference was notable for something else. The tension between the IMG supporters and the rest within the paper climaxed. For the IMG group the solution would be the *Black Dwarf*'s effective re-emergence as the paper of the IMG, in the same way as *Socialist Worker* was the paper of the International Socialists. This was not an outcome that others on the paper were willing to accept. The result was a split. It was one in which Ali was confident that his group would be taking away the title, and what was left of the goodwill of the paper.

'What are you going to call it, Tariq?' asked Goodwin.

'*Black Dwarf* of course.'

'I'm afraid you can't', replied Goodwin. 'I've patented the name.'

'It was the only moment of discomfiture for Tariq', recalls John Hoyland. But it left the *Dwarf* in a weak position. Goodwin was left as the main source of finance for a paper continually losing money. It left the paper searching for a printer – *Idiot*'s Larcular Press was one brief port of call – and it left the paper with only a rump of a staff. How was the paper to be sold? Ali and Pete Gowan had departed to Pentonville Road and had begun work on what was to be the IMG's paper, the *Red Mole*. The IMG had supplied some people for street selling. There had been times when International Socialists had, unofficially, sold the paper. By 1970 those days were effectively past; for IS members, enjoying a boom, *Socialist Worker* was the priority. The student tide on which the *Dwarf* had sustained itself had ebbed. Even an office was hard to find. By April its production was being conducted from a spare room in Goodwin's flat in the Cromwell Road.

A new recruit was Phil Kelly. Later he was to work for *7 Days*, in the *Time Out* newsroom, and by the mid 1980s he was to become the editor of *Tribune*. Then he was fresh out of the 'Red Guards' phase Young Liberals, and Leeds University, and took over as *Black Dwarf*'s distribution manager for £10 a week. It was depressing work, shuffling forms and lists of sellers left over from headier times, digging amongst his own contacts for potential sellers.

It was left to Goodwin and Barnet to make the editorial decisions, and, as autumn approached, it was clear that time was running out. The organization had to be refinanced, reorganized, and relaunched. That June the Conservatives under Edward Heath had ousted the Wilson government. The war in Northern Ireland was intensifying. New industrial relations legislation was in the pipeline. 'Woodstock' was number one in the charts, but the festival was a fading memory. Perhaps a new paper, drawing on the lessons of the last five years, was what was needed. By autumn the *Dwarf*, described as dormant, was dead. *7 Days*, its effective succesor, was just a year away.

Chapter 11

Getting straight

In Portobello Road Alan Marcuson had reason to feel that his adventure in the underground publishing trade was turning out better than could have been expected. It was the right place to be, a few blocks away from *Oz* – which he disliked – a stone's throw from John Hopkins's old home where, almost a decade before, Miles had begun his involvement in what was to become the underground.

The sound of a rehearsing rock band, Quiver, and Nick Lowe's bass guitar vibrated from the basement, shaking Pearce Marchbank's carefully arranged scalpels and pens from his drawing board. A stream of visitors dropped in. Some were what passed as street people. But the paper had arrived at a time when a new generation of university graduates was seeking a way into journalism. Local papers were boring, Fleet Street could be tricky, and the underground might pay badly but it was exciting. By 1970 Marcuson's age put him just above his new associates on the paper, and thus lent him – for a time – a certain authority. But Green was fresh out of Oxford, Marchbank not long out of Central, and others were to appear. Dick Pountaine was in the United States, but on his return began writing for *Friends* about his experiences of New York's Alphabet City, with its dope, overdoses, and violence, on the edge of Manhattan.

'We didn't have a policy of hiring and firing', says Marcuson. 'It happened. It was the *Zeitgeist* of the times. I wanted to do a magazine that was articulate, politically aware, more so than either *It* or *Oz* – which I thought was just a fuck magazine really – I was trying to do something that *emerged* from hippiedom. I thought you could take an underground magazine and make it acceptable to a wider audience. In the early days we were still in the grip of the music business and the mystics. Yet the less of a music paper we became, the fewer ads we got. The more political our content became, the fewer ads we got.'

But *Friends* at first followed a familiar pattern. William Burroughs provided a mystifying contribution; Michael Abdul Malik was interviewed from his 'Black House' near Highbury Corner in the Holloway Road; David Mairowitz, the *It* veteran, wrote on Amsterdam; and, despite Marcuson's wish to draw away from music, *Friends* did pull in small quantities of music advertising.

Films were occasionally advertised too, when the orthodox media stumbled to consummate its commercial romance with youth in revolt.

Other arrivals on the paper indicated that the British class structure was alive and well, and that Oxford, versatile as ever, provided a perfect training for a life within the underground press. Jerome Burne had read law there, but quickly switched to the more appealing option of philosophy and psychology. The university, having basked in play power for centuries, had the appropriate background for being relaxed and not appearing to work at anything. Combine that with the hippy ethos of being even more laid-back, smoking drugs, and regarding the establishment as a vast conspiracy, and a perfect recipe for paralysis had been concocted.

'There was at Oxford then a feeling that this new wave was coming through', says Burne. 'We all wore bell-bottom trousers and hipsters. We were that spirit, we thought, whereas these sports-jacketed hunting-shooting-fishing lot were all old, dead, and finished. We were going to sweep up the future. But it was much more to do with having a good time than anything else. There were drugs and acid, I'd read Huxley's *Doors of Perception* when I was about 16 and thought it sounded terribly exciting and wonderful.'

It was a training that made a career in the media appear the most favoured option, but not a recipe for immediate success, even in the London of the times. Burne took a job making antique furniture, another washing up, and then ran into the affable Jonathon Green. By the end of 1969 he had been installed as the new magazine's 'Kultur' editor. The Germanization of the language was a popular trait of the time, combining hints of Freud with the threat of some Strangelovian corporate state. Thus 'America' hardly ever survived the underground printed page. 'Amerikka' was the preferred spelling.

Burne got his first wage packet from *Friends* – £15. It was the last wage packet he was ever to see on the paper, he believes. He settled quickly into his work, reading books he found interesting and reviewing movies. He none the less took his work seriously. 'I thought it my duty to see all these movies – about forty minutes of a chair, or things to do with a sheet.'

It wasn't an attitude likely to impress older members of the underground. For Burne, Nuttall's *Bomb Culture* was overstated. *He* didn't feel overshadowed by the Bomb. For David Robins, developing his commitment to libertarian socialism, *Friends*, rather than underground, spelt another group of aspiring journalists looking for their start in the trade. It was, then, what he detested: the professionalization of the underground, a counter-career structure within the counter-culture.

Friends' style might be laid-back, but the paper did come out at fortnightly intervals. The finances might be haphazard, but the mix seemed to work. Perhaps *Friends* would be that underground paper that would surface. The phantom of the 1950s *Village Voice* was stalking Portobello Road.

Yet *Friends*, for all the ambitions for order, had a reality that left something to be desired. 'To me', says Green, 'the underground press was two things. One was going to Grosvenor Square in 1970 for the Kent State demonstration, and going back and watching oneself on colour TV. This did terrible things for my sense of irony and paradox. The other was the typical underground day. We would get up about 11 o'clock. We'd have a joint. Then we'd have a cup of tea. Then we'd have another joint. Then we'd ring for a taxi. Roll a joint for the taxi. Smoke the joint in the taxi. Get to the office, have a joint. Then I was the anomaly of the underground press, I'd go over to the off-licence for a can of beer. This was a major deviation. I *drank*. And then we could work through the day. I could type, then, stoned out of my mind so much I could hardly see, but faultlessly – I couldn't do that now – then we'd go on, go to bed about four in the morning having made lots of lists and plans. In the middle of this we would put the paper together.'

At the end of the line was Marchbank. He had no previous contact with the business side of magazine production. He knew no typesetters, so superb copy would return, complete with a vast bill.

But Marchbank learnt. Together with Green they began to see themselves as the professionals, committed to new concepts, like hitting deadlines. They both drank for a start and, Marchbank the exception, hated dope. This was, he suspected, a key reason why the paper came out. He became office-bound, experiencing the entire outside world through wet photographs and copy arriving in the early hours.

Marcuson continued with his lists and sped around London. Editorial meetings were disorganized. Copy tended to be over-lengthy and deadlines functioned as useful reminders to writers to think about starting work. They were the common problems of journalists learning their trade, but this time an entire magazine was painfully sharing the process, without the leavening of experience. Thus pages happened, rather than were planned, and copy would gatecrash schedules rather than couple harmoniously with them. Across the western world people who went on to be journalists, insurance salesmen, corporate executives, politicians, or dead, were going through similar processes.

But there was innovation. Some sixteen years later Rupert Murdoch's News International, having built up a complete printing works in Wapping, complete with direct input technology for journalists and the latest in printing equipment, sacked his entire printing workforce, broke the power of the print unions, and divided his journalists. A few months later Eddie Shah, having fought a similar, smaller-scale battle in the north at Warrington, brought out *Today*, a newspaper reliant from its inception on the new technology.

The same process had occurred on the underground press – and on some of the far left socialist papers – back in the late 1960s and early 1970s. *Friends*, improvising its way towards deadlines did just that. Committed to radicalism, devoid of unions, *Friends* was a direct-input paper of a peculiar variety. The journalists took over the IBM golfball typewriters with typeface instructions sellotaped on top. They set their own copy for paste-up. Green was enchanted by the idea. He would write his pieces, pull them out, and stick them on to Marchbank's pages. Thus around five stages on conventional newspapers were leapfrogged. Since headlines could not be expanded or reduced on a process camera Marchbank relied on recently invented Letraset. Pictures were rarely commissioned, but 'found objects' torn from magazines. Nothing had to be sent out, the boards could be written on, should the mood take the designer. Corrections were stripped on to the boards. And nothing could go wrong, unless tea, or something else, was dropped on the boards.

It didn't solve *Friends*' money problems. And arguments between factions within the staff flourished, as elsewhere. Marcuson's interests continued to widen. Some, liking him, despaired of what they saw as his quintessentially hippy approach to the paper.

And competition was increasing, while the market wasn't. In 1967 *It* and *Oz* had been on their own. For *Friends*, in a leaner world, one paper was soaking up the readership, advertising, and attention. By the spring of 1970 *Time Out*, still an A5 booklet, was getting plump. The bi-weekly was expanding, with advertising to match. Yet the design remained constricted. It wasn't just a magazine of lists any more. Verina Glaessner was writing film reviews and news. In February 1970 the price rose from 1/6d (7½p) to 2/- (10p).

Other papers took note. Early in 1970 at *It* £1,200 worth of advertising would be spectacular success. In 1969–70, with John Leaver covering ads at *Time Out*, Felix Dennis at *Oz*, and Sue Small at *It*, an informal support network developed, exchanging tips for potential advertisers. But increasingly it was Leaver who had the most saleable product, despite Dennis's skills. In February 1970 *Time Out* was 84 pages; by July, when advertising should have been declining for the summer, it was up to 100 pages.

And the ads weren't just the music sales that provided the underground press's financial lifeline. Cinema chains, noting the young market's disinterest in *What's On* and *Where To Go*, had begun booking. Venues, restaurants, travel, and clothes advertising was expanding. The transformation of the counter-culture was in the making. For some it was the fulfilment of the dream of 1967, the growth of an organism serving and being served by the young, the dissident, independent of the mainstream metropolis. For others it was hip capitalism, the wooing of the virtuous into an antechamber of the old gang. Visiting London in 1969, *Rolling Stone*'s Jann Wenner, asked what the 'revolution' was, had defined it as when his generation took over the running of Coca Cola. It hadn't been what Ginsberg, Burroughs – inasmuch as he noticed – Nuttall, or Hopkins had had in mind. Almost imperceptibly the process had begun and would bear fruit, and create problems, crises, and splits.

But in 1970 the views of Robins *et al.* had not greatly changed. *Time Out* wasn't really underground, but a harmless little magazine, making its producers a few bob. 'I regarded it as a redbrick university "what's on" sheet', observes Marchbank, the Shrewsbury public schoolboy, 'I hated the unadventurous way it looked.'

So did its founder Tony Elliott. Having established the magazine he could see by the summer of 1970 that it was bursting out of its confines. An *ad hoc* compilation in 1968 had given way to a design but it lacked either the iconoclasm of *Oz*'s fitfully brilliant design, the raunchiness of *It*, the imaginative tabloid approach sporadically attempted by *Black Dwarf*, or the cleanness of above-ground papers.

Or indeed, the increasing assurance that Marchbank was bringing to *Friends*. Flair, training, and bitter experience were turning him into a designer for the times. In the early 1960s magazines like *Town* had, with their use of 'creative white space', broken with the traditional model of upmarket magazines. The lessons had been applied on the Sunday colour magazines, particularly by designers like the *Sunday Times*'s David King in the mid and late 1960s. The classic clean 1960s format, from the *Observer* onwards, used bold sanserif typefaces, big pictures, bold black and white. It was a complete contrast to the *Oz* technique of creative nihilism and wild printing ink mixes. Marchbank made his own interpretation on *Friends*. A 'Whole Earth Catalogue', before the project petered out, gave him an opportunity not available amidst the normal chaos of the paper to implement some of his ideas. And the second issue of *Friends* produced in January 1970 previewed some of the style *Time Out* was to develop in the spring of 1971.

And while *Time Out* might be having problems with design, and with being taken seriously by some, others thought differently. For Michelene Wandor working for the paper, being able to write what she wanted was in itself freedom. But also the magazine was *creating* events via its network of information. Gradually, via its

Agitprop section, news – even if at a level of reporting on activism, rather than muck raking – was inching into the back of the magazine. At the front, after a rudimentary contents page, came film, the great mainstay. It was, as Marchbank noted, a stylistic mess.

So in other ways was *Friends*. Palace revolutions had begun to pall, he concluded, and began to drop out of the paper. A friend suggested to him that Elliott would 'give his right arm' if Marchbank would take over design at *Time Out*. He went to the magazine's new offices in Gray's Inn Road, near King's Cross. He had never seen, he reflected, so many people in ripped velvet jackets in his life. 'Take 6' jackets, he concluded, with torn lining.

Elliott was into expansion. An ill-fated attempt to produce, via Jeremy Beadle, a *Time Out North West* centred on Manchester was in progress. *Time Out*'s move to Gray's Inn Road spelt better, if more superficially squalid, times. 'It was literally rat-infested', claims Marchbank. 'You could have the rat catcher in and live with the smell of rotting meat for six weeks, and find droppings and dead mice on the typewriters.' Elliott disagrees: 'It was quite a *decent* environment. People all had their own desks and phones, we were trying to be fairly professional.'

After the first meeting Marchbank set off on a camping holiday in southern France. Elliott drove down, and they discussed the magazine. A complete reorganization had to take place, argued Marchbank. And new equipment was needed. No more the *Friends* techniques of pasted-up pictures from other magazines: a process camera, converted from a printing works, and probably the first installed in a British magazine office, was to be bought. Perhaps the new equipment would pay for itself. It could service the new fringe market. Why, the Royal Court Theatre where Jimmy Porter had once stalked the boards was then – to the probable disgust of John Osborne – to host an alternative theatre festival. The programme would need a new, in-touch, eye. So would the Place dance centre. There had to be a market. Marchbank signed on.

In November 1970 the new design was hastily implemented and the *Time Out* cover logo was changed to a style that has persisted to this day. It was done hurriedly, Marchbank recalls, on a Sunday afternoon, just before it had to go off. Its distinctive neon effect was, however, still considered a stop-gap, to be changed at some future date. The date never came. Elliott, despite suggestions from others, stuck rigidly to the design that was a key to the magazine's identity. Sections were picked out cleanly; 'creative white space' nestled into the listings. Leading the magazine, in place of the jumble of film listings, came *Time Out*'s own news section.

Once *It* had spun listings out of its cultural coverage, around its Ezra Pound exclusives, its reports on Marcuse and Mao, Ginsberg and Ferlinghetti. Now, falteringly at first, *Time Out*'s news and features took over the front of the magazine. It was a definitive step, spelling more trouble for the underground. David May was soon to be recruited from a local paper to provide the news coverage. Under the byline 'Hack Typewriters' May began to provide a section that not only undermined the old papers' erratic coverage, but even posed a faint challenge to the mainstream media's version of events, and its agenda.

Time Out's transformation had been planned for January 1971. Its hasty introduction in November 1970 led one angry reader to suggest a free pair of glasses with every issue, due to the stylistically neat but unreadably small typeface.

There were other complaints, other reservations. '*Time Out* offered a real service to a healthy cross-section of the community, called "student", "hip", "fringe", or just "discerning" ', wrote Peter Oliver, a main mover behind south London's flourishing arts centre, the Oval House. 'With the change of layout comes a definite blurring of the edges, and one suspects that your good intentions are weakening under capitalist pressure!'

Capitalist pressure was what was making the paper. . .

Chapter 12

Shattering the spectacle

At the end of February 1970 Indica, the bookshop that had started it all, closed. True, there were to be other alternative bookshops, notably Compendium up in Camden Town, but the hopes, diversions, and new adventures of the mid 1960s were withering in a colder decade.

It, meanwhile, was 'a monument to its own endurance', wrote George Meliesky in the paper two months later. '*It* is a great consumer, a great sewer of effects, it grinds on even when the gears aren't working smoothly. Why? Because it inhabits those castles still shrouded by the ghosts of old games.' Ghosts was the word, but plenty of sightseers were still attracted; the old verve might be missing, and some of the old personnel, but a new army of festival-goers, the latecomers at the 1960s ball, had been recruited. Yet the excitement was fading and by the end of 1968 Jim Haynes's contacts with the paper had withered.

The paper still reported battles far away – the *Rat* struggle, the Chicago conspiracy trial – but back home its reportage was of small meetings and tedious busts. The names that had been *in time* – Burroughs, Ginsberg, Trocchi, even John Michell with *Verbiage on Garbage: Philosophy of Pollution* – now tended to induce incomprehension amongst the newcomers, *déjà vu* amongst the older readers. Between the Decca ads the rock coverage flourished – with its Lennon and Ono interview, a Fairport Convention profile – but wasn't this moving the paper more towards an alternative *NME*, a battle that resources would ensure the latter won? And was it what *It* should be about? Miles returned on occasions to edit, and provided, *pace* 1966, another doomed plea for London to become the twenty-four hour city.

But there were, that summer, the festivals. 'Woodstock', Mark Williams observes, 'had a lot to answer for. It caused such damage because everyone tried to emulate it. And Woodstock, as far as I can gather, was a pain in the bum to be at. You were conned into thinking you were sharing this wonderful experience with sixty million other mud-crazed acid casualties – or mud *covered* acid casualties I should say. Ugh. . .'

Others disagreed at the time. For Williams's sometime *It* associate Mick Farren, Woodstock-type rock gatherings were proof that the new culture could work. That year, with rock as one of the few focuses for the freak end of the underground, he attempted to prove it. The location was near Worthing, in the heart of Conservative Sussex; the project was 'Phun City'.

The idea, according to Farren, although contested by others, was a festival that avoided the profit-orientation. In this it was a success. Failure to get any pay-booths installed ensured this. The weekend chosen was that of 24 July 1970. By mid July West Sussex County Council had applied for an injunction to stop the festival. Then the backers pulled out. A day later, on 16 July, while the organizers desperately sought fresh funding, the injunction was dropped. Even Ronan O'Rahilly, the one-time Radio Caroline boss, was approached. By the following Monday work, and rain, had commenced on the site. Campers drawn by publicity in *It* and other underground papers, and denunciations from the nationals, began to trickle with the deluge on to the site. Seeing a shelter from the storm they removed useful items of Phun City's construction material to establish their *ad hoc* nests in the nearby woods. By 24 July, low on finance, the organizers greeted the first of the thirty bands booked to play. The rain persisted. Showing the spirit of the times, most of the musicians agreed to play, despite the absence of cash, free. Free, whose 'All Right Now' was high in the popular music charts was an exception. It wasn't, and they wouldn't.

From *Friends* Jonathon Green arrived in their very own and Phun City. It had, he consoled himself, certain advantages, even if it was completely chaotic. Later indeed he was to regard it as one of the better things produced by the underground at the beginning of its Indian summer.

The police arrived, too, to supplement the Hell's Angels security operation. The Drugs Squad attempted to move anonymously amongst the bedraggled crowds. They were quickly identified and circles of campers formed dancing circles around them, singing and jeering. They were not attacked, but they were made unwelcome, and departed. The drugs remained, soaking the brains of the participants as surely as the heavens soaked their bodies. Drug dealers became generous in adversity. 'John the Bog' – so named because he usually ran a stall in Middle Earth's lavatories – sold dope until he had covered his costs. Then he gave it away.

Hunger stalked the woods. The Hell's Angels 'liberated' the wretched official caterers' supplies. A people's food stall was established and Green found himself briefly in charge. Across the churned earth the message crackled from the PA system. Free food was available. As one, the audience sprang to its feet and ran towards the stall. It was, thought Green, rather unnerving.

'Phun City', remembers Mark Williams, 'was disastrous in many respects – in most respects – but it was a great idea. I made it through the weekend. Horrendo! Bad acid and bad weather and bad music and fucking hell. I am just amazed that so many of us are still alive, the quantities of drugs that were taken.'

As the weekend concluded, the more privileged sections of the underground's largest – around 10,000 – self-organized army departed in cars and vans back to Birmingham and Bristol, Manchester and the Mersey, Notting Hill and Camberwell. Back in the woods the stragglers, and those who measured their commitment to the cause On the Road too during those years, slept on as the rain dripped from the branches. In the morning the Drugs Squad and the local police returned with reinforcements, and set about the business of searches, busts, and arrests.

Two weeks later professionalism and the revenge of Phun City had their hour, or days, with the Isle of Wight Festival. Jimi Hendrix had succeeded Bob Dylan as the star on a vast, expensive bill. He arrived on the island exhausted, straight from New York opening of his Electric Lady studios. It was early morning when he began playing a lacklustre set.

It matched the acrimony of the festival. There were the long-haired entrepreneurs and there were the groupuscules who identified the event as the battleground and the organizers as the enemy in the people's struggle against the Man, and the System. A nearby hill, which provided a free view of the stage, became the Spion Kop of the counter-culture, with fences, Alsatians, and security men to tease out the reality of the system of oppression. In America there had been the Black Panthers, revolution tinged with theatre, generating confrontation, tragedy, and pride. Their example produced the White Panthers centred around the curious figure of John Sinclair who managed the 'revolutionary' rock band the MC5, and doubled as founder-cum-'minister of information' of the White Panther Party. Revolt as theatre. In the summer of 1970, from the native farceurs came the British White Panthers. In place of Bolshevik demands for land, peace, and bread for peasants, soldiers, and workers came the demand for 'information, free music, and free food' for *It* readers, Hendrix fans, and hungry hippies. 'Performers are on that stage', announced the Panthers, 'because, and only because, of the People.' This truism left many of its recipients unimpressed. 'Don't be tourists', adjured the globe-trotting Joni Mitchell, dropping down from her helicopter. Fellow Canadian Leonard Cohen, said *Friends*, 'with his orgasm of despair represented the mood of the crowd'. It was the White Panthers who wanted to knock down the fence but, joked Richard Neville, 'that should be singular but no one dares reveal that Mick Farren is a one-man tribe'.

Eighteen-year-old Charles Shaar Murray had just been recruited into the underground press via the 'Schoolkids' *Oz*'. He was near to tears. 'It's all fucked. Hendrix was saying goodbye.' By accident or design the guitarist was. Eighteen days later he was dead of an overdose, in London, alone. The core of one of the 1960s parties had disintegrated.

After Neville's *Playpower* that spring, the autumn was to witness Germaine Greer's *The Female Eunuch*. *Oz* had been a gadfly, an early-warning system for ideas, anarchy, and one concept of sexual liberation. And its editor, together with Greer, had become a media celebrity. Two Australians had achieved what no British members of the underground had. Not everybody was pleased about the development.

'It's all too much like a handbook for a package holiday drop-out', wrote Martin Wright in *Friends*. In *It* Harvey Matusow was more generous: 'If John (Wilcock) is the father of the movement, then Richard Neville proves in this book he is the journalistic son of it.' But, as if *It* wanted to set the record straight, a supplementary review by Mark Williams appeared in the following issue. 'Richard is the underground whizz-kid', he wrote, 'the flash Harry of a mythical culture.'

Others were less dismissive of the flash Harry, notably Detective-Inspector Luff of the Obscene Publications Squad of the Metropolitan Police. In *Oz26* that February a note appeared: 'Want to edit *Oz*? Are you under 18?' A little more than a year later the replies were to put Neville in the dock of the Old Bailey. *Oz*'s role as a gadfly had always been one of its key functions, and at that time Neville was pulling back from the magazine, as he was to do with increasing frequency in the years ahead. He didn't, he recalls, get many ideas worth retaining while smoking dope, but the idea for the 'Schoolkids' *Oz*' was one exception. And when eventually the volunteers arrived at the ofice he was impressed. 'There was a whole debate about anarchism', he remembers, 'and I was really moved by the intensity of it. They really wanted to express themselves. But once they had gathered together I was effectively out of town. If I hadn't been I *might* just have done something about the small ads which caused trouble in court. I just might, but I can't be sure.'

When the issue came out in May 1970 it created little initial stir. It was just another edition to go alongside the 'Hippy Atrocities *Oz*', the 'Acid *Oz*' and, with the following issue another voyage into the stormy waters of women's liberation, with the 'Cuntpower *Oz*'. Luff's arrival at *Oz* came in early June, with Marsha Rowe the first contact the police made with *Oz*. It was just before the Election, which returned the Conservatives to power after six years. The 1967 conviction of Mick Jagger had provided a setpiece battle between the establishment and a youth culture at the late dawn of its life. *It* had passed much of 1970 awaiting its November trial. With the raid on *Oz*, Neville, the 'underground whizz-kid', together with Jim Anderson and Felix Dennis, formed a part of a movement which, moving towards dusk, was to be provided with an extended twilight.

In America that year the collapse of the Students for a Democratic Society into warring factions had led one wing, the Weathermen, to go genuinely underground and wage lethal if ineffective war on the Nixon administration and the Pentagon. In May four students at Kent State University were shot down by the National Guard, soon after the President had written off protestors as 'student bums'. In August had come the George Jackson Soledad shoot-out.

England had its echoes. At Essex University that May students were found guilty of a rather ineffective conspiracy to burn Barclays Bank in protest against its South African connections. In August had come the discovery of a bomb at Iberian Airways' London office. And outside Notting Hill's Mangrove restaurant in All Saints Road, centre of West Indian life for two decades 200 demonstrators were engaged in battles with the police which were to result in trials on into the winter of 1971. And in September a night-cleaner, May Hobbs, who had been waging an isolated struggle to improve conditions for women workers like herself, began to attract support from the new women's movement and the underground that was even to lead Richard Neville to join Louise Ferrier on the night-time picket line outside Empress State building in the dimmer reaches of Earls Court.

There was precious little to win votes for the Labour government in the General Election that June. Better the devil the electorate didn't know, the Edward Heath of the 'Selsdon group' committed to a revived free market, than the devil they did. Pragmatism and technological revolution evoked contempt and derision.

In America the underground produced strange blooms. The *Rat* women had challenged the paper's sexism, but it was but a pale imitation of the more calculated enterprises now emerging from the one-time sexual revolutionaries. The publication of sex-oriented personal ads had occasioned sporadic debate on the *Village Voice*; their publication in papers like the *Los Angeles Free Press* had provided a financial life-line. But the excuse of necessity proved the mother of invention. 'To make a bundle' was the reason cited by the *East Village Voice* when it launched *Kiss* in April 1969. Its publication was a response to the phenomenal success of Al Goldstein's *Screw*, which had been first published in November 1968, and was entirely devoted to sex, and to challenging, claimed Goldstein, the left's 'fucked up' attitudes to the subject. Referring to the 'much maligned' paper in *Playpower*, Richard Neville noted that 'obviously the refreshing irresponsibility of that approach will prompt a severe counter-reaction.' He was right, although the quarters it came from were probably to surprise him. Less enthusiastic was *Village Voice* cartoonist Jules Feiffer who labelled Goldstein's creation about as 'pro-sex as the clap'.

As the American underground press had set the irrepressible Jim Haynes in motion with *It*, so *Screw* re-energized him. In the summer of 1969 he had been deliberating with Bill Levy, fresh out of the *It* editorship, on an idea for another paper. He was, he wrote fifteen years later, 'becoming more and more aware of the pain and problems caused by sexual repression and frustration and ignorance'. So, they concluded, a paper about sexual freedom was needed. Thus he differentiated between *Screw* – which he labelled a male heterosexual humour magazine – and their new progeny, *Suck*, which was to represent the entire pendulum of sexuality. By the late summer he had enlisted playwright and poet Heathcote Williams and Germaine Greer to join its editorial board, and so began Haynes's last major essay into publishing. Since it was clear the venture would never get an English printer – or avoid legal action – it was published from Amsterdam. Subsequent issues were indeed to invite prosecution, as Compendium's owner was to find to her cost.

Partly it was back to the debate that had occupied Tom McGrath and David Mairowitz in the early days of *It*. It was the male voice of cultural, sexual subversion, and the debate been conducted largely within those terms, generating such slogans as 'dope, rock 'n' roll and fucking in the streets' by the later 1960s. With the exception of Greer, women had largely stayed off-stage in the debate, but centre-stage as symbols of hedonism. Dope, rock, and women were all, hopefully, dangerous, and the sign of good times. Thus *It*'s 1970 headline 'Tits, Ass and Hot Revolution' became less a parody of the American skin mags that provided its source material than an identical come-on. Yet for Greer *Suck* was, in its inspiration, a serious argument about sexual politics, an attempt to create a new kind of pornography in which there was no hidden anything, where, by going all the way, and avoiding mass-market pulp and glossy exploitation, they would get the entire western hang-up about sex over once and for all. It was a brave ambition, and it was not to be fulfilled.

Besides the tensions that later emerged within the *Suck* group, other forces mediated against its success, not that Haynes, going his Candide-like way, noticed. At the end of November 1970 he was helping get the first 'Wet Dream Film Festival' underway in Amsterdam. 'The four days long orgy of smut films featured entries from countries throughout the world', reported Los Angeles' *Candid Press*. 'The public was invited and they came in droves. Came, yes came. We're talking about genuine hard core flicks, not cock-teasing nudies.'

Candid laid it on the bottom line; others, including amongst the judges Germaine Greer, and Richard Neville, attempted to treat it with the seriousness which it deserved – rather less than *Candid* brought to the subject. The dialectic of sex was developing into a cacophony. While Haynes produced his festival, and the women's and gay liberation movements argued about their views, other hangovers from early R.D. Laing and the Dialectics of Liberation continued. In 1970 Kenneth Loach and Tony Garnett's *The Body* was released, a celebration of the same, made from a semi-Marxist standpoint, with a commentary by Vanessa Redgrave. The film made some fateful and farcical links. A mutual acquaintance of Loach and Garnett was Alex Mitchell, a journalist working for the *Sunday Times*. The film-makers wished to celebrate humanity with a tasteful act of coition, and Richard Neville was contacted to find a working-class couple, says the Australian, willing to give all for the cameras. It wasn't to be – and wasn't – a soft porn movie. Neville directed them towards Felix Dennis, who declined the offer. So did David Widgery and his then lover. 'Finally they came back and said we can't find anyone', recalls Neville, 'so they begged and pleaded for Louise and I to do it.' They did, and made an apparent friend of Mitchell at the same time.

The media interest in the underground was increasing, just as the movement itself set into slow decline. Thus it was in early November that David Frost, noting the arrival of Jerry Rubin on tour from the Chicago conspiracy trial, decided to put the 'new' movement on television.

Thus were the likes of Felix Dennis, Mick Farren, and Alan Marcuson invited to join Rubin and fellow American Stew Albert on what the *Daily Mirror* labelled the 'Frost Freakout'. While they sat in the audience the show began according to normal Frost style. Then the audience, or the more enthusiastic parts of it, occupied the stage, complete with one new participant squirting the wretched compère in the face with a water pistol. From behind the TV cameras Louise Ferrier, Richard Neville, and Caroline Coon quailed. 'I thought the whole thing was *absolutely* ghastly', shudders Ferrier.

The media meanwhile addressed itself to the underground with an enthusiasm it hadn't displayed since the 1967 Summer of Love, and 1968's May Events and the student revolt. 'Television chiefs will begin an inquiry today into the Yippie invasion of the David Frost show', wrote the *Mirror*'s James Wilson and Jack Bell. The 'yippies' – as the assembly found themselves described – were labelled, eccentrically, 'fellow revolutionaries' of Rubin, and members of 'an American-based cult'. Thus Bell and Wilson, like the many Bourbons of the underground, indicated that they had learned nothing and forgotten nothing in the ensuing years. The front man

for 1963's *That Was The Week That Was* – with its echoes of
American political humour – found himself hosting a gaggle of front
men, and the occasional woman, for an early 1970s satire on late
1960s values. The underground had set much store on wresting
control of the media. The result that evening was less Aquarius
rising, more traditional English fairground.

As an onslaught on the old order it was poor stuff, as sections of
the movement lurched further into self-parody. Post-Isle of Wight
the 'White Panthers UK' were officially announced in *It*. Their
immediate demands of the system responsible for Vietnam, Biafra,
and Richard M. Nixon included a £3,000 donation from the
producers of *Hair* to the 'community' they were exploiting.

Money was indeed needed, but less for the White Panthers than
for *It* itself. In November the *It* case finally came to court, with
Knullar, the owners, fined £2,000, while Graham Keen, Peter
Stansill, and David Hall found themselves with eighteen-month
suspended sentences and costs. They appealed.

New movements were forming. In December the process begun
by Stonewall in 1969 brought the Gay Liberation Front to London.
Briefly it comprised women and men, and, started by two men, it
grew rapidly during those winter months.

But another media event signalled key changes. Back at the
Albert Hall, where it had all begun, two strands of the underground, one present from before its inception, one partly growing in
reaction to it, fleetingly crossed paths.

As the underground drew on American influences, so did the
world it sought to challenge. Each year the Albert Hall was the
setting for the Mecca 'Miss World' contest. And in those days the
winner could expect a brief tour of the US Army secure bases in
Vietnam, in the company of the glazed compère, Bob Hope. The
event crystallized some of the things that the new women's
liberation movement was fighting to transform; and to a small part
of the ultra-left, it was also a classic example of the 'spectacle' that
enmeshed the world.

On 30 August 1970 a small bomb exploded outside the home of
the Commissioner of the Metropolitan Police. It went unreported.
The same happened at the home of the new Conservative Attorney-
General, Sir Peter Rawlinson, on 30 October. It also went
unreported. 'He who liveth off the people', said an accompanying
message, 'by the people shall he die.' The night before the Miss
World contest a small bomb was planted in the BBC transmission
van outside the Albert Hall. The police became aware that they
were dealing with some new, and unidentifiable, movement.

Separate, and rather more easily identifiable, was the Women's
Street Theatre, which had grown from the new women's liberation
movement. It was partly out of that theatre group that the

subsequent intervention at the Miss World contest was to come.

As far as the organizers were concerned, Miss World – Vietnam, Republican Mr Hope, Conservative Mr Morley, and all – was not political. True, the Indian government had been infuriated when an Indian winner agreed to tour Vietnam. 'She received cheers', noted Hope, 'in spite of being coloured and wearing a sari.'

Yet that kind of politics still wasn't the essence of the Miss World protest, which was to grab rather more effectively at the headlines than the Frost freakout. Beauty contests were about traditional paths for women to follow in the wake of 1945, and 1970 was a year when some of them were setting off on another route. 'Pretty girls', added Hope, 'don't have these problems.'

The women took their seats in the hall, scattered around the auditorium and in the balcony, with smoke bombs, flour bombs, stink bombs, whistles, rattles, and leaflets concealed. The stage was within easy reach, the security was lax, and so was the comedian. The brisk liberal of the 1940s had given way to a dull, stale performer reading disjointedly from cue cards. The women moved in. Flour, smoke, noise, and mayhem engulfed the organizers and judges. Hope fled. The show lurched out of control.

In a few minutes order was restored and the women's movement established itself as part of the 1970s, unlike the Frost show participants, fighting a rearguard action for a lost decade. The media had already discovered shorthand ways of treating the subject. The bra-burning myth had been useful; so had Valerie Solanas's *Scum Manifesto* and attack on Andy Warhol back in 1968, but Solanas had been an oddity from the closed world of New York's avant-garde; Anne Koedt's *Myth of the Vaginal Orgasm* had stirred fears amongst men within the movement and occasioned pieces in the leisure sections of the heavy papers; and Greer's *Female Eunuch* had put the subject on the review pages. But the Miss World attack symbolized values challenged. Hope understood this as he returned to the stage, dragging the turmoils of the 1960s into his, for once, unscripted monologue. 'These things can't go on much longer', he told a surprised audience. 'They're going to have to get paid off sooner or later. Someone upstairs will see to that. Anybody who wants to interrupt something as beautiful as this must be on some kind of dope.'

Nobody upstairs could really sort it out, as the decade proved. And for once, out of the counter-culture came people who weren't on dope. It was a long way from that evening back in June 1965.

But there were curious echoes. In the wake of the night a pamphlet 'Why Miss World?' was published by supporters of some of the defendants. 'We are poisoned by the spectacle', Raoul Vaneigem wrote in the Situationist's *Totality for Kids* back in 1962. In the pamphlet the writers noted that 'the spectacle is vulnerable.

However intricately planned it is, a handful of people can disrupt it and cause chaos in a seemingly impenetrable organization.'

'To the passivity imposed on the dispossessed masses', wrote Vaneigem, 'is added the growing passivity of directors and actors submitted to the abstract laws of the market and the spectacle.' 'The spectacle', said the pamphlet, 'isn't prepared for anything other than passive spectators.'

The avant-garde dreams of Trocchi, the art world of the 1965 sTigma exhibition had metamorphosed. The heat and the turmoils later in the decade had transformed the environment and produced different movements. Now, in the cold of the beginning of the new Conservative decade, politics as art had become art as politics. The women were bailed. By December they made their first court appearances. In January they returned to court, but by then the situation had changed. Some of them were picked up immediately after the hearing for questioning by the police investigating the Angry Brigade. The 'spectacle', noted the sharp-eyed Detective Sergeant Roy Creamer, was a term that recurred in Angry Brigade material, and the women had used the slogan 'We're not beautiful, we're not ugly, we're angry.' Angry, equalled Angry Brigade? It was too neat a correlation, but the cultures interconnected. The women meanwhile were eventually fined, discharged, and bound over to keep the peace for two years.

Suddenly *Oz* was out of step, and behind rather than ahead of the times. '*Oz* doesn't reflect the official women's liberation party line', editorialized its 'Cuntpower' issue that autumn. But there was no party line. There were socialist feminists, radical feminists, separatist feminists, even quasi-situationist feminists. 'Everyone digs the ideas of the new female militancy', it added, whistling in the dark, 'so long as all it does is demand things from men. Rejecting that workshop mentality *Oz* argues that if anything will free women it will be their own peculiar force. Read on fatherfuckers!'

'It is time to dig *cunt*', wrote Greer, 'and women must dig it first.' It was a different, and increasingly isolated, perspective that she followed. While her book captured the popular imagination and turned women to feminism its author remained isolated from the movement emerging in all its different manifestations; from Miss World to the night-cleaners, from Ruskin to consciousness-raising.

'In the early 1970s', says Michelene Wandor, 'political energy took over from cultural energy in the avant-garde.' It was an energy that had little time for *Suck* magazine or Phun City, freak-outs or wet dream festivals. Yet parts of that 1960s cultural energy had been retained, with good, and occasionally catastrophic, implications for those who possessed it. The Situationists, born of a theory of the long boom where the problems of production had been overcome and the problem of consumption had become paramount, began to find their politics translated into action at the very instant that the economy began its long slide into the recession of the 1970s. The Miss World protest had clear echoes of the 'Sits', but it had been part of the cultural spectacle. So, more emphatically, had the Angry Brigade as they drew on other traditions to create a disastrous brand of isolated, elitist, revolutionary politics. Having romanticized the criminal and the lumpen as the only true outsiders in the years after 1956, some of the Angry Brigade were to find themselves cast very neatly into that role in the spectacle that surrounded them.

Oz had, perhaps, been right about the 'peculiar strength', if nothing else. 'If there was a radicalism about *Oz*', says David Widgery, 'it was predominantly a sexual radicalism for men. When women took it up, or took its premises seriously, or asked what it was promising for them, it was hoist by its own petard. The "Cuntpower" issue managed to flatter male chauvinism. *Oz* always found movements very threatening. It meant there was a form of organization that undercut their particular patch. They didn't like the left, and they liked the women's movement even less. The women's movement wasn't trying to humiliate men, but unfortunately people who live by the cock, die by the cock!'

It is a view that Neville disputes, up to a point, '*Playpower* wasn't influenced by the women's movement, there were great sexist paragraphs in it, but at that time I remember seeing the Living Theatre and being influenced by that, and a lot of very interesting American women were arriving. I can't actually pinpoint my reactions to feminist ideas but they began to seep in with the damp in my basement. After the *Oz* trial something wasn't right for me, and the women's movement did add to that sense of confusion. It made enemies out of friends to some extent. There was this element of "are these women having their revenge on us?" It was the beginning of a break-up of solidarity because in the early stages of the underground there was this tremendous feeling of solidarity and harmony. It may have involved women getting exploited but there was this great friendship between men and women – exploited or otherwise – and the change was part of a general fragmentation.'

'When their secretaries and "chicks" started meeting independently', argues Widgery, 'there was an audible gasp of paranoia.' The meetings were to begin in 1971. The paranoia extended outside the confines of *Oz*, and was already around.

Chapter 13

Professional problems

Ninety per cent of the criticisms of the underground press are
right; it is just clothes and dope. The underground press has
created a scene that for the most part is just the emergence of hip
middle-class intellectuals.

(Alan Marcuson, on quitting *Friends*, 1971)

By the standards of the underground press it had been a
spectacularly promoted project. Yet it was a desultory launch. The
staff trickled out of the offices in ones and twos and made their way
down Princedale Road towards the restaurant. It was a sunny
afternoon in May 1971 and the venue was suitably upmarket, if a
little desolate for the new style of paper that London – and Britain –
was supposed to take to its heart and off the newsstands.

But as it was launched, *Ink* had big problems. It no longer had an
editor for a start. After the meeting with Alex Mitchell about *The
Body*, Richard Neville had kept in touch, and with plans for the new
paper Mitchell seemed just the man for the job. He had worked in
Australia, which seemed a good omen, and he was an experienced
Sunday Times journalist with a good radical track record. He surely
would break with the sloppy traditions of the underground press.
True, Neville found him a trifle *elusive* at times, but he was out
getting stories after all. And Neville had seen him working, he knew
he was a quick, professional writer, the man to produce a paper
combining the muscle of the *Village Voice* with the better parts of
the underground, and the professionalism of Fleet Street. Then on
the big day he had upped and left. It took some time for the stunned
staff to locate him. Mitchell, or 'Mad Mitch' as Neville was to label
him in imitation of the Colonel who had presided over the bloody
British departure from Aden, had decamped to Gerry Healey's
Socialist Labour League. The SLL was the graveyard, or transit
camp, for many would-be revolutionaries over the years. In the
wake of the Hungarian tragedy the *Daily Worker*'s Peter Fryer had
enlisted with the SLL; in the midst of the *Ink* farce Mitchell did the
same.

Amongst those attempting to prevent the 'bridge between Fleet
Street and the underground' subsiding into the crevasse was
Richard Adams. He was a designer from Birmingham who had quit

127

that city in 1969 to put his graphic skills to work in a place where they could, he thought, have some political and cultural meaning. Down in London he shared a church-cum-studio in Acton to produce his own work. But for money he worked at Decca Records' design studio. In the autumn of 1970 he had picked up a copy of *Oz30*. Allende's recent triumph in the Chilean elections was being analysed; Greer was noting the inevitability of Hendrix's death. Travel was prominent as hippies headed east to the lands popularized in print in the previous decade. Travellers to Iran and Afghanistan, where ayatollahs remained in mosques, the Shah on the Peacock Throne, and the Red Army across the borders, provided their reminiscences for the people back home. And there was an advertisement inviting designers to get in touch with the magazine. Adams did.

Meeting Felix Dennis he was surprised. He had expected a hippy; true, Dennis had a beard, but also a suit and tie. He wasn't the designer's idea of what people within the underground press were supposed to look like. Perhaps, suggested the uncharacteristic hippy, Adams would like to work on *Oz*? Adams agreed, but the work would have to be out of hours. Daytime belonged to the corporation by Waterloo railway station.

Thus at evenings and weekends Adams climbed Princedale Road stairs to *Oz*'s first-floor office, and an entry to the rest of London's underground press. Writers, good, bad, and indifferent, were two a penny, designers weren't. He worked at Endell Street with *It*, in Portobello Road with *Friends*. There were street-sellers and fans, people with stories and people with dope, concert promoters and community organizers; a spiral of activity surrounded him and sucked him in. He produced record sleeves, the cover for the new edition of *Playpower* and, while at Decca he was earning good money – £32 a week – the job's always limited attractions had evaporated. He leapt at the offer of £20 a week from Neville. Perhaps, with the support of his wife's wages, the job would be feasible.

Martin Sharp, whose illustrations had, as much as anyone's, set the tone for the underground in Britain, the United States, and Australia was moving back to his homeland. Jonathan Goodchild, the early *Oz* designer, had found a more lucrative outlet. In California Jann Wenner's *Rolling Stone* had given birth to Straight Arrow publishers and Goodchild had been recruited. But a band of roving designers had emerged. Marchbank was, in early 1971, established at *Time Out*; there was Barney Bubbles's spectacular work at *Friends*; and, throughout the underground, David Wills and a new generation of women designers began to emerge, particularly around *Time Out*.

At *Oz* Adams worked closely with Jim Anderson. Racks were

piled high with comics, collages, cartoons, illustrations sent in by the ambitious, the dedicated, the dope-heads. It gave the designer an exhilarating freedom.

The freedom would naturally be redefined for the more orthodox adventure that was to be *Ink*, it was assumed. In the autumn of 1970 *Oz* explained that, while launched by the magazine, '*Ink* newspaper will be entirely independent in character.' It would be open to all who shared the magazine's boredom with Fleet Street's inability to provide news relevant to the new culture. And later it was explained that *Ink* was being carefully planned, financed, and treated with a professionalism commensurate with this most serious of publications.

Much of the impetus for *Ink*'s birth came from the discussions between Richard Neville and Ed Victor. The Australian, tiring of *Oz*'s erratic monthly deadlines, yearned for something more immediate, and by then there were the examples of not only the *Village Voice* and the American underground papers but the increasingly professional *Rolling Stone*. Neville had held preliminary meetings with others within the underground, but little came of it. Then, one day, having lunch with Victor, Neville briefly snapped at Victor that he was tiring of his 'fashionable discontent'. They parted; later that afternoon the American called Neville. His phrase, Victor said, had really stung him. He intended to quit Jonathan Cape and join the new paper, *Ink*. Once there, his enthusiasm, thought some, exceeded Neville's, particularly as the latter was sucked into the preparations for the *Oz* trial. And there was the new editor, Alex Mitchell, chosen via Neville, Victor, and Andrew Fisher.

Soon Anna Coote was recruited to the news section. A former editor, like John Lloyd, of Edinburgh University's *Student*, her clashes with the one-time Rector of the University, Malcolm Muggeridge, won her national publicity. In 1968, heralding the backlash of the early 1970s, the former editor of *Punch* had claimed that all the students advocated was 'pot and pills. It is the most tenth-rate form of indulgence ever known. It is the resort of any old slobbering debauchee anywhere in the world at any time, "dope and bed".' It wasn't a position with which Coote had any sympathy.

Another person interested in the venture, as the staff list climbed towards twenty and the bills extended, was Michelene Wandor. Neville was sympathetic, her husband wasn't. It was frightfully *unhippy* of him, she thought. That winter of 1970–1 her marriage had effectively ended. John Lloyd applied too, and again Neville was sympathetic, but there was no money for a parliamentary correspondent, as Lloyd had proposed, so perhaps he could just contribute.

As the staff grew, so did the pressures on organization. *Ink* had, it was realized, to break with the sloppy ways of the old underground. A democratic structure, or at least an accountable structure, had to be evolved. Regular meetings were instituted to refine the process. They were rarely a success; increasingly it seemed to many that the core decisions were being made by Fisher, Neville, and Victor on their own. And for Neville, with the *Oz* trial looming, there were more pressing concerns.

Marsha Rowe was another recruit to the paper. She had finally followed Ferrier to the ship in Sydney harbour in 1968. After quitting Australian *Oz* she had eventually joined Conde Nast's *Vogue Australia*. The money was bad, but for the future co-founder of *Spare Rib* the experience was to be vital. It was an apprenticeship in production and layout. And it was, she found, a refreshing change from the underground, where she had been patronized and ignored. But, ultimately, *Vogue*'s concerns were rather far from hers.

Arriving in England Rowe, the political naif, promptly shipped out to Greece as a cashier on a ship, and picked up a lesson in politics in the country of the Colonels. Their coup and dictatorship were just a year old.

She decided she had to get involved. But back in England she met Australian expatriates, stoned musicians, then Richard Neville again, who suggested she rejoin *Oz*. In another echo of 1963 the man she was living with in London counselled against it, again she ignored his advice.

She hated the new job. The magazine seemed to have become a more formalized place. And she felt too old to be on her knees clearing up, or taking dictation. There were breaks in the routine, as when on 8 June 1970 three policemen arrived to bust the 'School-kids' edition. It was, she thought, quite like old times. But the rhetoric of *Oz*, with Greer promoting the idea of women as individuals, didn't seem to match the reality. She renewed her friendship with Louise Ferrier, a central figure in the forthcoming *Oz* defence campaign in which Rowe too was to be engaged.

The approach of *Ink* offered some possibility of change. But, as the meetings began to take shape, she found herself saying little. And ideas for a collective were quickly pushed to one side. Her confidence in the project began to ebb. Neville suggested she might do editorial work but her confidence flagged. And the presence of Coote, rather than strengthening her resolve, weakened it. There was, she felt, an enormous gulf between the properly university-educated graduate, employed to write her thoughts about the world, and Rowe, there to serve the world. She moved into production.

The weeks leading up to *Ink*'s launch began to expose the problems of setting up such an ambitious venture. And spirits weren't raised by the news that *Time Out*, in the week of *Ink*'s launch, was to change again. Gone would be the A5 booklet, in its place an A4 magazine, and, worse still, it would be a weekly, just like *Ink*.

'We all knew we had to go to a weekly frequency some time', says Tony Elliott. 'The magazine was so thick the printers could hardly bind it. But the arrival of *Ink* was a shock to the system. They made no bones about the fact that they were going to run an information service.'

Marchbank got to work revamping the design. Again. *Ink* put out feelers, but the designer spurned them. *Oz* might be a wonderful magazine, but the idea, the thought, of any newspaper of importance coming out of that group was ridiculous. For the first time within the underground milieu something perilously close to a newspaper war was breaking out, but the competitors were unevenly matched. *Ink*, gambling, was planning a 50,000 print run, but it was wildly optimistic – or just desperate. In 1969 *It* had approached that kind of figure, but times had changed. The *Time Out* of 1971 was a very different magazine, and the culture that had sustained *It* was withering.

And other, nagging resentments frayed tempers and damaged morale. Ed Victor's style could be irritating, he was clearly quite out of type with the foot soldiers of the underground: he drove a Morgan sports car, used an expense account, took people out to lunch. Spending money to make money was beginning to be a keynote of *Time Out* too, particularly later in the decade, but the habit rankled with many of *Ink*'s staff. So did the sudden arrivals of staff catapulted in from Oxbridge and Australia. So, most of all, did the increasing pressure of the *Oz* trial.

It came together – and fell apart – as the talk and plans of months telescoped into the nightmare of producing the first issue, with four days and nights of work sucked into a deadline. Limitations became all too visible. The art director was skilled, but his forte had been advertising design, and *Ink* was a newspaper and it was beginning to tell. Thirty people worked on, some fuelled by pure commitment, some by coffee, some by amphetamines, many by all three. And there was always the lead story. Nobody, except Alex Mitchell, knew what it was going to be, but it was known it was going to be a hot scoop, and that, as the staff wilted, was a morale-booster.

Two days before the deadline the art director cracked. The pressures of transferring his skills into a new area, and one in chaos, had taken their toll. He was discovered, crouched in lotus position, in the lavatory at five in the morning. With two days left *Ink* was surviving on a thread. 'We were speeding and confused', says Adams. 'Nobody knew what the fuck they were doing. Nobody had slept. I had been up for about fifty-six hours straight, with no sleep.'

But there *was* the lead story. The headline had already been partly set, 'The Great —— Robbery', and Mitchell had mentioned the word uranium, which cheered Neville, since nuke stories were supposedly good stories. Then Mitchell let the turkey out of the bag. 'The Great Uranium Robbery' detailed the theft of five uranium bars from the Wylfa nuclear plant in Anglesey, Wales. The theft – if theft it was – had taken place in July 1970. 'The theft has been ignored by the national press', wrote Mitchell, 'because of its explosive political and security implications.' The story's explosive element was confined within the paper, particularly when it was realized that it had already appeared, downpage in the *Times* a couple of weeks before. 'Then', recalls Neville, still angry after all these years, 'he disappeared. I was so naive and trusting, it took a while for the penny to drop.'

Frantic phone calls couldn't locate him. Neville meanwhile switched his attention to helping Adams with the design of the front page. 'I am not', says Neville, 'a great designer.' Gloom settled more deeply over the paper. Adams was called in to design the front page. Exhausted, it was pasted up, as Fisher and Victor fed him grapefruit to help keep him awake. It finished, he collapsed. Neville, Victor, and Fisher presented him with 200 Rothmans and packed him off on the bus. He fell asleep, to wake in the cold morning light, way beyond his stop, at Acton bus garage.

Judged by some of its future issues the cover of the first of the revamped *Time Out*s was nothing spectacular. It featured the newly familiar symbol of the women's liberation movement, and accompanied an informative if pedestrian feature on the subject. And James Baldwin was interviewed, and John Ford wrote on Jane Arden and the Holocaust Women's Theatre's, 'A New Communion for Freaks, Prophets and Witches'. It was a competent issue, balanced with advertising and crucially accompanied by the magazine's key weapon – its listings – which by now meant not only that it was draining the staid *What's On*, but pulling in mainstream magazine readers as well.

Ink had a scoop which was no scoop, and an issue without form. Tempting fate, Neil Lyndon provided an obituary for *Idiot International*. And *Ink* fell down in any attempt to compete with *Time Out*'s listings. For *Ink*'s listings editor, Wynford Hicks, the task verged on the impossible. He was competing, effectively alone, against a paper whose entire *raison d'être* had been the provision of such a service, which filled the bulk of its issue with them, whereas he had just three tabloid pages. The staff of *Ink* contemplated their rival. There wasn't, thought Adams, even any comparison. Elliott breathed a sigh of relief. 'With that lead story', he says, 'they destroyed themselves in one issue.'

The aftermath was almost as bad. Having produced one issue,

the experience had to be repeated, and repeated. Worries about internal democracy, about planning gave way at *Ink* meetings to discussions about production, about just how copy, typesetting, layout, and printing could somehow be co-ordinated. And the rivalries continued. Rowe found her status within production eroded by the arrival of what she saw as another Australian whizzkid. Taking a holiday she found on her return that her carefully worked out arrangements had been ditched, that her new recruits had been fired. She had found the paper foul from the start, she realized, and resigned in protest. Nobody noticed.

With Mitchell gone Fisher and Victor assumed the editorship. Fisher had occasionally edited *Oz*. His skills were not primarily journalistic, and Victor wasn't a journalist. Neville's attentions were elsewhere. Coote and Andrew Cockburn – younger brother of the *Black Dwarf*'s Alex, and son of Claud Cockburn – worked on. Issues continued to come out. It might remain a horrifying experience, but, to a point, *Ink* appeared to be stabilizing.

But it was doing so as a newspaper with little news, falling into the pattern of covering stories that nobody else could be bothered to print, intermingled with arts stories of the kind enjoyed by their writers and ignored by the readers. The paper had no position, no line, it offered no service, rode no new wave; its design was orderly, but dull. It provided a meeting point for the fringes of the art world, the more depressed parts of the underground, and some of its political refugees. It was a paper for people who had nothing very much else on; 'Academic Freedom in Ghana' might have enlivened the pages of *The Times Educational Supplement*, but left readers unmoved, as did 'Hailsham's Economies Threaten Defendant's Rights'. Some *Oz* veterans resurfaced in its pages, as did others swimming away from the other leaking ships of the counter-culture, but few could have expected the voyage to last for long.

The peculiarities of the time, trapped between revolutionary withdrawal and recession, were well captured in an interview conducted in Algeria by Sally Beauman, some years away from the financial rewards of her novel *Destiny*, and Eldridge Cleaver, some time after the royalties for *Soul On Ice* had run out. On the run from the FBI, and denounced by his one-time allies in the Black Panthers, Cleaver cut a curious, if pathetic, figure, still tied in the once-optimistic, but now doomed politics of the 1960s movement. Still unwilling to accept that the time had passed, he locked himself into the revolution via those other 1960s fetishes: technology and the dispossessed.

He wanted to reach the criminal element, he told Beauman: 'I'm sure you have some criminal blacks, some criminal students, some criminal workers. We want to reach the lumpen – perhaps stimulate the assassination of the Queen.' Did she find such a scheme relevant? She could think of more relevant targets, replied the hapless Beauman. 'Like who, Heath?' queried the faltering revolutionary. She tactfully changed the subject to his extensive video equipment.

The prophet of black power detailed his plans for insurrection via a console-worth of flashing lights indicating global 'liberation movements'. As the light of insurrection began to go out on the American radical movement, so it twinkled on Cleaver's dreamscreen. It was a neat symbol, and the love affair between affluent radical chic and one-time street fighting men was becoming tiresome.

If so, where did it leave *Ink*? Any dreams of a *Village Voice* revamped and politicized for London in the 1970s were fading almost as rapidly as the lights of Cleaver's Algerian hideaway and the memory of Mitchell's tenure. Elsewhere within the British underground bedraggled armies of new recruits stumbled across sodden English fields in search of Woodstock's holy grail, two years too late.

And at *Friends*, even before the first issue of *Ink* had dribbled on to the streets, Alan Marcuson, editor, founder, and 'South African playboy', had parted company with his creation. The months after the departure of Marchbank had not been particularly happy ones. Jonathon Green had followed his old school friend to Elliott's paper for a short and ill-starred sojourn, and others whom Marcuson had relied on had begun to drift away, leaving the paper dividing into two loose camps. Marcuson saw *Friends* as a paper that should, he thought, develop its politics, as the Irish struggle, the Angry Brigade, and the economic dislocations of the early 1970s intensified. Some, it has to be said, regarded his aims with some scepticism, but against that general position were ranged what Dick Pountaine was to label the 'flying saucerists'. Saucery implied a retreat to the great hippy nostrums. Some of Marcuson's friends noted, meanwhile, that the editor, in his life-style and interest in dope, gave a more than passable performance as a hippy himself, albeit an increasingly paranoid one. Yet if paranoia implies a belief that people are out to get you then Marcuson's position was understandable. They were.

For Marcuson the limitations of covering events far away – in the United States, Vietnam, Biafra *et al.* – became more irksome. He was, after all, from a country that had witnessed the power and violence of the British version of empire at first hand, and just across the water was the old country's first colony. Being fairly anti-British it seemed, he observes, a wonderful thing to beat the Brits with at the time. 'And it was natural stuff to cover if you were interested in magazines the way I was. None of the other magazines were covering it. They were all into peace and love and group sex, which was never terribly attractive to me as a way of life, or a political philosophy.'

For Marcuson his dream remained, he says, a left-wing magazine without connections with the labour movement – of which he knew little – or the Trotskyist left which he despised. It wasn't a very secure position, particularly given the paper's disorganization, exhaustion, and the departure of many of his closer associates.

And there were other arguments. A women's issue was suggested. He didn't think there were many women writers around and greeted the proposal with little enthusiasm. Worse, there were ideas that the editorship might be taken from him for the issue. As long as he *was* editor, he thought, his ass was on the line, and he was going to be taking the final decisions. It became another irritant.

But Ireland, allegedly Britain's Vietnam, became the spot where Marcuson's trip on the underground arrived at Waterloo. In late February 1971 he was visited at the Portobello Road offices by a seemingly irate Irishman who brandished a sawn-off shotgun from beneath his overcoat. Marcuson was about to undergo the Jim McCann experience.

With his tales of his very own Northern Irish Liberation group, 'Free Belfast', the Irishman made an immediate and favourable impact on the South African. Free Belfast, he told Marcuson, policed and defended the city. 'Their main influence comes from the people', he explained – that great, solid, and completely anonymous force. 'We're gonna have Great Britain's Sharpeville.' The editor ran the verbatim interview with his Irish revolutionary under the heading: 'Interview with a Belfast Fighting Man'. The street-fighting man, Jim McCann, says Marcuson, 'took me in, like he took everybody else in. He gave that wonderful interview, there wasn't all that much historical fact in the story but it read remarkably well. The boy does have the gift of the gab and was bloody convincing. I'm not the first person to be taken in.' Nor, as McCann's career unfolded over the rest of the decade, was he to be the last.

The real McCann, if such a person could be said to exist, was at that time a small-time crook who had worked with a variety of dubious characters. These included a property speculator in Brighton, Nicholas Hoogstratten, later imprisoned. It was that curious time, slipping between periods, between conflicts, when such characters could emerge and be taken seriously. Sometimes they took *themselves* seriously.

Once printed, McCann's story developed a momentum of its own. True there were sceptics, but there always are. Since McCann was clearly at the centre of this struggle in Northern Ireland's imperial city it was important to take McCann's advice that 'you've got to send people to Belfast!' It made enormous sense at the time when many so-called radical journalists were sitting around in London, far from the front, *talking* about the action. This was *it*. 'It made the black movement in this country – which we had toyed with for a bit – look silly', says Marcuson.

The man for the job was Felix de Mendelsohn, veteran of the underground press almost since its beginnings. As Felix Scorpio he had been writing for, and occasionally editing, *It* for years before the arrival of *Friends*. Off he went to Belfast, and such was the fervent climate of the time that others from *Friends* followed, who all, reflects Marcuson, 'wanted to get on the bloody bandwagon. I said: "For God's sake, *report* the story. Don't get involved in political activity. *Bring it back*." '

They did, but not in the way that Marcuson had intended. While his Irish team went to work he was left with a magazine with a tottering circulation, bad advertising revenues and the occasional help from his relatives. Meanwhile John Lennon and Yoko Ono, having first been united by their meeting in Indica all those years before, were then at the height of their revolutionary phase. Coming into contact with the *Black Dwarf* via Hoyland, and later to grant an audience to Tariq Ali and Robin Blackburn of the *Red Mole*, they seemed a possible source of finance for *Friends*, the ailing radical paper. Thus Marcuson set out one winter day late in 1971 to explore financial backing with them. On the way he saw a newspaper billboard. '15 Anarchist Bomb Gang Members Arrested', it proclaimed. Marcuson paused. Clearly the Angry Brigade, then at the height of its activity, had been picked up, and, in the radical spirit of the times, he spared a second's sympathy for their plight. Then he bought the paper. The entire *Friends* contingent had been arrested. Including, he noted, his wife.

McCann, faced with the problem of making the revolution within the revolution without any revolutionaries, and needing to provide a story, had attempted to recruit the *Friends* contingent. A farcical incident at Queen's University Belfast had ensued, with home-made petrol bombs. The police had moved in. It was, even by the free-and-easy standards of London's counter-culture, a catastrophe. A police raid was an unpleasantness, the disappearance of almost the entire staff behind the bars of the strife-torn province was rather more. Reality had intruded in a most painful way.

Marcuson flew into Belfast and contacted lawyers. He organized the release of some of the staff, and as spring gave way to summer found that the problem of getting the remaining defendants out of Crumlin Road jail occupied more and more of his time. McCann didn't present any problem. True for once to his revolutionary protestations he escaped. 'I had got to know Jim a bit by then', says Marcuson, 'I knew he was a really dangerous character, a liar, *more* than a liar. I'd spent time with him, found out certain things, but I was still pretty much in awe. He has a mega-personality. He pulled the wool over the eyes of the best of us.'

Marcuson had indeed come some way from concerns with peace and love, and also from *Friends*. He was losing his interest and grip on the magazine. The women's issue did little to re-enthuse him. Returning from Belfast he found that what he saw, as a coup had taken place. Gone was his little office; in its place was a tacky, make-shift *collective*, circular desk. It didn't cheer the editor, but then not many things did in those days. 'I put my hands on it. The whole fucking thing collapsed.'

The arguments got worse. Marcuson tried firing dissenters. They dressed in sacks and walked the sidewalks of Portobello Road: 'We've been given the sack', they waggishly proclaimed. The editor lasted a few more weeks. He was talking to the bank managers, lawyers, and conversation with the staff was becoming increasingly fractious. They wanted joint decision making. He didn't. Meantime he raised money for the Belfast case.

In its seriousness it changed his attitude to London. 'Here it was all bullshit. There it was serious stuff. I came back determined to throw the magazine more behind the Irish situation.' In London they were less enthusiastic.

Attempts were made to restore harmony. Harvey Matusow suggested that the principle protagonists should retire to his place in the country for the weekend. There they could drop acid, sit together, and work out harmoniously just what it was they were failing to communicate about. 'The suggestion', says Jerome Burne, 'was greeted with horror and distress.'

One evening when arguments seemed to have started early and gone on late Marcuson went home and made a decision. He picked up the books of T.F. Mutch Ltd, the ill-fated concern behind the *Friends* publishing empire, and went for a walk. 'I threw the books in the fucking canal', the retired editor recalls. 'Then I went in the following day and said "you can have it".'

There wasn't that much to have. The absence of the books may even have been therapeutically useful, since T.F. Mutch was around £18,000 in debt. Burne, arriving at the *Friends* office where he had been accustomed to seeing around fifteen more or less smiling faces, discovered five glowering visages left. From then on, he remembers, 'it was real amateur night in all directions. Anyone who had ever done anything elsewhere was throwing their hands up in horror at the chaos.'

It appeared to be the death of *Friends*, and it was. *Ink*, the purported dynamic new voice out of the underground, was moving towards its launch. Once there had been brief discussions between *Friends* and *Oz* on the possibility of jointly starting a new paper, now it appeared all was ashes around the *Friends* campfire. *Time*

Out was thriving, and announced the departure of Marcuson and his ally Charlie Radcliffe in their relaunch issue. *Oz* definitely wasn't short of publicity; and *It*, as ever, was surviving. Yet the residue of the staff of *Friends* felt that somehow the paper should keep going. They contacted a prominent young radical lawyer who had already been working with the paper around the Belfast case. Yes, he explained, if the paper got a new name and a new company, then production could continue. Thus T.F. Mutch (Too Fucking Mutch), complete with its debts – to the struggling Larcular Press and the unfortunate Douglas Gill amongst others – expired. But out of the ashes sprang Echidna Epics Co. Ltd and its progeny *Frendz*. Echidna was a spiny anteater, Burne told his colleagues, which he had read about somewhere. Its hearing apparently expanded at a tremendously rapid rate.

The same could not be said of the new paper. 'We were stumbling about', confesses Burne. 'We addressed ourselves to the immediate disaster and hoped everything else would come alright. I don't even know who the rent was paid to.'

New staff as always had begun to materialize. An early arrival was a 20-year-old drop-out from the University of Kent, Rosie Boycott. She had no previous journalistic experience, but she was living with Jonathon Green. Since Green knew Burne, well maybe a job could be provided. It was. Off *she* went to interview John Lennon.

George Snow, with *Idiot* – his launch into the world of the underground press – started helping with design and layout. So, as the year advanced, did Richard Adams. And the magazine finally got round to producing its women's issue. Burne, by dint of being there and being more organized, became *de facto* editor. Perhaps the paper could convey an impression of greater political serious-ness than *Ink* with its flashy £25,000 raised by Neville's business acumen. '*Ink*', says Burne, 'seemed to be a bit of a sell-out. There was all this talk of professional journalists and proper people – it didn't seem ideologically sound. There was too much money, and they were talking about being a sensationalist paper and grabbing attention. To us it didn't seem proper. It seemed to be straying from the true path.'

Thus *Frendz* lurched off on its uncertain trajectory. Rock revolutionaries and street people grabbed issues and attempted to digest them, with Burne and others trying to hold on to some form of course. To some it projected an image of a movement going completely off its head.

The problem extended to within the paper. The first benefactor, a former inmate of a mental hospital, arrived with £300 but, having donated the cash, she moved her mattress into the office. Six months later she suffered a relapse, and talked of Leonard Cohen and of a monk being given a blow job by a nun. Returning to the office she removed her clothes and toured the office with a bedspring, which she used to slash the artwork. It proved a harrowing test for the staff and their commitment to popular theories of anti-psychiatry. In her madness she was, after all, only expressing the insanity that defined the society against which the magazine was attempting to wage war. On the other hand the staff were, with the best will in the world and against overwhelming odds, attempting to get the paper on to the streets. As on *It* in 1969 the police were called and an ambulance took the unfortunate woman away. 'That was the last we saw of her', says Burne. 'it was all a bit upsetting.'

For Marcuson, meanwhile, losing *Friends* proved a trickier business. While creditors might be fuming and a new staff going elsewhere, the authorities were not prepared to let him go. In Ireland there was the continuing struggle for the remaining three members of the unlikely 'Belfast Four', still rotting in jail. Not until July were they acquitted and released. And to add insult to injury he was notified in early June that he too was to be prosecuted 'for posting obscene publications through the post', namely three issues of *Friends*. It was, it seemed, just one damn thing after another.

It was, however, his opportunity to stand up and fight the forces of an oppressive state, as *It* had done, and *Oz* was about to do. It wasn't an opportunity which Marcuson had any wish to avail himself of. Did he wish to fight on a landscape defined by the authorities' displeasure at the paper's coverage of Jim Haynes's 'Wet Dream Festival'? Or indeed for a cartoon published by *Friends* that Marcuson himself found vile? He didn't, despite the urgings of others to fight on. Neville might be a wonderful self-publicist, thought the retired editor, but his interest in publicity was dwindling; a spell of private life – perhaps in southern Ireland – was more appealing. He didn't want to become a famous obscene publisher, he even found obscenity *irrelevant*, for God's sake.

In court he refused to plead, made an unsworn statement, and was fined £150. 'It had something to do with *Friends*', he says, 'but nothing to do with me.'

The judge, the jury, the defence campaign, the liberal establishment, the media, and the defendants thought otherwise about *Oz*.

Chapter 14

Time of trial

At 2 p.m. on Wednesday 23 June 1971 Richard Neville, Felix Dennis, and Jim Anderson finally made their trial. In arraigning the three men in Court Number Two the authorities had, perhaps for the last time, rallied that broad army of the 1960s which stretched from liberal progressives through the underground to the farther shores of the left. And it preserved a culture that was already beginning to decay in the artificial environment of the Old Bailey. Neville was to defend himself; representing Anderson and Dennis was John Mortimer QC, playwright, and journalist.

That process hadn't been simple. Originally Tom Williams MP, another QC, had been approached to do the job being performed by Mortimer. Less than two weeks before the trial began he had quit. The defendants applied for an adjournment for three weeks. The judge, Michael Argyle, turned the plea down. Five days before the trial began they approached Basil Wigoder QC. He seemed enthusiastic, wrote Tony Palmer in his book on the case, *The Trials of Oz*; within an hour he had refused. A further plea for a postponement was made to Judge Christmas Humphries, which cheered Neville, since the judge was famous for being the only Buddhist on the bench. 'He was the one, I thought', says the Australian, 'he had written these books on Buddhism and Zen, so I knew he wasn't going to be insensitive.' Neville was quickly disabused. Not only did he turn the plea down, the judge briefly had the three taken into custody while their briefcases were searched. 'He was absolutely *outrageous*.'

The legal wrangles were already taking their toll, the search for barristers and the battles with the judges. 'I was pretty nervous', says Neville. He also remembered the sheer boredom of sitting in court in Australia watching the legal profession go through its routines. He didn't want a replay, which was one reason why he decided to defend himself. 'But I also took seriously some of the precepts of the counter-culture, and one of them was to take control of your own life', he says. 'Part of that was controlling what was said about me in the courtroom. I was prepared to take the chances and if Mortimer did the other two defences it seemed like a good strategy.'

A lot had happened since the schoolkids had finished their issue of *Oz*, in the last month of the Wilson Government. Edward Heath's Conservatives were still embarked on the radical phase of their administration, the era of the new Industrial Relations Act, the rhetoric of free competition and an end to 'lame ducks', and, in a decade when illusions of empire had faded, another application to join the Common Market. But the resistance they met was from sections of a community still acclimatized to the long post-war boom only then drawing to a conclusion. Plans to close Glasgow's Upper Clyde Shipbuilders met with resistance and a workers' occupation; in January the Industrial Relations Bill had brought tens of thousands out on London's streets to oppose it. In the 1960s it had been primarily the students and the young middle classes that had marched; at the dawn of the new decade the majority came from other social groups. And talk of lame ducks hadn't prevented the Government from nationalizing Rolls Royce in February 1971 when the company's ambitious RB211 engine programme brought it down. The 1970 birth of the Provisional Irish Republican Army had added a dimension to the conflict that rapidly made itself felt on mainland Britain.

The day that the trade unions had marched in London against the Industrial Relations Bill had posed another, more personal, threat to the Government, and, indeed, the state. At the north London home of Robert Carr, the Employment Minister, there were two explosions. 'Robert Carr got it tonight', announced the Angry Brigade, 'we're getting closer.' A day later Detective Chief Superintendent Roy Habershon launched a series of dawn raids. Two months later two men, Jake Prescott and Ian Purdie, were arrested. On 1 May the Biba boutique in west London was also attacked. 'The only thing that you can do with modern slave houses called boutiques is wreck them', said the communiqué. At that point many on the left, and within the underground, who may have had sneaking sympathies with the group began to reassess. The group had said they intended to attack property, not people; but despite the warning given, many felt that of all the wrong targets, this was a particularly crazed choice. As a surge of militancy built up amongst sections of the organized working class, so this strange manifestation of commitment from the fringe of the counter-culture further chilled the political atmosphere.

As the *Oz* trial got underway Richard Handyside, publisher of the *The Little Red Schoolbook*, was also on trial. In July the book, originally published in Denmark and designed in Scandinavian style to advocate tolerance and an open attitude to sexuality, was judged obscene. On 21 June, *Nasty Tales*, a cartoon magazine out of the underground, was seized by the police. At the end of July *It* had its appeal against the sentences of the previous December rejected. If Cleaver's dream-screen had lights for Britain, they were going out.

Not that the *Oz* defence campaign would have accepted such a view. Having quit *Ink* Marsha Rowe joined Louise Ferrier on the campaign, which brought together some of the sharper, and sometimes more eccentric, movers within the underground.

There were stickers and balloons, benefits and demonstrations. A spectacular press kit was produced by Richard Adams, while Sue Miles, wife of *It*'s co-founder, was amongst those giving her services. A key figure out of *Frendz*, as an organizer, was a Yugoslav Australian, Stan Demidjuick.

Perhaps more than anyone else in that west London milieu of the early 1970s 'Stan the man, the plastic man' symbolized activist and at times farcical hippiedom. Amidst that swirl of posers, drawing-room revolutionaries masquerading as street people, and rock idols manqué mouthing about the revolution, Demidjuick stood out. He gave every impression of believing the rhetoric. This was his appeal, and won him a large circle of bemused friends. 'What a star!' remembers Jonathon Green, 'leather from head to foot, hair down to his arse.'

Green's first encounter with Demidjuick had been while still at *Friends*, when he had crashed in, uninvited, and suggested a confrontation at Harrow Road police station. Marcuson and Green had followed the plastic man back to his flat, and uneasily upstairs to Demidjuick's residence. Any plans for confrontation with the police were diverted. Sounds of shouts and screams from above heralded their arrival. They found Demidjuick wrestling with his unhappy landlord, Richard Branson. They separated the combatants, and the tenant and landlord terminated their relationship.

He brought a similar abrasiveness to his work for Friends of *Oz*. It helped ensure that a crowd, large or small, could invariably be found outside the law courts, or marching to and from Lincoln Inn's Fields as the case edged through July.

Until the trial Ferrier had been pulling back from *Oz* and had played little part in *Ink*. But she flung herself into the trial, working with another Australian, a Rhodes scholar and young lawyer, Geoffrey Robertson, who was crucial to planning the *Oz* defence, and to advising Neville. Lists were compiled of potential defence witnesses, copies of the offending issue were sent out to them, meetings arranged, strategy planned. It was a well orchestrated campaign, aimed to hit the headlines and keep them. For some around the defence the choice of Argyle as the judge was fortuitous. His politics and style were such that the defendants had a good chance of irritating him sufficiently for him to slip up, and thus it proved. The prospect of going through another *Oz* trial for Ferrier – having sat through the Australian performance – wasn't appealing, but she was certain about the final outcome. 'I knew Richard's capacity for making headlines', she says. 'In the end I always knew they would get off. People took up Richard's cause because they really liked him. He had this talent for getting sympathetic publicity and getting people to work with him.'

Out of London's academic, literary, and post-Bohemian worlds came forth the host to testify on the magazine's behalf: George Melly, one of the signatories to that 1968 letter calling for a 'Cohn-Bendit for Britain'; Professor Hans Eysenck, whose appearance raised eyebrows across the spectrum, since his views on inherited intelligence had made him a despised figure on the left; Michael Duane, the progressive one-time headmaster of Islington's Rising-hill School; Ronald Dworkin, the American Professor of Juris-prudence at Oxford; Mervyn Jones the writer. Aside from the defendants and the schoolkids themselves the nearest the court got to see of the counter-culture were comedian Marty Feldman and disc jockey John Peel, both of whom testified on *Oz*'s behalf.

Against them was prosecuting counsel Brian Leary. He was skilled, urbane, and – compared with Mervyn Griffiths-Jones at the *Lady Chatterley* trial back in those distant days of 1960 – worldly. Above them all was Judge Michael Argyle, a former Conservative parliamentary candidate and Recorder of Birmingham. By then an 'additional judge' at the Old Bailey, he was moving smoothly to the high plateau of a career that was to continue to be dogged by controversy into the late 1980s.

It was a hot summer and a long trial. Outside, the Friends of *Oz* continued their demonstrations. Amongst their trophies was a twelve-foot-high papier mâché model of 'Honeybunch Kaminski'. Honeybunch, a character from the American underground cartoon-ist Robert Crumb's considerable repertoire, boasted a vacant expression and large breasts. A fixture at the trial, her spirit was to pervade the lucrative career ahead for one of the three.

Within the court it was Neville, conducting his own defence, who put in the most impressive performance of the three defendants. But his background gave him the advantage. Against Dennis the prosecution wheeled on traditional upper-class condescension towards one of the lower orders; against Anderson the tactic seemed to be to wheedle out an admission of his homosexuality.

'I felt most sympathy with Jim because he'd been much more undermined', says Marsha Rowe. 'Felix got blustery, but both he and Richard were more confident. Jim, because of his identity was less of the establishment. He found it very hard to deal with the structures of the court.'

'He had a terrible time in the box', says Ferrier.

Meanwhile she continued to search out potential witnesses. Sometimes, although she got sympathy, she didn't always find a willingness to testify. One particular cartoon in the issue, featuring Rupert Bear in sexual congress with the underground cartoon figure

'Gypsy Granny', provoked particular qualms. Rupert, the long-time children's cartoon from the *Daily Express*, meant little to Rowe, who hadn't been in England long enough to know who Rupert *was*. For her the airbrushed women on the cover, with their whips, made her uncomfortable, but for her in those days there were no words to explain just what it was she was concerned about.

Another potential witness did know Rupert. Having talked to Louise Ferrier she indicated that she couldn't take the stand. She felt bad about it; and they were, she thought, quite offended and hurt, but Rupert, she brooded, was one of her childhood *heroes*. 'I think in many ways my character was partly shaped by Rupert Bear! My memories were being violated. The arrogant, male, aggressive style of the drawing that appeared in the name of revolution worried me. It brought into symbolic shape areas of male antagonism to women that were completely covered up in the old socialist style of the movement. It awakened our antagonism to the way men had the arrogance to portray sexuality in *their* terms.'

Not that it had been Neville, Anderson, or Dennis who had provided the drawing, and it was to be a criticism that Neville was to note in the future. Meanwhile it was their futures that were in the dock. And there the reservations of feminists were not the stuff of Leary's attack on *Oz*, or of Argyle's summing up. The judge told the jury that they had to look at the 'double standards' of the 'so-called expert witnesses'. It was not, he concluded, 'a case of the Government trying to crush some small magazine because it frightens them. The defendants are not being tried over this issue of the magazine because, as individuals, we may think its contents are nasty or dirty, but because it is alleged that these articles and the magazine as a whole, infringe the obscenity laws of the country.'

The jury retired and returned twice. The first time was to query the definition of obscenity, the second time, to Argyle's annoyance, to say that they couldn't reach a unanimous verdict. They didn't have to, he told them, but it would be good if they could. They didn't on four of the five charges. On the charge of conspiracy the jury found the defendants not guilty. This was a small advance, for it pinpointed what had been a success for the Crown in its case against the *It* trio. But on the charges of publishing an obscene article, sending it through the post, and having 'such articles' for profit and gain, majority verdicts found them guilty. Ferrier, furious, rose to protest, and was ejected from the court. 'We *had* – I had – to say something', she recalls.

Had deportation papers been served on Neville, asked the judge. They had. Argyle then, to the angry surprise of the defence, had the three defendants remanded in custody pending 'prison, medical, and psychiatric reports'. Apart from outraging many, it also mystified the defendants. Looking back now, Neville suspects that

Argyle thought the trio were junkies. And there had been other curiosities during the case, such as the judge's bizarre references to 'bomb threats' from supporters of the three defendants. Later, says Neville, a court official was prosecuted for making 'false and malicious' statements. 'He and his wife', the editor claims, 'had Argyle to dinner just before the trial and she was so nervous about the occasion that she invented this story about threats. It might explain why Argyle was so peculiar, because he was working under false information.'

Two days after the remand an appeal for bail was turned down, but three appeal court judges ruled that no more than a week could pass before the defendants were sentenced or released on bail. In the intervening period the authorities ensured that their own peculiar form of vengeance on upstart youth – or receding youth, since Neville was 30, and Anderson 34 – was taken. Anderson and Neville were separated from Dennis and they were told they were going to get prison haircuts. Neville sunk into a rage. 'I wasn't going to have my bloody hair cut', he says, 'but when we met Felix he was in a chair with all his hair shorn. My resistance completely evaporated. Now whether this was from cowardice or the feeling that I couldn't *not* have a haircut when Felix had, I don't know. I was just so upset I went like a lamb to the slaughter. I don't know if they would have tied us down, but we were certainly never given the option.' It was to prove – when leaked to the press by Geoff Robertson – a crucial symbolic move by the forces of the law, and a brilliant publicity coup for the defence, but, insists Neville, its implications escaped him inside jail. 'I didn't think of it except in terms of my own vanity. I know how dreadful I look with short hair, especially when cut by prison barbers.'

'Mr Neville you are a man of very great ability and very great intelligence', Argyle told him. He was then given fifteen months and a recommendation for deportation. Anderson got twelve months and Dennis nine. The judge also labelled Dennis – spectacularly innaccurately as it later transpired – the 'least intelligent' of the three. Subsequently they were released on bail, amidst a continuing storm of protest from liberals and the left, and amidst smiles of quiet – and occasionally noisy – satisfaction from sections of the right, for whom, perhaps, the Chatterley trial tide was at last being turned. It was to be three months before their cases came to appeal. Yet fortune had worked in their favour. 'If we'd had a more liberal judge we might have got shorter sentences and we wouldn't have got the mass public support', Neville speculates. 'By going over the top he forced the liberals of the press to make a choice.' Five years before, Peter Cook had burned the inaugural *Oz*, five years on he prepared the cover of *Private Eye* that castigated the verdict. Yet times were changing, as Neville wrote at the time; there was an inch of difference between a Conservative and a Labour Government; in that inch the underground survived.

The Festival of Light didn't need the *Oz* case to spur it into action, but the verdicts doubtless added fuel to the flames. With the authorities on the offensive, the Festival signalled that another grassroots movement was following them, and digging into new redoubts. On 9 September 1971 the Festival, a fundamentalist Christian crusade against the decadence of the times, held its inaugural rally at Central Hall, Westminster. Lord Longford, the Dowager Lady Birdwood, Cliff Richard, and Malcolm Muggeridge, who had lit the torch back in 1968, were all there. Others came too: the Gay Liberation Front, plus freaks, mice, bogus nuns, and stink bombs materialized, reported *It*. At the end of September the Festival had followed the Vietnam Solidarity Campaign and the Trades Union Congress example and marched to Hyde Park. So too had the dissenters, who by now included a new editor within the underground, John Lloyd.

The trial aftermath had left *Oz* and *Ink* in a state of exhaustion. *Ink*, post-trial, and without Neville, announced it was suspending publication until the end of September; the *weekly* was effectively dead. But *Oz* had been the *raison d'être* of the battle and one of the pivots of the movement. It had to survive. Thus three more editors were recruited to keep the magazine on the news-stands: Jonathon Green, Pearce Marchbank, and David Widgery.

The choice made sense, of a kind: Marchbank, the key designer, a main mover behind *Time Out*'s success, and a long-time admirer of the magazine; Green, by now established as a journalist from the less political, more hedonistic end of the underground; and Widgery, *Oz*'s house Marxist and more than capable of playing the media tricks so beloved of Neville's approach. Indeed, on one occasion Widgery had even played Neville.

Asked, as he often was, to deliberate on the key issues of the underground, by Harlech Television, Neville felt as loath to turn down the offer as he was to make the long trip to Wales to perform. So he asked Widgery to attend, as Neville. 'This is', brooded the scourge of the underground's lack of perspective, 'the most irresponsible thing I've ever done in my life.' It didn't stop him taking the morning train and appearing at the studio, to be greeted by a large audience of the concerned of south Wales, local dignitaries, and a Conservative MP. Wasn't his hair a trifle *short*, asked the interviewer. There had been problems, pointed out the medical student, and, anyway, skinhead fashions were percolating into the underground. Well, didn't he lack the distinctive Australian twang? Maybe, replied Widgery, but he had been in England a long time, which was indeed true. Thus the programme disappeared into the video can, and thus the following weekend *The Sunday Times* revealed the awful truth, and despatched the can unshown into the dustbin. It was a good trick, and it kept on working. In 1969 the *People*, anxious to float the tide of moral outrage, had sent a reporter to interview the infamous editor of *Oz*. Neville, describing himself as the 'office boy', obligingly furnished a Rasputin-like American hippy, Lee Heater, who proceeded to fulfil, in his guise as Neville, all the worst/best fantasies of the luckless journalist. The paper published a suitably vigorous denunciation of the magazine and its hirsute editor Heater/Neville, complete with a chilling picture the following Sunday. The piece was a great success, so much so that *Oz* reproduced it in its next issue.

Widgery and I tried the same trick, but without Neville's verve, in the post-trial issue. Since Ronald Biggs was much in the news, perhaps an interview with the notorious train robber would be a shrewd move. Since no one at that time knew his whereabouts imagination was called for, and I read copiously of the felon's activities and escape before subjecting myself to an interview – as Biggs – with Widgery in Princedale Road. So taken with the role was I that I even adapted an appropriate accent to go with the part and waxed lyrical on my fictitious exploits post-escape from Pentonville. It was a good stab at the story even if I did locate the escape in south-east Asia rather than Brazil where he in fact was. Thus 'Ronald Biggs, the Most Wanted Man in the World' graced *Oz37*.

The issue was labelled the 'Angry *Oz*', in keeping with the times, and there was, post-trial, certainly a market. Stan Demidjuick reported from Clydeside on the workers' occupation and realized there was a real, radical world outside west London and its freak community, and the acquittal of the 'Belfast Four' was covered. But the editorial mix was short-lived. Green and Widgery regarded each other with some circumspection, and Marchbank returned, post-issue, to *Time Out*. The duo lasted little longer, with Widgery by November sending in a letter of resignation. He disagreed strongly with the way the magazine was being run, he said, and labelled the current issue 'no more left-wing than the *Daily Sketch*'.

There was more to it than that. The magazine could ride the punches, even delight in them, but the world had become a more serious place. The strike wave was continuing; eight men and women were behind bars on or awaiting Angry Brigade charges; the previous summer had seen internment without trial in Northern Ireland and Operation Motorman to destroy Republican strong-holds such as 'Free Derry'; and, within the underground, there was another issue – women.

'The underground can't go on seeing every nipple and ripple and grunt as an attack on capitalism', Widgery had written. '*Ink* shows how little is left when *Oz* is shorn of the porn. It's simply not enough to publish a perfunctory "women's issue" and still be saying, like that lovable little piglet Tony Elliott: "An extra 5,000 copies if we put boobs on the cover." The underground can no longer go on evading the issue, with the aid of the token woman and the whole reactionary super-groupy sludge, any more than the left can think the promise of socialist revolution is the reason to stop women's liberation now.'

However *Oz37* had featured an excellently airbrushed Monroe figure with her skirt up, brandishing a vibrator – a new sign of the times – and a joint. Early in 1972 *Oz* published a letter from Rook Ashover: 'Dear *Oz*, I thought of you the other day and realized sadly that you had nothing to say. Once affectionately yours. . .'

Widgery's attacks on sexism were, suddenly, only one of many. 'we are attacking you, straight male freak', a Gay Liberation Front representative told *It* in September 1971. 'We are telling you that until you get out of your whole male-superior life-style of "chick screwing", your mentality of "making it" as if "it" were an ego achievement, then you are our oppressor. . . . The real pornography is not just Vietnam and Bangladesh, but also every image or picture that tries to keep the idea of man/woman stereotyped, whether it's *Playboy* or in the supposedly liberated sex sections of the underground press.'

Out in the sticks, as a succession of provincial correspondents had told *It* and *Oz* over the years, nothing had changed, and the late arrivals to London brought the message with them. When Muggeridge had made his 1968 Edinburgh outburst John Lloyd had been amongst those picking up the message. The old man was, he thought, identifying a mood brewing in the city, and drawing on cultural roots deep under John Knox's old stamping ground.

Graduating in 1967 Lloyd had worked his way up to sub-editor on the *Scottish Daily Mail*, but the Edinburgh-based paper could no longer match its Glasgow-based rivals. He quit and followed the familiar *emigré* path to London and a job as a warehouseman in West Hampstead. Initially his only friend in London was another associate from university days, Duncan Campbell, by then an advertising copywriter. It was an isolated time: solo trips to the great 1968 demonstrations, nights at the warehouse. But, through another acquaintance, Lloyd met, and moved in with, a group sharing a flat/quasi commune off Oxford Street. It included a cartoonist working for *It*, Ralph Edney, and his sister Margaret. Soon Campbell moved in too, and shared with her jibes about 'working in the belly of the beast' since only they had anything approaching 'proper' jobs. Lloyd, taking Antonioni as the new role-model, signed on at the London Film School.

But the flat was the core of their lives, hardly political at first, but gravitating towards a species of anarcho-communalism. It was a familiar pattern of London student and post-student life, but one tinged with the particular mood of the times. In all-night dope-fuelled rap sessions they examined each other, analysed each other and, as was the fashion, set up a street theatre group. Hippies' successors were no longer just doing it for themselves, they were attempting to do it for other people, moving towards the political frontiers. The group even played at the January 1971 anti-Industrial Relations Bill march as it wound through Marble Arch, while, in north London, the police were sifting through the wreckage of Robert Carr's front door. There were no problems with careers, none were planned. It was a *déclassé* group, without constraints, or in revolt against them. There were books and magazines to read, psychiatry and anti-psychiatry, and *It* and *Oz*. For Lloyd his Scots Baptist upbringing still meant that *Oz* was disturbing, but impressive too. Shocked by its promiscuity, its energy, its flouting of convention, he sought to emulate it.

And he sought an entry into that world. A meeting with Haynes when the American was still working with *It* yielded an invitation to drop in, but he never summoned up the courage. But by the time that *Ink* was announced he was less reticent. Meeting Neville stirred memories of the Haynes of Edinburgh, the easy style, the charm, the crowd of admirers. He began writing for the paper and enjoyed its atmosphere, even if others didn't. But he wasn't one of the group, his lack of self-confidence still found him more at home in the commune.

Then one day in the summer of 1971 Ed Victor rang and invited him out for a Chinese lunch off Gerrard Street. Victor, by then in the thick of *Ink*'s trial chaos, offered him the editorship, for £30 a week. Lloyd accepted eagerly, unaware that at least ten people had already turned it down. 'They knew what was happening', he says, 'I didn't.'

He arrived as the announcement of the suspension of publication had been made. Yet issues still came out. In mid August John Gerassi, the Dialectics of Liberation, *Time*, and *Newsweek* alumnus, edited a 'Repression in Britain' issue, and a follow-up appeared in the first week of September. *In extremis* the paper was developing the glimmerings of a style, a verve, a cutting edge. And yet again, out of the underground, another new staff emerged.

Although Andrew Fisher and Felix Dennis remained, the 'new professionals' had gone. Their replacements mixed the sadder, wiser, and increasingly politicized of the old underground with recruits like Lloyd for whom politics had either been ever-present in the background, or unavoidable as peace, love, and demonstrations finally gave way to anger, bombs, and women's liberation. The women on the new staff were no longer just Christian names; designers Judy Grove and Claudine Meissner worked with David

Wills and Felix Dennis, and they were joined by Sandi Sparrow, Diana Shelley – and Sue Small.

Her relationship with *It* had ended in the summer of 1970. After a Manchester underground press meeting she had stuck around, made friends and, after a subsequent visit to that city, had returned late to *It*. Dave Hall had fired her and nobody appeared to respond to the sacking of the veteran loyalist. Later she quizzed Mick Farren about the abruptness of the action. He laughed sympathetically and explained that 'Dave fired *everybody*. We all used to come back, but when you didn't, we thought you *wanted* to go.'

She returned to Manchester, becoming briefly Farren's White Panther chapter in that city, and worked at trying to sell ads for the local alternative paper *Grass Eye*. If *It* ad selling was difficult, on *Grass Eye* it seemed virtually impossible; she also got cancer of the cervix. She quit and returned to London in the summer of 1971. When she heard of the *Oz* sentences she rang Felix Dennis, who asked, would she sell ads for *Ink*? She accepted.

By now the paper had left the offices in Princedale Road and shifted to the fringes of Covent Garden, off Leicester Square in Great Newport Street. It was a very different set-up from the *It* she had known, which by then had also moved, to Soho's Berwick Street. And there were some resentments from the other paper. She had gone over, if not to the enemy, to a different world on *Ink*, a paper apparently in its death throes but still competing for the dwindling underground market. And she wasn't entirely comfortable there herself. Selling ads wasn't much easier than it had been on *Grass Eye*. The frost was forming over the underground.

Despairing of *Frendz*, Dick Pountaine had switched his allegiances. *Ink*, thought Pountaine, was a great place to work even if his job designation as reviews editor was a trifle vague. At the paper too he came across David Robins, completing the long march from the days of small magazines, Beats, and Bill Levy back in the mid 1960s. Back from eighteen months in Canada, Robins was all the more concerned with his concepts of libertarian politics as the class struggle intensified. And, at a time when the personal being political became a popular women's liberation catchphrase, he split with his lover. Her departure, he says, forced him to 'face new sexual and political realities.' Or, to put it another way, 'I was off my head.' On *It* he had worked on a 'Daily Grind' supplement, his last real contribution to the paper, a libertarian manifesto, a critique of the underground and its growing embroilment with what he saw as hip capitalism. The Grind highlighted the new movements mushrooming in the London of the early 1970s: the community groupings, the claimants unions, which had replaced the easier alliances of just a few years before. 'My contributions to the underground press took on a decidedly intransigent tone', he observes. 'I shed the last vestiges of beatnik floridity. In my head I was rejecting academic discourse, Marxist discourse, hippy bingo.' It wasn't just the 1960s that were being buried, it was that earlier tradition going back to the 1950s and even Kerouac's New York of the 1940s that was vanishing, or being deluged with the detritus of a would-be rebel culture.

And his work changed his views: teaching day-release kids, the people the underground had passed by, except to provide an occasional stage army for rock festivals. Under the dazzle other forces had been at work. Working-class youth culture had proceeded separately and unevenly in the world of Tamla Motown rather than Pink Floyd; dead-end jobs rather than drop-outs. There had been changes, he reckoned, that the underground press had never reflected.

After the two 'Repression' issues Lloyd had effectively moved on to the paper, although the post of editor bestowed on him by Victor wasn't one the rest of the staff – if staff they were – were particularly happy to recognize. The first of his issues was the 'Alternatives' *Ink*, a stop-gap between the old and the new.

If Lloyd was regarded with suspicion by the staff, the feeling was mutual. The business manager, Mike Radford, was a man whom Lloyd saw as an 'absolutely ruthless Stalinist who would deliver the most devastating attacks on all of us, what we were doing, all we had ever stood for, and all we'd ever amount to. He had a tremendous mind, and I was very admiring of it, but slightly frightened of him.'

Sue Small felt out of place with most of the staff. It seemed upmarket for her conception of an underground paper. The *It* crew had been in comparison hedonistic and undisciplined. 'The *Ink* people were much more political. I wasn't. I hadn't thought things through.' Half the time she didn't even think she knew what they were talking about. Movements outside that world in Endell Street had passed her by; so had women's liberation in its first evangelical phase. She had never got on with women. 'It took me a long time to realize how important female friendships were. I was the only girl with the lads, desperately trying to keep up with their drug consumption and their conversation. I spent a lot of time feeling inadequate. Looking back I think they were talking bullshit a lot of that time, but I assumed they knew what they were talking about. I thought myself very fortunate because I was exposed to ideas and conversation that I wouldn't have been if I'd stayed a south London bank clerk. I found it absolutely enchanting.'

In that respect, *Ink* was different. Women were writing, and men appeared to behave differently. Robins and Lloyd appeared to take an interest in what she thought. She started thinking.

It was through the 'Alternatives' issue that Robins came into the paper. He provided an article on the underground press. It had dreamed some beautiful dreams, he suggested, and they had been stolen by the system, corrupted, and defeated. 'If the underground wants them back – and wants them realized – it will have to fight for them with all the fury of the dispossessed.' The language was overblown perhaps, but within it was the changing message. A part of the London underground, swayed by larger movements outside but *within* Britain, was stumbling to find a base: one that didn't centre around knocking down fences on the Isle of Wight, or even enraging Judge Argyle, but made some links with larger struggles, and yet brought with it some of the issues that the movement in its brighter, and darker, moments had stumbled across. Women's liberation, gay liberation, and, yes, hedonism too fitted into a broader movement for change. It wasn't a lesson that the Labour Party under Wilson, or the far left glowing in the renewed industrial struggle wished to take on board. The issues would surface, and not in a way that Robins would particularly like; they would become the stuff of Labour Party resolutions and articles in *Cosmopolitan*, stolen, but not altogether forgotten in the ensuing years.

The 'Alternatives' issue was indeed a stopgap, but showed a movement on the cusp. Wynford Hicks, freed of his ill-fated *Ink* week listings, interviewed Robin Blackburn of the *Red Mole* and the ubiquitous Mick Farren of the White Panthers on politics. Blackburn delivered his version of proletarian revolution, and Farren his alternative society. David Cooper, veteran anti-psychiatrist, wrote on psychiatry. Jim Haynes provided his *Suck* manifesto. John Wilcock wrote on travel. Vince Hines wrote on race. John Peel on music. It looked forward, but also, and predominantly, it drew on the past. And it was entirely written by men, just like the old days.

But the 'Alternatives' issue had shown just that: a new route for *Ink*. The subsequent issues developed on similar lines. Next came 'Futures', then a 'Working-class' issue; an Irish issue; by mid November it had got to 'Who owns Britain?' The paper had made a virtue, and a policy, out of necessity.

The paper was still ploughing through the debts of the early months, the staff was broke, the 'bridge between Fleet Street and the underground' had receded into the realm of fantasy. The paper became, says Lloyd, 'an expression of what we were about, or thought the world should be about'. That in itself wasn't new. The same had been true of *It* all those years before, but for the first time in the 1970s a paper had seriously attempted, in the oft-repeated cant of the end of the previous decade, to size the time. Times were tougher, harder. The Festival of Light, rather than peace and love, was on the streets.

So were the counter-demonstrators, amongst them the Women's

Street Theatre, and, amongst them, another Scot, a former art student and poet, Alison Fell. The theatre managed to get itself arrested for providing a *tableau vivant* of the family for the benefit of the assembled moral majority. She wrote an account of the day and sent it to *Ink*.

Lloyd had moved out of Baker Street, and into a north London house where the politics took a more formed variety. He commissioned an actress and theatre director, Pam Brighton, to write a piece on why middle-class women's liberation wasn't going anywhere, and why it was the economic system that had to be changed. He felt he needed a counterblast. Fell provided it. Subsequently he offered her a job: £10 a week, seven days a week.

She joined an underground paper on which, as usual women did the layout; Felix Dennis did the design, Sue Small did the advertising, and men did the writing. But Lloyd had been exposed to the new influences of the women's movement, and Fell became the woman in editorial.

She also carried some of the seeds of the American sexual liberation movements with her. That year she had crossed the United States, as the movement shifted gear from the old militancies towards gay and women's liberation; and in the US they were further, she thought, along the road. Thus her role as token woman was strengthened. This had occasionally unfortunate results. Her contribution to *Ink*'s Gay issue – complete, to her fury, with a lipsticked Che Guevara on the cover – for example, was a long interview with a married couple which comprised a male transvestite and a woman. They were, they reckoned, engaging in a neo-lesbian relationship. 'It gave me the chance to make an absolute idiot, a complete arsehole of myself.'

Fell's role on *Ink* wasn't the one that Greer had had on *Oz*, or indeed Coote had on *Ink* in its first incarnation. It was closer perhaps to the role that Rowbotham had tried to carve out on *Black Dwarf*, but that had been coming out of the Marxist, and not this new libertarian left. It meant that women's angles were supposed to be her speciality, whether the issue be rock or Ireland, or sticking up for women with the collective. Not that, with some of the women within the design staff, this was always a task that had to be performed alone. But it did mean clashes, as with Felix Dennis, whose views remained closer to an older, dying underground. They took, she suggests, an immediate dislike to one another. This she followed up by desecrating the portrait of the elegant hippy blonde amidst the daisies adorning his wall. With that old guard the relationship was always going to be spiky. 'They obviously thought I was your ultimate knee-jerk leftie', she recalls, 'and I thought they were your ultimate hippy decadents.'

Within the paper the clashes proved salutory. 'A bloke wrote on the wall', recalls Lloyd, 'that one of the women on the staff "was good, tell your friends". It was one of those male lavatory things. Alison went for him tooth and claw. It was the first time I had seen a feminist argument deployed. He was completely lost, blushing to the roots of his hair, looking round to the other men for assistance, and of course we gave him none. None of us would have done it, but none of us would have pulled him up for it – not necessarily because we were any less sexist than him but because we knew better than to put it up. None of us could, or would, give him support. It was a graphic instance of just where the old hippy, almost *Playboy* philosophy broke and you met a feminist anger at that kind of unthinking sexism.'

The change had finally, and too late, come to the underground. And as issue followed issue the circulation began to creep upwards. But the paper's problems didn't dwindle; indeed they grew. Another group of visitors started dropping into the office. Down the road, across Leicester Square, the new collective had finally formed around the wreckage of *Black Dwarf*, and this time it was to be different. No more the cramped, pictureless pages of the *Dwarf* – or indeed papers like *Frendz* – but a new lively and exciting paper: again to be professionally produced, but based on months of forward planning, carefully mapped-out decision making, and political *theory*. *7 Days*, after all those months, finally hit the streets on 27 October 1971. And, as *Ink* noted, the final product wasn't bad. Since the previous winter the editorial group had indeed met, and an attempt had been made to evolve a collective means of working. Its staff largely came from a tradition outside the underground, a tradition drawn from the new left of the 1960s – with a heavy Oxbridge bias – and from the new movements that had emerged within the universities. Thus David Triesman, an alumnus of Essex University, was on the paper, so, from *Black Dwarf*, were Alexander Cockburn, Anthony Barnett, John Hoyland, and Phil Kelly. And women like Judith McFadzean-Ferguson, Maxine Molyneux, and Rosalind Delmar meant that many of the old battles about the role of men and women within the radical press should have been some way towards solution. But many suspected that what was going to be on offer was a revised, downmarketed version of the *New Left Review*. It was an accusation about which the paper displayed mixed feelings.

'Add *7 Days* to your week and the new audience to your media schedule', said the hand-out for the advertisers. 'They want change, a new life. . . . We know there is a new young audience demanding new papers that talk to them in their own language.'

Maybe, but if there was *7 Days* had considerable difficulty in locating it. In its use of photography and its more open layout the paper did indeed make waves, at least amongst the more staid parts of the socialist press. And in its use of writers like Tom Nairn, Fred Halliday, and Gareth Steadman-Jones it went some way to challenging the staidness of the established mainstream radical press. But none of this went anywhere to finding the new audience that *7 Days* was talking about. If it was the industrial militants the paper wrote about they remained locked into the *Morning Star*, or occasionally the papers of the far left such as *Socialist Worker* and *Workers Press*. If it was the underground, then *7 Days*' language and style ensured they stayed on the outside, despite the paper's forays into rock coverage. If it was the new left then, yes, progress was made, but the new left was thin on the ground, and not a target that the advertising industry was likely to be too concerned about.

Yet there was, with the pre-planning, and the £15,000 raised – with many an old Communist who had done well called upon – optimism as the paper launched. For the *New Left Review* sympathizers within the paper it was to be their chance at a populist intervention, combining the best of the style of the *Picture Post* in its 1940s heyday with the content of the new, Marxist left.

Yet scepticism greeted its launch, which was attended by a handful of underground journalists and just three from the nationals which the new paper was attempting to challenge. 'There is no paper in this country which would run an analysis of Chinese foreign policy and an article on gambling and sexuality in the same issue', claimed foreign editor Fred Halliday. 'That's what's new.' Perhaps, but maybe no readers wanted such a mix. And the readers that *7 Days* was pitching for, the young, were going in other directions.

But there were some grounds for optimism. It seemed to Phil Kelly – who resumed his role from *Black Dwarf* – that the embarrassments of that paper were a thing of the past. The new distributors, after all, believed they could shift 50,000 copies a week. The distributors, it transpired, were thinking indeed of a new *Picture Post*, and *7 Days* with its first lead of 'SS Reunion in Bavaria', its reviews of new works on realism, its 'ideas' page's conclusion that Marx, unsurprisingly, was right, was not it. The back issues began to pile up. Rather than the brave 50,000, sales began to settle at, at best, around 10,000 to 15,000, which meant that a product aiming to break out of the *Black Dwarf* ghetto rapidly found itself back within it. And, with a larger staff, it meant larger overheads, and increasing friction between members of the collective soon emerged. And it did so at a time when the staff still fondly believed that their paper was selling, if not 50,000, then at least 30,000.

7 Days was regarded with mixed feelings. For the rest of the far left, the paper seemed too flash, too detached, another product of the elitist left; and there was considerable and, as events turned out, justifiable scepticism about its sales potential. For the underground, too, suspicion was prevalent. Yet for David Robins on *Ink* the paper was wonderful, if an over-ambitious rival to his last underground contribution. *Ink*, with its developing libertarian leftism, and *7 Days*, coming out of the Marxist left and flirting with similar ideas, gravitated towards sympathy as well as rivalry. 'My biggest concern', recalls Lloyd, 'was that it was going to wipe us off the map. As it transpired, there was no map for either of us.'

But initial contacts indicated that *Ink*, far from its £25,000 of the summer, was the poor relative, financially and theoretically. *7 Days* could give the impression of depth, but in one crucial area it was weaker than *Ink*. Apart from Alexander Cockburn it possessed few journalists with any long-term track record. Indeed, as the two papers struggled into 1972, Lloyd began to receive overtures from the other side of Soho that perhaps he too might like to enlist. And Cockburn's supposed status, too, was a source of internal friction; debates about the right line on Ireland could be intercut with arguments about 'professionalism' – was it necessary? And had the paper despite its commitment to the women's movement actually changed relationships? But perhaps most crucially of all, was the paper selling? If there was uncertainty about that, there was little about the other crucial aspect of its success, advertising. There, even more than other papers within the underground, it was failing on a spectacular scale.

If *7 Days* was one forum for arguments about sexual politics, there were plenty more elsewhere. By mid 1971 Michelene Wandor's marriage was effectively over; *Time Out* was providing a regular source of limited income and a method of intervening in a world which, after the eruption of the women's movement in the eighteen months since the Ruskin conference, had become far more exhilarating, far more challenging. She had a play of hers put on within what there was of the Fringe in those days, and she had done poetry readings; she was no longer the graduate mother of 1966, she was becoming a crusader. And leaving aside her new sisters within the establishing women's movement, there were plenty of other women within the underground. On *Time Out* there was Verina Glaessner; there were Sue Miles, Cassandra Wedd, Claudine Meissner at *Ink*; Louise Ferrier at *Oz*; Tessa Topolski, Rosie Boycott at *Frendz*; Pat Bell, Anna Coote, and Marsha Rowe. Something should be done.

Rowe had her suspicions. Michelene, she had heard, was this crazy woman who was messing up Ed Victor's life. But, seeing her, she seemed interesting, and she was a friend of her friend, Louise Ferrier. Through Wandor, Ferrier, and Rowe, meetings of an underground press women's group were set up. One, Wandor recalls, took place at the London Film Co-op, a child, by many devious routes, of the Arts Lab of Jim Haynes. Others took place at

Louise Ferrier's flat in Palace Gardens Terrace. They began as restrained affairs, with Rowe and Ferrier wondering just why they had set them up, but beginning to speak on how, within the underground press, women were permanently assigned to secretarial roles.

The meetings persisted. Boycott continued to go, so did Rowe. But for Wandor, closer to home, there were also meetings for women organized within *Time Out*. And also the tenor of the meetings seemed wrong. 'There was', she says, 'a positive lack of interest in reading Shulamith Firestone and talking about being women – which I was dead keen on – so I drifted out.'

The winter of 1971–2 was the time of the first major clashes between a Conservative government and the National Union of Mineworkers. On that occasion, as in 1974, the miners were to emerge victorious. It was the time when the nine defendants in the Mangrove trial – triggered by battles around that Notting Hill West Indian restaurant – were fighting, and showing signs of winning, their case. It was the time when the *Oz* defendants finally emerged, in November, with the threat of jail, and in two cases deportation, lifted from them. But it was the time when, in December, Jake Prescott and Ian Purdie finally listened to the verdicts in the cases against them. Prescott was found guilty of conspiracy – having addressed envelopes used to send Angry Brigade communiqués – while Purdie was acquitted of charges of bombing the Department of Employment building and the home of Robert Carr, Employment Minister. Prescott was sentenced to fifteen years. Purdie was detained pending charges on cheque fraud.

It was a time for paranoia. But it was also, for the women still meeting out of the underground press, a time when a different type of activism became appealing. No one at that first underground press women's meeting had thought of setting up a paper. For Wandor the movement itself was the preoccupation; and anyway, there were papers, pre-eminently *Shrew* which was still coming out, still circulating between the groups.

Perhaps she felt more involved in *theory*. Out of the birth of *7 Days* had come an awareness amongst some who regarded themselves as politically naive that they had to get educated. 'My politics were closer to *Ink*'s', recalls Phil Kelly. 'I wasn't a Leninist, my perspective was much more libertarian. I hadn't done any serious Marxist reading until this phase – it was a *Capital* reading group set up by David Triesman on *7 Days* that was where I started.'

Another arrival at Triesman's group was Wandor. And she went to a women-only group with Rosalind Delmar. The journalists might have ambitions to change the world; suddenly that winter, they set about trying to interpret it. John Hoyland attended the

Triesman group too, and so did his then wife. And *she* went to Delmar's group as well. For Wandor, too, there was another magazine, *Red Rag*, looming on the feminist horizon, committed to socialism, probing Marxism, proclaiming feminism.

No such certainties existed for Rowe. She had seen *Rat* – which in common with most of the underground press arrived at *Oz*'s office – and she had noted the women's takeover of the New York weekly. But they, she thought, were proper women, women who had something real to confront, and were of the New Left. Not that she then even knew what the New Left was. And Boycott, amidst the confused politics of *Frendz*, was in a similar position.

But what Rowe had was expertise, more perhaps than other women within that loose grouping, at the *trade* of putting magazines together. And other women within the group had talents that were under-recognised, misunderstood. By then the meetings had moved to Louise Ferrier's home.

'There was an American woman, Bonny Barton', remembers Rowe. 'I think she came because she knew Ed Victor, and she was friendly with Rosie Boycott. And she said, "why don't you start a magazine?" And I thought, "why not?" '

It was far from Wandor's purpose in organizing the first meetings. 'Looking back it was an absolutely logical thing for that group of women to do. It was where their skills were, and it was like taking control of what they were doing anyway. It *had* a political dimension, but my recollection is that it wasn't discussed in any political context at all. It was more like "Christ we don't want to sit round talking man, we gotta get up and *do!*" '

And Rowe, recalling *Rat* and contemplating her supposed ignorance, had qualms herself. 'I felt we were just waffly and with a sort of feeling of mess and confusion with a real inability to perceive the world for what it was.' But Rowe and Boycott proposed the idea, and interest was plentiful, if volunteers were few.

'That was December', says Rowe. 'Six months later, in June 1972, we did it.'

Chapter 15

We are all angry?

'The phrase "Now we are all angry" sums up the reaction of all radicals and revolutionaries', said *Time Out* on 10 December 1971. 'For unlike the *Oz* trial, there is no middle ground. No liberal indignation.' The magazine was commenting on the first two verdicts in the cases of the Stoke Newington Eight, the group accused of being the core of the Angry Brigade: Ian Purdie's acquittal and Jake Prescott's fifteen-year prison sentence.

They had been picked up in March, and Detective Chief Superintendant Roy Habershon claimed that he had caught the Angry Brigade. But in that month Ford's administrative building at Dagenham was bombed. In May Biba and the Scotland Yard computer centre at Tintagel House in south London were hit. In June Ford was hit again, and the police labelled the group public enemy number one. At the end of July another government minister, John Davies, had his London flat bombed. In mid August an army recruiting office in Holloway Road, north London, was hit. Then, on 21 August and 22 August, the police swooped again. Six arrests were made in Stoke Newington. The police had wanted to try all eight cases together. In that they were to be disappointed. And in October the Angry Brigade claimed another hit, this time at the Birmingham offices of a building firm, Bryants, then involved in an industrial dispute.

Time Out was right about one thing. There was no liberal indignation, no pillars of the establishment were to step forward for the defence. And on the left there was anger, but much of it was directed as much to the anonymous perpetrators of the bombings as to the establishment. By January 1972 seven people, other than Prescott and Purdie, were being held by the police, and one was bailed. Two were freed that month. But for the orthodox far left the Angry Brigade's actions, rather than complementing others' struggles, were a suicidal diversion from them, which, one way or another, would be crushed by the power of the state. But as that left blurred into the underground the arguments intensified. There was no conspiracy, asserted the Stoke Newington Eight Defence Group in the wake of Prescott's conviction. The perpetrators of the Carr bombing were part of a movement 'every second of their lives; every time they feel great, every time they run and laugh and fuck together; they are part of a movement when they work with other revolutionaries doing countless other things. Being part of their revolution they are sensitive to the needs and desires of the revolution. On 12 January 1971 we had a one-day strike, we went on huge marches all over the country, we planned strategies for the future and we bombed Robert Carr.'

It was a neat but sloppy formulation, a perfect mirror image of the far – and not so far – right's view of the underground and the left. Queasily the left indicated its support for the accused, while damning everything they were supposed to have done. It was amongst the underground that the Angry Brigade's politics struck a deeper resonance. Again a small group were doing something, but even within that milieu the 'we' was disconcerting. Many of the 'we' had no jobs to strike from, had tailed huge marches; rather than plan strategies they had wondered what to do next; and they hadn't bombed Robert Carr. Out of the turmoils of 1968 movements searched for short cuts and encountered brick walls, and sometimes bars.

Thus was the irony of *Time Out*'s position. One part of it pursued consumerism briskly, another went to radical cultural politics, and another combined radical news coverage with the belief that the 'we' were indeed angry. There was anger, but it was undefined.

Within the underground and its press, time and money were tight. There were ways of making out, selling soft drugs was one way, opening stalls was another. For Richard Neville, finally safe from deportation, there was a place as the 'alternative voice' on the London *Evening Standard*, the paper that had first noted *Oz* six years before. His slot in what was then the mouthpiece of liberal Conservatism earned him £70 a fortnight and raised eyebrows from some within the underground. It was a move he could, and did, defend: it freed him to write for *Ink* and *Oz*, he told *7 Days*, and it removed the financial pressure. But Neville, an expert within the media circus, was himself becoming jaded. Post-trial he got the good tables in restaurants, the invitations to parties, but it was beginning to ring false. The trial itself had forced what he regarded as an unnatural polarity. 'The trial wasn't about sitting down and discussing points of view, it wasn't about civilized discourse – which I'm quite good at – to pursue the contradictions of the underground. By that time I'd known people who'd died in the streets from shooting up heroin, I'd probably realized there were a lot of complications about the black movement here, about sexism, and I was aware of the problems of proselytizing about free love and feeling jealous simultaneously, but that was *privately*. Publicly I had had to go into a witness box and fight for my freedom in the context of defending a culture.'

It hadn't really improved after escaping the clutches of the law. He wandered around the city he had been drawn to back in the mid

1960s in a daze. 'I had an invisible megaphone attached to my already voluminous mouth and I felt I wasn't really being my true self.' Back in *Oz* for its fifth birthday issue he reported from New York. Al Goldstein, *Suck*'s editor, was planning a new paper *Mobster Times*, he noted, which was to be sold with the slogan 'crime does pay'. Jerry Rubin, meanwhile, was conceding that the movement was in bad shape. The Australian also observed a 'revival of blood and guts fetishism' which was, he suggested, the real obscenity.

It became popular in London too. In January 1972 Stanley Kubrick's film of Anthony Burgess's book *A Clockwork Orange* opened, pulled in large audiences and intrigued *Ink*'s reviewer. In its depiction of Alex, 'a young man whose principal interests are rape, ultra-violence and Beethoven', the film leapt the gap from its birth as a novel in the early 1960s to take a more chilling meaning in the new decade.

A year before, Donald Cammell and Nicolas Roeg's *Performance* with Mick Jagger had been belatedly released. Finished in 1968–9, the film industry, like the law, had difficulty in keeping up with the progress or degeneration of the underground. *Performance*, perhaps more by luck than judgment – or perhaps by a sensitivity to sub-conscious mood – had captured something of the flavour of those late 1960s days: a fascination with androgyny, an underground flirtation with *organized* crime and violence, a taste of Notting Hill, and a lot of drugs. *A Clockwork Orange* seemed a lifetime away: in place of the criminal entrepreneur on the run came the dispossessed working-class young out of the council estates, terrorizing the world of money and of easy liberalism from which they were excluded. It was a sketch similar to the world that others reassessing working-class culture had been looking at within the radical underground. For most of the children of the middle classes violence was something to be theorized about, romanticized in the abstract, toyed with as a vehicle for revolutionary change. The violence that Kubrick depicted was shocking, a hobby, the means were the ends. It was a philosophy going nowhere, except into the popular consciousness. And it did, with Alex's 'droogs' filtering into popular style via the innocuousness of Slade and the Bay City Rollers, and into right-wing demonology as the source of the problem.

Alex's gang, suggested *Ink*'s anonymous reviewer, was the 'logical conclusion of the ideologies currently peddled by the underground and the left: the one glorifying indiscriminate violence . . . the other ignoring subcultures as irrelevant or trying to "politicize" them into its own tired image.' The reviewer found it hard, she or he wrote, to say anything nice about the film, except that the reviewer liked it.

'Maybe', Neville had added in his *Oz* piece, 'we're all secretly hungering for a world war of our very own, just like dad's.' It was a new current, one to swiften on its progression into the 1980s.

In the absence of the world war within the British Isles there was the Irish conflict which took Fell and Lloyd to Ireland for *Ink*. Ideologically the conflict put *Ink* on the spot, and 'Britain's Vietnam' caused problems on *7 Days* too. The left within the underground was being forced to pick up the tab for the politics it had once espoused more easily. For *Frendz* a generalized hostility to the British presence in the north was usually enough; for *Ink* it didn't prove so easy. But it did give the paper the chance – under an effective banner of support for the Provisional IRA – to produce, finally, good reportage, to extend the possibilities at last of underground journalism.

'I now blush to think about that Irish issue', says Lloyd, 'but it was my first exposure to real, hard-nosed reporting. I was absolutely taken up with it. I was lucky, I got an introduction to an essentially IRA family who, unusually, were rather trusting. I didn't abuse their trust, they took me in, put me up and introduced me to lots of people. It was a time when it was all beginning to flare up, but before there was a real clampdown. There was a bit of freedom in the Republican communities and I was captivated by it, uncritically captivated. When I began to think it through I changed radically my position.'

Dick Pountaine sees Ireland as the 'killing ground' for discussion on *Ink*. 'We couldn't decide a line on it at all, and the one we finally went for – "conditional support for the IRA" – was cowardly, inept, awful.' Both Lloyd and Pountaine were impressed by Radford's fierce denunciation of their equivocation, and, indeed, their brand of libertarianism. Radford's position, which remained an eccentricity on the far left, was the 'two nations' line; that Northern Ireland contained, with the Protestant and Catholic working classes, two national struggles trying to get out of – or stay in – the same country.

For Pountaine the paper had become part of a 'struggle for the hearts and minds of the new left. We represented a libertarian tendency as opposed to *7 Days*'. It was a loosely linked tendency. 'There weren't two people on the paper who agreed with each other, it was one continual argument.'

Yes, agrees Fell, it was one long meeting, but 'we were a pretty solid bunch of lefties compared with the shit-heads elsewhere in the underground.' They were also a pretty broke bunch of lefties. By the time Lloyd was off to cover Ireland he – and the rest of the staff – were down to £10 a week, a long way from the princely £30 that Victor had offered him that previous summer. The staff took teaching jobs to supplement their income, as Mike Radford and

Andrew Fisher juggled with the figures, coming out with progressively gloomier results. As January gave way to February there were signs that the circulation was beginning to pick up. For Fell, *Ink*'s rivals were too druggy, too louche, or, while *7 Days* might command respect, it was *too* respectable. *Ink* seemed to be in the vanguard of new ideas, concepts moving beyond the underground. 'It was very Angry Brigade-ish, anti-imperialist, it had black voices, women's voices, it really did represent that new libertarian/situationist nexus of politics.'

And as such it rubbed shoulders uneasily with the other survivors of the underground press. A joint meeting between *It*, *Frendz*, and *Ink* indicated that friction between them. Its aim was to consider any possibilities of pooling resources and increasing liaison. It failed. Meeting in a pub, drink and political differences took their toll. For Lloyd *It* was just staggering on, and *Frendz* seemed hopelessly drug-oriented. By the end of the gathering fist-fights seemed the most likely item for any other business.

Another meeting at that surviving bastion of the student left, the London School of Economics, had underlined other divisions. John Hoyland represented *7 Days*; Fell and Lloyd came from *Ink* together with Felix Dennis. For Fell, the *Oz* one-time defendant, confronted with a new brand of student militancy and feminism, looked in that setting, out of his time, from another era. His was an underground that was defensive about sexism and talking about the 'sexual revolution', a lost cause, rather than sexual politics. 'It was about sucking and fucking and screw everything that moves. Women were supposed to do it too, we were "all equal".' For her it had no structure, and defined as puritan all those arguments about women as sex objects. Perhaps in one sense the old guard was right. A decade before, Richard Hoggart had defended *Lady Chatterley* as very much a puritan book, morally serious, about life and sex. 'Yes', she says, 'there was that strand to it, but it was all that they could see, and it threatened their privilege.'

Ink meanwhile addressed itself to the new movements. On 21 January 1972 it was reporting the announcement from the women within the Gay Liberation Front that they were quitting the movement. The GLF had been a broad alliance out of the counterculture, its division was another indication of new priorities and of growing fragmentation. The terrain was fissuring. And the paper responded too with a new section, 'Gay News'. Then came a 'Romantic Love' issue, which drew on more women writers – including the poet and novelist Michele Roberts – and found the underground finally trying to be funny about sex in a style and content that didn't relapse into the sexism that had gone before. But it was to be a brief encounter, for that issue was *Ink*'s last.

Many schemes to fend off creditors had been tried. There had been the obligatory pursuit of Jagger and Lennon; Radford won admiration for his financial juggling; Sue Small pressed harder on a dwindling number of potential advertisers. She and Lloyd went on a tour of record companies. There were the old hippy executives, one even made a deal, for £25-worth of advertising. Mostly it wasn't the polite refusal, it was the closed door.

The big companies had their own reasons to pull back. Cultural dissent during the twilight of the long boom in the late 1960s had been one thing. The sellers of the product, caught with arthritic old music papers stumbling after the youth culture, had felt impelled to use the underground press, to an extent, and weekend hippies had peopled the press offices. But in January 1972 the number one record was the then Coca Cola jingle, the New Seekers' 'I'd Like to Teach the World to Sing'. 'We are the children of Marx and Coca Cola', the French New Wave film director Jean Luc Godard had said back in the 1960s; the big companies could now dispense with the former, particularly as the atmosphere of industrial militancy intensified. And the music press had begun to recruit writers from the underground too. The mainstream was developing its own canals into the counter-culture.

Small and Lloyd returned to their office. Even that, for a paper on the skids, was too damned large. But they were tied into a lease and extinction was the only way out of Great Newport Street. The faint signs of recovery couldn't outweigh the debts accumulated during the previous ten months. And there was the unpaid National Insurance bill. 'On *Oz*', remembers Pountaine, 'it was the telephone bill; you couldn't argue with the GPO, as it was then. On *Ink* it was the unpaid contributions.' Radford was running out of ideas.

There were further desperate trips to raise funds, but after a week came the shareholders' meeting. Neville reappeared. It had been a struggle by dedicated people, he said, but this time the establishment had been too much for them. They would be back, he said.

'I was very upset', says Pountaine. 'Everybody was. I was more upset by *Ink*'s closure than by any of the others. No tears were shed when *Frendz* went down really.'

Neville too was saddened. Sixteen years on he still believes the paper might have been able to survive, had not the disastrous launch crippled it, and, like those more closely involved in its later days, he shares a pride in the product. Perhaps, he thinks, they should have gone in harder, perhaps Dennis's preoccupations were beginning to move towards other avenues.

There were, suggested Dennis, other possibilities: there was some work available on *Oz*. Not for Fell: she returned to her communal life in north London, a world of libertarians, food co-ops, squatting – and uncertainty. The underground she had come into had been dying during those months. Once drugs and music had *seemed* important, they had been part of her heart, part of a cultural intervention in that city. 'We were all becoming heavier politicos, into activism. We were leaving something behind. It was certainly a lot poorer. And the underground was connected to capitalism, and we were certainly getting snooty about *that.*'

But she had been writing. Some of her unpublished Northern Ireland work later resurfaced in *Spare Rib*, text and pictures. She had worried then about her role as a woman photographer, and it had distracted her attention from the real, physical dangers. Correct handling of the zoom lens had been more important than the armoured cars, the rubber bullets. Gradually the writing was to take over her life.

For Robins too it was back to north London, to writing and to teaching. But Pountaine took up Dennis's offer. He stayed with the magazine for six issues. Neville was still around, just, with Felix Dennis, Andrew Fisher, and Jim Anderson still soldiering on for a product which was showing serious signs of its age and changing times. It wasn't Pountaine's kind of magazine any more either, but *Oz* had always been eclectic, liberal in its policy, and, even if he and Dennis disagreed on everything, they still got on, and respected each other. Dennis took care of business, while Pountaine concentrated on technical matters.

Lloyd meanwhile got a call from Tony Elliott. The paper was beginning to show signs of prosperity, but the balance between the staff remained erratic. There had been talk of turning it into a co-operative, an idea which Elliott opposed, and so did many of the staff, with the newsroom beginning to push for the idea. The previous October Neil Lyndon had brought his pragmatism to the magazine, and in December Marchbank had relinquished his post, to reappear in the new year as 'design consultant'. Would Lloyd, asked Elliott, like to join the paper? He wouldn't, the Scot replied, but he would write for it from Northern Ireland. He was touched by the bug; it wasn't the IRA, or even Ireland, but reporting. Elliott provided the money for a Pentax and Lloyd headed back to the province. In May he was reporting from Derry, in June he produced a massive feature on the Loyalist community. But by July he was co-editing features with another university associate of Tony Elliott, John Fordham, *Time Out*'s then jazz correspondent. By September Lloyd had completed the leap from *Ink*, as *Time Out*'s acting editor.

There was another recruit from his old paper. Despite its visible success *Time Out* had, by the end of 1972, accumulated heavy – between £30,000 and £39,000 – losses. Via Louise Ferrier, says Tony Elliott, Mike Radford was brought in to sort through the magazine's finances.

Between the left and the further shores of the underground 7

Days had effectively only had *Ink* as a rival but, with that paper gone, the group in Shavers Place, near Piccadilly Circus, were in little better shape. By then there were around seven people, all on £20 a week, and it was a good distance from the days of planned collectives and into the world of desperation. 'I had two small children by then', recalls John Hoyland. 'My wife was active in the women's liberation movement and was very angry that I never saw the children.' The personal and the political had become just that. *7 Days* had become the number of days he worked each week, and at the end of it the cash on the table wasn't enough.

With enough capital, or, as with *Time Out* during its rockier moments, sympathetic printers, the crises might have been ridden, had the formula of a committed radical picture paper had time to evolve. It didn't. After seven months the stark truth about the circulation bled into the consciousness of the staff. They went back to the old Communists and the other benefactors who had put up the cash. They appealed to their readers. A tense shareholders' meeting took place. 'They were quite straightforward', recalls Kelly. 'They said admit defeat. It can't work and we can't give you any more money. Stop before you run up bad debts.'

They suspended publication. Then, as the National Liberation Front of South Vietnam began to close on the US supported regime, the staff put out one last issue, for May 1972, on the war. With a wit sometimes lacking in earlier editions it featured a US helicopter with GIs cramming on board on the cover: 'Who for the Chopper?' was the headline. The answer was the US Army and *7 Days*, the 1970s' most ambitious attempt at a radical newspaper. They had appealed for a further £20,000; by 1 May they had received £8,000 and a large number of letters of support. But support, even when accompanied by cheques for £5 and £10, didn't get the paper out of the red, or the ditch into which it had sunk. With May Day, *7 Days* too was dead.

'We in Britain have to create the revolutionary politics that is appropriate to this country', stated the paper's final editorial. The argument was the tautology of people caught in a cul-de-sac. 'To have to cease publication at this moment is a bitter frustration for us. But either as separate individuals, or in some ongoing form of collective work, we shall be continuing to assist the creation of such a politics.'

Facing it was a page of condolences, contributions, and demands that the paper survived. 'You were the first paper I found that lifted women's rights, position etc. out of what was traditionally the women's pages in newspapers', wrote Wendy Edmond, enclosing £10. She couldn't believe that the 'rich lefties of this fair land will let you vanish'. She was wrong. Tom Driberg, whose curious brand of leftism had persisted since the days of Claud Cockburn's *The Week* in the 1930s, also sent a tenner; and John Lloyd and Alison Fell, 'ex-staff, ex-*Ink*', sent £5. But the rich lefties, after six years of erratic donations to the counter-culture's causes, were pulling back.

'Looking back it was a good paper', says Hoyland. 'But it was too academic, it wasn't open to the left's diversity. The trade unions were loosening up, it was the beginning of community politics, if we'd built up a base we might have sustained ourselves.'

And there was no 'ongoing form of collective work'. Soon Cockburn was to cross the Atlantic – with his younger brother still occasionally surfacing in the London underground – and eventually reappear where it had all started, as a columnist for the *Village Voice* into the mid 1980s.

'*Frendz*', Bill Butler told the paper in May 1972, 'for the most part has wandered around trying to find out where the hell it was supposed to be going. And it has never decided. Every issue is different.' Butler, an American veteran of the English under-ground, and the man who had preceded Miles into Better Books back in 1965, was being interviewed on his life and times, which by then meant a Brighton alternative bookshop. Perhaps its very confusion helped *Frendz* to outlast Marcuson, *Ink* and *7 Days*, but only just. The coterie on the paper fluctuated, as did its concerns with Ireland, through workers' occupations, to the standbys of music, and the festival culture that sustained the illusion that the underground had survived.

Two tramps became regular visitors, begging, hustling, becoming almost part of the office's entourage. Its financial fortunes were helped more by the arrival of a drop-out accountant. His Christian name was Donald, he was Irish and, because he kept talking about the need for a cashflow when nobody else knew what such a thing was, he earned the name of Donald O'Cashflow. By Christmas 1971 Richard Adams appeared, out of *Oz*, to do some of the design; from *Idiot International* came George Snow.

The results were mixed. With the political events of 1971 *Frendz* attempted to put together what the staff hoped would be a heavy political issue for Christmas. It addressed the Irish issue, and the Mangrove trial, just concluding, which pitted west London's West Indian community against the police. The issue would be something special, thought Adams, as he planned the design. He painstakingly put it together to bring out the reality of life on the streets of London and the ghettos of Northern Ireland. Type was to be set against a background of grey, gritty brick walls. It came back from the printers. 'You couldn't read a sodding word', remembers the designer. 'It was just black on black. The environment encouraged mistakes like that.'

Frendz' financial support still spurted from odd sources. Marcuson, long gone from the paper, had introduced Jim McCann

to Howard Marks. What Tony Elliott had done to build a magazine,
and Richard Branson was to achieve via records, was accomplished
by Marks in the field of dope sales. He provided the illicit segment
of the triptych of hip capitalism for the times. In 1972 he even threw
a little money *Frendz'* way by backing a new record label, Lucifer.
Its first release was to be 'Fuck You'. In March Lucifer took a page
in the paper to promote 'Fuck Rock'. 'It's a love song', claimed the
ad copy, 'but the record companies won't touch it, the BBC won't
play it, and the shops won't sell it. They think the words are dirty. If
you buy it this way we can finish the album.' The offer concluded
with an application form for copies of the disc. The record, selling
1,500 copies, was a flop, but then Marks had other more lucrative
priorities.

So did Burne. Tramps, the occasional threat of physical violence,
the offices in Portobello Road were taking their toll. So were sexual
politics. Rosie Boycott's new, if unstrident, feminism seeped into
the paper, but *Frendz*, in February 1972, found itself the junior
partner in another venture in which feminism played a more
forthright role.

Time Out, the Other Cinema, and *Frendz* rashly co-sponsored a
conference on 'freedom and responsibility in the media'. The
venue, once again, was the Roundhouse.

'Whether it's hippies, drug busts, demos, blacks, striking miners
or the IRA, what the media says and what actually happened is
often very far apart', *Frendz'* plug for the gathering had suggested.
'Everyone welcome. Meet the men who make the news.'

That day it wasn't the men. True, worthy had followed worthy:
The Sunday Times's Geoffrey Hodgson; film-maker Peter 'War
Game' Watkins; Northern Ireland's socialist and civil rights
campaigner, Eamonn McCann. . . . Morning gave way to afternoon. And a leaflet was distributed by women from WITCH, Gay
Liberation, and the Women's Liberation Workshop. It centred its
attack on the one with, as they assumed, the money. '*Time Out* is
irresponsible in the extreme. It is extremely opportunistic, totally
uncommitted, designed to reach the widest possible range of trendy
liberals possible and sell them radical politics as one more item on
the list of goodies for the good life. Cashing in on the good life is
total hypocrisy.'

The written attack on *Time Out* was just one part of the
onslaught that followed. Around fifty women stormed the platform.
It had been a gathering blithely concerned with serious male issues,
and women hadn't featured on the written agenda. They did from
then on. 'We're here and we're staying', said one. 'If you try to
move us we'll smash the fucking microphones.' What the subsequent discussion lacked in coherence it made up for in vehemence
about subjugation, separateness, discrimination. The birthplace of

the underground's first paper became the venue for the revolt of its underclass. Marsha Rowe had arrived to distribute questionnaires about her new paper, *Spare Rib*; she stayed to join the occupation of the stage, as did Alison Fell. Neither had planned it, both were impelled to join it. For Rowe, shattered and confused in its aftermath, it seemed to mark some kind of turning point, and it was.

Others were noticing the change. Following the emergence of the women's underground press group, Neville indicated that he too had revised his views on *Oz*'s attitude to women. The paper should think seriously about how women felt about their graphics. '*Oz* had always been an uninhibited magazine', says Richard Adams. 'It was one of the reasons why people were drawn on to it. If one wanted to use pictures of naked women or naked men, nobody had given it a second thought. But after that people did start thinking seriously.' Well, some did.

For Jerome Burne his main thought soon after the Roundhouse was departure. A woman friend gave him a choice: move to New York with her, or stay in London without her. America, even in the year of Nixon's re-election, seemed the promised land where there was real revolution, real hippies, and Tom Wolfe's Pranksters. Andrew Cockburn, noting his departure in his 'Underground Dave' column in *Private Eye* – the bi-weekly did make attempts to keep up with the times – suggested Burne had decamped with *Frendz*' money and retired to the Bahamas. Money, thought Burne, what money? What Bahamas?

By May *Frendz*' remaining staff found the problem of keeping the paper going was proving too much. Yet attempts were made to sustain it. They had started with nothing, and produced thirty-two issues. By August they had run into major problems with printers, who complained about that common underground trait of not paying. The collective announced they were setting up a mail order business and hoped to produce *The Great British Catalogue* to rival the American underground's ecological handbook *The Whole Earth Catalogue*. And from then on, they announced, *Frendz* would be monthly and distributed by them. It wasn't and it wasn't. The paper was dead, a long way geographically and politically from its one-time parent – although it would blush to consider it – San Francisco's *Rolling Stone*.

Eight months before, that paper had celebrated its fourth birthday. 'As long as there are bills to pay, writers who want to earn a living by their craft, people who pay for their groceries, want to raise children, and have their own homes', wrote founder Jann Wenner, '*Rolling Stone* will be a capitalist operation.'

And as *Rolling Stone* dominated American youth culture, so *Time Out*'s stranglehold on London was growing. Now only *Oz* and *It*, the first two, survived of the old underground press within the metropolis, but the fringe theatres were expanding rather than contracting, so were the music venues, cinemas, restaurants. The less radical young of 1968 were beginning to accumulate cash and – with stereos bought – contemplating the first mortgage. And more disposable income spelt more business opportunities, miners' strikes, or no miners' strikes. For others, community politics became an issue, as the Garden, the Gate, the Grove, and the Farm began to change. Groups formed in localities, with only the women's and gay movements and the political groups – and *Time Out* – retaining a London perspective.

The trickle of writers and designers into *Time Out* continued. By the time Marchbank had relinquished his full-time post there women increasingly dominated the art studio. There was Ellen Dale to take over from him, and later Carol Warren. Women were in charge of production, typesetting, photo research; the female proletariat was still there, but they were moving to some power within the kingdom. On the editorial side Michelene Wandor remained, and was to do so into the 1980s, as was dance editor, Jan Murray. Future TV journalist Carole Barnes had a shorter stay. But while part of the changing underground had effected the change, *Time Out*, too, was flowing towards a mainstream already changed by the move of women into higher education in the 1950s and 1960s. Within the newsroom the tensions remained, but it was a fatter, richer paper than the one Marchbank had joined – even if one that still left him sceptical. Once there had been bogus British bands like the Flowerpot Men singing of going to San Francisco from recording studios near Denmark Street. To the designer *Time Out* had that same faint flavour of having been manufactured. But he had, in another way, been one of the people doing the manufacturing, and it had been a big project. There were to be few more out of the London underground.

Chapter 16

Ribs, rads, and bombs

After a spell at Louise Ferrier's flat the underground press women's meetings had moved to the *Oz/Ink* offices in Great Newport Street, early in 1972, by which time Rosie Boycott and Marsha Rowe were working seriously on *Spare Rib*. Getting money, getting support wasn't easy. It was no time, amidst a floundering underground, to be thinking of setting up a magazine, let alone a radical women's magazine. Small sums dribbled in. The planning group moved again, this time to the flat that Boycott then shared with Jonathon Green. His own tenure on *Oz* was short-lived, and, having assisted in Boycott's placement at *Frendz*, he now found himself in a subsiding underground while his partner embarked on a new and almost exclusive venture.

Who was to design it? Kate Hepburn, then at art college, was planning her finals display, and she took it on as her project. A friend of Rowe's from *Vogue Australia* provided advice. The questionnaire was prepared for the ill-fated Roundhouse media conference. A larger meeting was called where ideas were solicited. So was money. Ideas were forthcoming, few produced results and just £2,000 was raised to launch the magazine. But publicity began to trickle into the underground press.

'*Spare Rib*, the alternative women's news magazine will be published in June', *Oz* reported. '*Oz* warmly wishes them well and urges readers to check it out. Two of their staff have been closely associated with *Oz*. Pat Bell once our business manager now belongs to *Spare Rib*, which is our loss. Marsha Rowe was the first "secretary" *Oz* ever had – way back in Australia almost ten years ago – then she rejoined the London team and later *Ink*. Marsha has written bitterly of *Oz* brutishness, so we can claim some credit for goading her into this venture, which we think is likely to be the only women's magazine of any relevance to stoned chauvinistic freaks like you.'

Out of *Oz*, it was going to be very different to *Oz*, resolved Rowe. *Oz* had reached a narrow audience within the underground, and despite the sporadic rhetoric had been elitist. Out of the first women's meeting had come the idea that the magazine had to reach women who weren't like them, who didn't have their life-style. Women like, amongst others, their mothers.

There were practical considerations. Where was the magazine to be based? Marchbank provided the answer. He had decided to quit his design studio in Newburgh Street, just off Carnaby Street, and the new magazine moved in. Rowe sought out the people who had supported *Oz* during the trial the year before. The theatrical impresario, Michael White, gave his old office chairs. With the collapse of *Ink* some of its old equipment came their way.

A dummy issue was produced for advertisers and potential backers, itself a startling break with underground traditions of launching blindly into the unknown. The founders' desire to pitch towards the mainstream was underlined by the image, a picture of the *Guardian* journalist Jill Tweedie, taken by a young feminist photographer, Angela Phillips. Sixteen years later, remarks Phillips, she is still awaiting payment for the picture, as it circulates Fleet Street. Rowe, picking up lessons from the glossies, had liked the contrasting paper quality on *Harpers*; a similar technique was adopted on *Spare Rib*. They adopted another habit from the mainstream: there would be no more of the vagaries of the old male underground, they were going to come out on time, every month. And coming from *Vogue Australia* she was at last going to be able to plan production effectively. They budgeted on returns, sales, printers. They would, they decided, do two-colour-only issues. The distributors disagreed. To get a decent sale, they argued, the magazine would have to use full colour. It nearly crippled their finances. Yet the groundwork was done, by people who had learned silently in the background. 'But I think women do that', says Rowe. 'They get more obsessive about the details.'

Newburgh Street was obviously unsuitable for a launch party; instead they chose the Place, just off Euston Road. By then Pat Bell had been forced to drop out. On publication day, she had twins.

It was a warm sunny June evening. The guests drew on the underground, and, even if the magazine had an uncertain future, well, all papers out of the underground had an uncertain future. The orthodox media showed up, and one of the Jay Twins, celebrities at Sussex University in the ancient 1965 days of swinging London.

Some people gatecrashed, including a group of radical feminists. They were no ordinary radical feminists. They were men. It was just after the division of the Gay Liberation Front and on the verge of the production of the first issue of *Gay News*. As, indirectly, *Spare Rib* had been born of – or in reaction to – *Oz*, so *Gay News* was partly to emerge from *Ink*'s short-lived 'Gay News' section. In the winter of 1971–2 Richard Adams's design expertise had led Denis Lemon to ask him to help with the projected new gay paper. It had also introduced him to the movement's more eccentric sections. One of them was the 'Radfems', based in a Bethnal Green commune, and a point where street theatre crossed over into life.

Adams found himself reminded of that moment in *Psycho* when Norman Bates emerges to stab a victim dressed in his mother's clothes. 'That', he says, 'is what they looked like. They were just outrageous. One of them used to drive a lorry from London to Norfolk dressed in a gold lâmé evening dress, high heels, with shoulder-length hair, and deliver bricks to building sites. There were these acid sessions where they would drop a tab of acid, then hit the street, dancing, performing to anyone they came across.'

That night it was *Spare Rib*'s turn. Adams realized it was going to prove a difficult evening when he arrived and found Lemon being punched on the face by one of the group. It set the style for the evening. In view of the 'radical feminists' ' own style their key complaint against the magazine proved somewhat ironic. They complained about a make-up ad for Woolworth's in the launch issue. It was, the men told the women, a case of compromising feminist principles and, dressed in their 'gender-fuck' drag, they tore up the magazine amidst shouts of 'sexist rubbish' and 'stamp out sexism'.

The co-founders were mystified by the onslaught. It didn't conform to Rowe's previous experience of gay men, or of gay liberation. It did fit into some familiar patterns as the evening gave way to violence, mingled with traditional male exchanges of 'cunt!' and soon-to-be traditional shouts of 'sexist pig!'. *Oz*'s ad manager, wearing a Gay Liberation badge, made efforts at conciliation, and tried to kiss one of the protesters. 'Right now', reported *Oz* the following month, 'he still has a chunk of his top lip missing.'

They were, thought Rowe, a parody of women, yet appearing to be more like women than – women. It was, she thought, another example of men telling women what they weren't allowed to do.

It was a neat male coup, symbolically engaging more than an angry grouplet within GLF. Heterosexual men within the underground had been in overt retreat from feminism for more than two years. Women's liberation was knocking away many of the ideological props that had supported the broad movement since the mid 1960s. And it left some heterosexual and gay men in danger of being caught with their pants down. Having proclaimed liberation for humanity, it was difficult to deny it to 'old ladies' and 'chicks' now briskly redefining themselves as sisters, although some made the attempt. Gay men were oppressed by the system, which often gave them an affinity with the women's movement, but that system didn't deny them the familiar streak of male chauvinism. And in that Radfem outburst there was indeed that, together with something else, a last throw within the dying underground of a particular male view – men could do anything better, including being women.

The level of farce too was familiar. It had surfaced the year before at the Skegness meeting and rally of the Women's National Co-ordinating Committee.

There an obscure Maoist sect had attempted to take over the gathering. It had been led by a man, with his wife as deputy. He had threatened physical force to hold the microphone, but had lost it. In doing so he signalled the end of men at women's liberation meetings. The Maoists did succeed however in taking over the workshop. The women responded by deserting the WNCC, leaving the victor with a handful of dust. Times had indeed changed.

And the more intelligent, sensitive – or adept – men recognized the fact, waving their sisters off to the front. Widgery, with his contacts with Rowbotham, had been an early arrival at the railway station. By January 1973 Neville had joined him. In 1969 feminism had won no mention in *Playpower* as Boycott was to point out, but it was a comment not so much on Neville, as on men. Three years later in *Oz* he was noting that 'any woman not involved to some extent in the women's movement is either stupid or masochistic'.

Women didn't need the waving handkerchief, and looking back Rowe regards his observation with some scepticism as more of a stance, a move to be *au fait* with current ideas. If so, it was a leap to new ground that many others followed with greater or lesser conviction.

Neville, meanwhile, retains a pride that *Spare Rib* appeared, whether as a child of, or a reaction to, *Oz*. 'I was thrilled by it', he says, 'I may have behaved like a sexist during that period in terms of my sexual colonization but I also really liked strong independent women, and I completely respected Marsha all the way back to our meeting in Sydney. She wrote articles about how I used to throw pots of tea at her because they weren't strong enough but I took them in good grace. They had an element of truth. . .'

Spare Rib's first issue sold, and the magazine continued to sell, pushing past 20,000, and hitting its monthly deadlines. The *Red Rags*, *Socialist Women*, and *Shrews* persisted too for a while, and in other forms lasted into the next decade. But *Spare Rib*, born out of persistence and what some imagined to be a naive confidence, effectively became the national magazine of the women's movement. It had located an audience that outlasted the underground from which it had come, but against which it had reacted. Boycott left within two years, and after four years Rowe too quit, at a time when the editorial staff had stabilized and finances improved. It was just when, she thought, it would have been easier to stay.

The sexual politics of *Spare Rib*, good, bad, and erratic, were tailor-made for the decade. *Suck*'s brand of sexual liberation was too much, too late. In 1972 Jim Haynes was teaching at the University of Vincennes on the outskirts of Paris. With Bill Levy he was still producing the paper but, at least for Germaine Greer, *Suck* had not been a success. Her unhappiness culminated when a plan was agreed that all the editors of the magazine would appear nude in one issue. For Greer, as she was to explain in 1987, it was a serious argument about sexual politics, about demystifying male and female bodies, and about making a new kind of pornography in which nothing was hidden. It would not be professional models doing it for money, it would be the editors, and it would, was her argument, go the whole way, and get it over with once and for all. She was also concerned that, unlike the naked pictures of Yoko Ono and John Lennon then circulating the world, the pictures would be impossible to mass market. So she devised a pose where anus, vagina and face were in juxtaposition. Unfortunately *Suck* didn't run a picture of all the editors, ir ran a picture of just her.

Greer was outraged, and wrote a furious letter of resignation from *Suck* to Haynes. 'No indication is occurring that the snotty elitism and smirking, hypocritical love-thy-neighbour journalism is getting any better, and the only part of the thing that's genuinely exciting to most people is the sadism', she argued. 'Therefore I regard the whole paper as counter-revolutionary. . . . My action was never meant to be a piece of exhibitionism on my behalf. It was meant to be a group action on the part of the editors of *Suck* magazine. The fact that it wasn't is just a further example of the spuriousness of your pseudo-revolutionary aims. Yours in name only, Germaine.'

'I don't believe there's anybody on earth who can blast as well as Germaine can blast', wrote Haynes in *Thanks For Coming*.

Possibly true, and it also helped ensure the end of *Suck*. As she insisted, Greer's letter was published in full. Haynes also provided another naked picture of Greer. In his book Haynes concedes that the fracas with her was a factor in *Suck*'s demise, but maintains that he and Levy had decided from the beginning that the paper should be killed at its height, 'instead of trailing off into squabbles and mediocrity'. If that was their intention, they failed. Greer in full flight transcended mere squabbles, it was true, but the paper's scrappiness, incoherence, and tackiness reflected the mediocrity of its vision. Having followed that early *It*'s concern with sexuality and sexual freedom, *Suck* remorselessly pursued its logic into a different decade, a different mood. It was not a male chauvinist paper, insisted Haynes. Perhaps not, but it was a paper that had learned nothing from the women's movement, and forgotten nothing of 1966. It 'helped transform the puritan climate of the time', he added. It did not; the climate changed, and *Suck* shrivelled.

Alongside *Spare Rib*, the emergence of *Gay News* that summer underlined the way that the old underground was giving way to specialization. It was a curious parallel with the fate of the great

American general interest magazines. As *Life*, *Look*, and the *Saturday Evening Post* had faded, so magazines like *Fortune*, *Sports Illustrated*, *Playboy*, and, out of the underground, *Rolling Stone* had risen. So too the broad papers of the counter-culture gave way to the new, more specialized products. *Spare Rib* and *Gay News* were to survive into the 1980s; *Let It Rock* a serious, sometimes too serious, rock music monthly, did not. And another spin-off from the underground, capitalizing on its use of artists like Richard Crumb to develop a new style of cartooning, were papers like *Nasty Tales*. Prosecution brought notoriety, acquittal brought respite, but costs awarded against it brought the magazine down.

Gay News meanwhile drew on the first wave of enthusiasm around the Gay Liberation Front, and the energies of people like Jim Anderson, Warren Hague, Andrew Lumsden, and Denis Lemon. With his design expertise Adams was well qualified to play the role of 'token het'. A week after the *Spare Rib* fracas the Radfems trashed *Gay News*'s Paddington offices, but the paper, like *Spare Rib*, survived the experience. Yet the tensions that had split GLF persisted in *Gay News*. Women saw their role as token within a predominantly male gay paper, and it was on those lines that *Gay News* was to develop. Again the ubiquitous Mike Radford was called in to provide financial advice, and, under Lemon's editorship, the paper began to expand. But it wasn't an atmosphere in which either Adams – who fell out with Lemon over his style of editorship – or Radford felt happy. They both quit.

It was a very different terrain. In *Oz44* Dick Pountaine reflected on the Notting Hill he had known, and the new, upmarket area that it was becoming. 'Back in 1966 rooms were cheap and it seemed like an exciting place to be, there was dope around on the black scene, there were musicians and poets and no one cared very much what you did. 'A sort of momentum built up, people moved in and it got more exciting and so more people moved in. . .'

And by then people were starting to move out – the people who had made it exciting. By November *Oz* itself had found a new owner. Honeybunch Kaminski, the cartoon character-cum-effigy for the trial, had given her name to the Felix Dennis-instigated company, H. Bunch Associates, which was to see *Oz* through to its demise. '*Oz* itself I read more out of a duty than pleasure', wrote Neville in the magazine in January 1973, '. . . lazily regurgitating second-hand slogans, a harmless peacock posing as a gadfly to the state and still searching for the perfect orgasm in the manner of Winnie the Pooh behind the stairs with a flashlight.'

It had indeed become a celebrity, but an old, jaded one, and when one of the *Oz* defence counsels, Geoff Robertson, put together a play on the trial off Broadway, the *New York Times*'s drama critic, English-born Clive Barnes, called it 'the dullest thing to have come out of Australia since the koala bear'. Ever since the fifth birthday issue premature obituaries and retrospectives had become a staple part of the magazine. Instead of indictments of straight media, the magazine turned on itself, whether the author be Auberon Waugh or David Widgery, Neville or, later, Dennis himself. 'There was this old Australian tradition of dame Nellie Melba having endless farewell appearances', says Neville. '*Oz* had a bad case of the Melba syndrome.' As the year ended the magazine was again promoting *Spare Rib* which 'gets better all the time and, unlike any other alternative publication, comes out regularly and is sold by W.H. Smith'.

Spare Rib was the exception, a magazine out of – but not part of – the underground, and serving a national audience, as the old London papers failed. Yet there was still growth, but in different places. Within the capital local community papers like the *Islington Gutter Press* had emerged as far left libertarian voices, and outside London the underground had already dug its tunnels.

In Manchester in the late 1960s Dave Clark – later the main mover behind the late 1970s *Leveller* – had set up *Grass Eye* as a paper with a strong political edge. Across the Pennines the *Leeds Other Paper*, established at the same time, was to survive until the present day, unlike the *Eye* which folded in 1970. Before it closed it had been joined by *Mole Express*. By its second anniversary *Mole*'s Mike Don was telling *Oz*'s reporter, Roger Hutchinson, that he was trying to produce a paper 'somewhere between straight community papers like the *Cardiff People's Press* and the underground press. The national underground papers in Britain exercise too much influence.' They weren't to for very much longer. Yet, with a mix reflecting a poorer readership, the papers out of virtue and necessity attempted to deal with local politics, local concerns, while still drawing on what was left of the culture nationally and inter-nationally. The Underground Press Service's material out of the United States was regularly used; John Wilcock's 'Other Scenes' column was a fixture, for a time; so too was an often critical coverage of the London underground. Thus regrets about the outcome of the *Oz* trial had been mixed in *Mole Express* with reproofs at the paper's sexual attitudes.

The papers emerged in far outposts, to the surprise and outrage of local dignitaries and media alike. Thus by November 1971 even Rochdale boasted its own *Rap* (Rochdale Free Press). Two months earlier yet another paper had come out in Manchester. Triggered initially by a strike on the *Manchester Evening News*, the *Manchester Free Press* avoided the underground tag entirely, settling into the city as a radical monthly out of the Manchester Free Press Group.

To the west there was the *Liverpool Free Press*; further south

Birmingham provided fitful births, and deaths, to *Grapevine*, the *Birmingham Free Press*, and the *Street Press*. The 'North-East's Alternative Press' was *Mother Grumble*, out of Durham. In Scotland, from the late 1960s a series of papers appeared and vanished, but as 1973 dawned Dundee had 'Scotland's Alternative Magazine', *Inside Out*, while farther north was the more severe *Aberdeen Free Press*. On the south coast there was *Brighton Voice*. In Barnsley during 1971 there was Roger Hutchinson's own paper, *Styng*.

If anything the separation from London intensified the radicalism at the expense of hedonism. Being a freak could be a more isolated and dispiriting business outside the capital, thus the mood was tougher, even if often couched in the cosy excesses of London's – and the United States – radical purple prose.

For many of them the trial that ended in early December 1972 was a watershed. Four of the eight defendants in the Stoke Newington Eight trial were acquitted, but four received ten-year prison sentences. 'The Verdict of an Uneasy Majority', said *Time Out*'s cover, displaying an equivocation that had been absent the previous December in 'Now We Are All Angry'. In the north-west the line was simpler: 'None of us is free while our brothers and sisters are in jail', claimed *Mole Express*. Suddenly one trip out of the underground had crashed against a wall.

It was doing so while proclaiming the unity of disparate struggles: squatters, claimants, the unemployed, and the organized working class. But it wasn't a link that the old, or new left were happy to make. That summer five dockers engaged in 'secondary picketing' had been jailed and a strike wave rolled across the country in the wake of the move. The Heath Government had discovered an obscure legal apparatchik, the official solicitor, who was empowered to free them. It had been, claimed the left, a demonstration of what mass action could do, and an answer to the Angry Brigade's blind alley. Not so, said the Stoke Newington Eight Defence Committee. While skirting round the question of who *had* carried out the bombings it emphasized their complementary nature to the other actions.

In other quarters the distinctions were seen as academic. Realizing that their traditional map of left-wing activism was out of date, the police and security services tried to find entry points into the new left and the underground. Papers like *It* had been raided, to no avail; the International Socialists were planted with an MI5 agent; some affluent middle-class associates of the far left were discreetly sounded out on whether they would be prepared to keep an eye on their friends within the left and the underground. Sections of the far left and the far right developed mirror images of one another.

The case was part of that continuum that stretched back to the beginnings of the 1960s. Scattered acts of dissent and defiance against the status quo were inevitable, a welcome part of the regeneration of the body politic. But after 1968 a group for whom the old solutions, the old accommodations were not enough remained and they appeared then to have no place to go. There had been the literary/cultural clashes from *Lady Chatterley* through *Naked Lunch, Last Exit To Brooklyn, It, Oz, The Little Red Schoolbook, Nasty Tales, The Mouth*.

There had been the drug cases, from the Rolling Stones and John Hopkins in 1967–8. There had been the Cambridge House trial in which undergraduates had been jailed after breaking up a Greek travel reception in that town. There had been the battles and cases around the Mangrove, around the case of black activist Tony Soares. Suddenly in the early 1970s, against a background of the largest wave of industrial militancy witnessed since the war, they merged together in parts of the popular conciousness, in parts of the media, and in parts of the left and right. While the underground itself was dying, splitting into political, cultural – and religious factions, even – the mass of discontents blurred together. 'They were young. They were bright', commented the *Sun*, post-Stoke Newington Eight. 'And very, very big-headed. Arrogance was their inspiration. Arrogance proved their downfall'. It was not alone, and the London *Evening Standard* made what it assumed were the right connections: 'These guerrillas are the violent activists of a revolution comprising workers, students, teachers, trade unionists, homosexuals, unemployed and women striving for liberation.'

Out in the provinces the popular image of the underground was reinforced even more clearly. 'Landlord tells of cottage orgies', reported the *Evening Gazette* in Colchester, where two of the defendants, Anna Mendelson and Hilary Creek, had shared a cottage. The landlord summoned up spectres that would have delighted the *News of the World* reporter browsing in Indica five years before. He had seen 'men and women dressed only in white sheets taking part in strange rituals', and while 'unable to verify reports that revellers had indulged in the sacrificial killing of birds' did recall 'sacrificial orgies, bizarre sexual activities, anarchist-type-meetings, drug taking and unpaid rent bills'.

It was some distance from the reality of the post-Situationist, post-1968 libertarian politics of the defendants and their supporters dotted through the decaying inner cities of Britain. One of the acquitted defendants, Angela Weir, told *Time Out* that week that, while the organized left had paid too little attention to the trial, the libertarians had, if anything, given it too much importance. 'Now I'm much more convinced of a proper Marxist understanding of the situation, and a strategy which comes from that, and of the need for proper organization.'

And, post-trial, Granada TV's *World In Action* networked a special on the Angry Brigade, including an interview with Anna Mendelson. What, it concluded, had been the achievement of the Angry Brigade? 'Achievement, in terms of change, it hasn't achieved anything, anything at all', she replied.

So, amongst Marxists, squatters, claimants, freaks, followers of the Bhagwan, the Guru Maharaj Ji, rock fans, feminists, Situationist theorists *et al.*, where was there room left for an underground?

Chapter 17

Around the corner

We'll be publishing alright. *Oz* volume two is just around that
proverbial corner.

(*Oz47*, April 1973)

Al, Steve, and the 'Communal Raincoat' were voicing complaints in
Oz's letters page in April 1973. The magazine had dropped its
welcome line in obscenity, they reckoned, and followed their
observation with a string of expletives. Some alumni of the school of
underground press journalism disagreed, muttering that the late *Oz*
was veering perilously close to a skin mag. But the previous year
had been accompanied by increasingly plaintive if briskly worded
complaints from the traditionalist element of the male readership,
like Al and Steve, complaining about the declining values of the
magazine.

The old staff had begun to pull out, leaving Dennis *in situ*. Even
in 1970 Richard Neville had become bored by the paper, and by
1973 he had effectively withdrawn. And the old relationship
between Neville and Dennis had changed. The one-time street
seller from Surbiton had a different vision to Neville's, and an
element of rancour had intruded. The Australians began to pull out
of London: Martin Sharp, Louise Ferrier, and, very soon, Neville
himself.

A sign of the times in that April 1973 *Oz* was a feature on the
lyrics of Cole Porter and the golden days of song writing. It was a
tribute to the man who, as he had put it, 'found that the fountain of
youth was a mixture of gin and vermouth'. Too much space had
been devoted, *Oz* suggested, to 'temporary tin-pot rock morons'.

Dennis extended the revisionism the month after the Cole Porter
feature. *Oz* wasn't an underground magazine any more, if it ever
had been, he suggested. Nostalgia for the 1960s was a bad idea, so
the paper would return in June, revived and changed. It didn't. In
reality Neville and Dennis were exchanging angry letters about
whether the magazine should ever reappear. Neville felt that his
friend was trying to perpetuate *Oz* too long and exploit its name.
Summer gave way to late autumn before another issue was
published, and it was something that Neville, from a distance, had
to be talked into.

By now *Oz* – or rather H. Bunch Associates – had moved to Goodge Street, north of Soho, in the heart of the Greek restaurant belt, round the corner from a long-closed UFO club within a long closed Irish Blarney club. The issue, finished on 31 October 1973, marked the end of the magazine. Dennis and his production manager, Dick Pountaine, had to find other avenues for their talents.

Some were available. Kids liked comics. The underground supposedly liked comics, even if it didn't seem to want papers with words any more. So *Cosmic Comix* poured out of Bunch's offices. But no big money came back in return. Some issues were innovative; some specials were, thought their producers – which included Adams – spectacularly good. But the money was thin on the ground.

For *It*, too, the outlook was bleak. The last edition of *Oz*'s 'Spike' section had been edited, for old times' sake, by Roger Hutchinson. Back in 1971 he and a few others had put together a little paper in Barnsley, *Sad Traffic*. Having quit college following a battle with the authorities it seemed a good idea to expand the magazine. The title – a line from a Brian Patten poem – was, thought Hutchinson, terrible. If it was to expand, something more punchy should be devised. 'I had got a taste for publishing', says Hutchinson, 'and I wanted to do something more adventurous.' The result, in the spring of 1971 was 'Sad Traffic Yorkshire News and Gossip' – *Styng*. They had a printer, talent, the Leeds–Sheffield college belt as a market, and it did well. So well that the police took an interest. It was July 1971. In Glastonbury the first Free Festival was taking place, linking those obsessions of John Michell and the early *It* with the mysticism of old Albion and the 1970s wave of rock festivals. In France Jim Morrison was dying; at the Old Bailey *Oz* was on trial; and in Barnsley, alerted by the vigilance of the local press, the deviants of *Styng* were raided by the police. If Barnsley had developed an underground – outside the coalface – was anywhere safe? *Styng*'s printers were also visited. Did a reputable company *really* want to produce a paper like this, they were asked? 'They were really surprisingly crude', says Hutchinson, 'at the time we thought it was all part of the glamour, what happened to every underground paper, so we were delighted to be a part of that.'

And there was news to be covered in the area. The Huddersfield 'rhino whip' case, in which police had been exposed for brutality – by the local paper – was a memory; and in Leeds a black tramp, David Olulwale had been beaten to death by the police. And, nearby in the county, the Poulson case of municipal corruption was making waves.

The police went to the extent of threatening prosecution under the Obscene Publications Act. The subject was some of *Styng*'s cartoons. One of the paper's – anonymous – contributors and cartoonists was Jeff Nuttall, fresh from *Bomb Culture*, resettled back in the north, and working at Leeds Poly. 'I don't think we ever paid him, although we talked about it', Hutchinson recalls.

But, despite the fact that by the autumn the paper was selling a respectable 7–8,000, there were problems. If distribution was difficult for London papers it was worse for papers like *Styng*. The retailing couldn't be centralized as it was for London's papers through the ubiquitous Moore-Harness. 'There were so many different outlets', he says, 'every penny that came in went straight out again.' There was advertising, but the core group of four or five couldn't rely on any wages out of the venture. But, through Styng, Hutchinson had come into contact with the London underground, on his visits to the city to organize distribution there. He met people from *Frendz*, Jonathon Green – and Felix Dennis. 'He was the only person who went out of his way to show real interest in *Styng* and us, was Felix, he was absolutely tremendous from the first day. He taught me an awful lot about the business side, about design, about putting magazines together. I would never have learned it anywhere else. He did it too when he was involved in the trial.'

By November 1971, after seven issues, *Styng* went into that familiar underground sleep from which there was no awakening. And on New Year's Day 1972 Hutchinson received a telegram from Dennis, asking him to ring. With the triumvirate of Marchbank, Green, and Widgery at an end Dennis had problems with an ailing *Ink* and a short-staffed *Oz*. So Hutchinson quit Barnsley and headed for London to help Dennis in *Oz*. They worked together on the fifth birthday issue and into the next, a crime issue, that stirred memories of Neville's tales from New York of *Mobster Times*.

The impermanence of the arrangement meant that Hutchinson needed to look elsewhere. At *It* Mick Farren was pulling out. The *NME*'s move to absorb the talent of the underground was drawing him in. So would Hutchinson be interested in coming over to Berwick Street? The *Oz* work was uncertain, the *It* job less so, and by the spring of 1972 Hutchinson had switched. *It* moved, even briefly lodging with *Oz* in Great Newport Street, before taking rooms in Wardour Mews back in Soho. It hadn't just been *It*; *Frendz* had approached Hutchinson too. For the *ingénue* from Yorkshire it was quite flattering.

The *It* staff regrouped. From *Oz* Chris Rowley had come to cover advertising. Joy Farren and Caroline McKechnie continued to provide *It*'s administrative backbone and typesetting. Duncan Campbell and Jonathon Green contributed; so did Miles.

The finances remained bad. The paper was selling 12,000 to 15,000 a fortnight. 'But it was obvious that the underground wasn't going to survive in anything like its old form', Hutchinson says. 'I hadn't been in on the thriving years. It was a strange situation. But I thought – and do – that it was an important branch of publishing. I was excited by being a part of it. I was getting an education, a stimulation, but it was no longer 1967.'

The old and the new came together. Once, back in 1952, John Wilcock had set out from Sheffield destined for New York. Twenty years later Hutchinson had again quit South Yorkshire for London. Both men came together on another Wilcock-edited *It*.

By the summer of 1973 the situation had become hopeless, the staff concluded. They decided that *It*, the doyen of the underground, had finally to close. Meanwhile *Oz* was about to die, but *Time Out*, glossily, and in colour, was about to celebrate its fifth birthday that October.

Tony Elliott's brainchild was selling 42,000 a week, had substantial advertising, efficient distribution, and a staff that agreed on little except that the paper wasn't underground. The complaints of the women demonstrators at the Roundhouse the previous year had a truth. *Time Out* then, and ever since, was dogged by complaints about its consumerism, its schizophrenia towards radicalism, and that glossiness which was a sin both for those out of the underground and for those brought up on the stern verities of the left. But in one sense the critics missed the point. If *Time Out*'s effective slogan was agitate and consume – or enjoy the spectacle, as the Situationists might have put it – then the thinking behind it was far from Machiavellian. The mix was a product of that ultimately irreconcilable tension between the two souls of 1968. It was to snap when people – most of whom knew little of those days – finally locked into combat in the next decade, under a very different government from the floundering corporate Conservatism of Edward Heath.

Souls, slogans, and spectacles aside, *Time Out* paid, even if its wages system had, for a long time, remained haphazard. 'We were paid £20 a week, I guess', says the then jazz editor John Fordham, remembering the early times when Elliott would wander the office dishing out little brown envelopes. 'Then one week we found £25 instead of £20. We all thought, what a wonderful gesture.' These acts of virtue by stealth passed as the trade union-federated chapel (branch) was established and the magazine was forced to rationalize its relationship with the Inland Revenue.

It was a state of paranoia, and within the magazine the struggles were reflected. If the Angry Brigade had ceased its operations, others hadn't. The Derry events of January 1972 had left thirteen unarmed demonstrators dead at the hands of the British Army. In its aftermath *Time Out* news had argued that: 'There is an army in Ireland fighting the British. We must lend that army our support and we must give them money.' It wasn't a position that made friends at MI5.

The arrival of John Lloyd at *Time Out* tended to be seen by some within the newsroom as an attempt to change the weekly's priorities. His arguments with Radford, and his experiences reporting from the province, had changed his politics. It didn't make for an easy relationship.

The Agitprop collective – that group descended from 1966 – had continued to provide listings. As 1970s militancy accelerated, so, increasingly, it was the target of attention from the authorities. Thus, while probing the Angry Brigade, the most astute of the police investigators, Detective Sergeant Roy Creamer – 'the smart boy of the Special Branch' as the AB's supporters called him – made a point of dropping in on the Agitprop bookshop in Bethnal Green, checking out anarchist and Situationist publications. Other visits took him to *Frendz* and to *Time Out*. At the magazine Tony Bunyan out of Agitprop was drawn into the newsroom, and soon he was effectively running it with David May. Another arrival was Phil Kelly, jobless after the collapse of *7 Days* in May 1972. 'There was', suggests Kelly, 'a huge left-wing cuckoo in Tony's entertainments nest.' The result had been the isolation of Elliott from the newsroom, and, to a lesser extent, the isolation of the newsroom from the rest of the magazine. 'We were reporting hard left politics from a libertarian milieu', Kelly continues, 'we had almost nothing to do with the Labour Party. The rest of the underground was drifting away, and the rest of the magazine, to us, was selling on pure consumerism.'

It isn't a view that Elliott accepts. The argument about whether or not the paper should become a co-operative took its toll, and with Lloyd's arrival he was persuaded to withdraw from the day-to-day running of the magazine. The move was even endorsed with an official paper drawn up via the ubiquitous Mike Radford. But, he says, the argument wasn't about the political coverage as such. 'I wasn't at odds at that stage with the general ideological tone of the news. I supported our political stances on the Angry Brigade.'

In May 1973 Lloyd quit as editor. There followed, for a matter of days, a farcical interregnum with the appointment of a new editor, who, in an effort to win goodwill within the magazine, presented the female staff members with roses. The publisher compounded the error. 'Not only did I appoint him – on advice – but I decided, in an act of sheer vindictiveness and stupidity, to fire Phil Kelly and Chris Bunyan at the same time.' The sackings were withdrawn. So was the ill-starred editor. Elliott returned, and situated himself in the newsroom. 'It was terrifying', he says.

Elliott's progression up and down the magazine's masthead, sometimes as editor, sometimes as publisher, sometimes above the staff, sometimes below, became a useful barometer for *cognoscenti* of the state of struggle within *Time Out*. For that fragment of the new London intelligentsia from the new and redbrick universities of the 1960s, with the underground almost gone and industrial and political struggle at new heights, *Time Out* became almost a world of its own. Unkind critics on the left and right began to label it 'Noddyland' or 'Toytown'.

That it was a potential goldmine was also clear and nuggets were beginning to surface amidst the dust and dross. Its success was noted in New York and triggered a half-hearted attempt to topple it in 1973, using techniques largely left over from the early 1960s and incapable intellectually or financially of cutting into the new seam. In New York, publisher Clay Felker had made a fortune from his *New York Magazine*. In 1974 he was to buy the *Village Voice*. In the spring of 1973 he was in London, and dropped by the *Time Out* office. Some have suggested that he wanted to buy the paper, but was put off by its labour relations. It is a suggestion that Elliott denies, and he was, anyway, unwilling to lose what he – if not others on the weekly – saw as his baby.

Peter Elman, the former editor of *Campaign*, the advertising trade paper, had other ideas: an overground rival to *Time Out*. Through his friend Clive Irving, Felker had met with Elman and with David Frost, who quickly pulled out. But Felker, it was suggested, could put money into Elman's project, *Inside London*, while leaving the Englishman with overall control. Around £175,000 was needed, it was projected, to get the magazine up and running. Later Felker indicated he wanted an increased say in the new weekly; Elman said no, and went ahead on far lower funding. Its first issue appeared on 11 October 1973. It was glossy and it had some competent journalists. It was also dull, out-dated, and under-financed.

'Can you trust this man with your city?' asked the front cover, above a picture of the then chief of the Metropolitan Police, Sir Robert Mark. Possibly not, but by the time the third issue appeared it was clear that Londoners didn't trust the magazine too much either, and the staff were not greatly enamoured with Elman. It was as if the late 1960s, now a fading memory, had never *existed*, as if London had leapt from *Time* magazine's vision of swinging London in the mid decade, from the times of Len Deighton's *London Spy* colour supplement-style guide of 1966, to the early 1970s without noticing anything in between.

The style of the magazine – compared with a *Time Out* just going through another of Pearce Marchbank's spectacular redesigns – was pedestrian; and the listings, a craft which the Gray's Inn Road staff had now almost perfected, were woefully inadequate. Amidst acrimony and recriminations *Inside London* became outside publishing. It was another stiff in the graveyard already containing *Town*, and, from 1963, the Peter Cook/Nicholas Luard-sponsored *Scene*, born out of *Private Eye*'s success. *Scene*'s insatiable appetite for money nearly brought down its parent publication. Its promoters were not to be the people of the late 1960s, but even then it was born and died too early. *Inside London*, a decade later, was born too late. Having seen off the entire underground, *Time Out* had now effortlessly rolled over the first attempt at an orthodox challenge to its grip on young – and, increasingly, old – London.

While *Inside London* collapsed, *Time Out* was celebrating its fifth birthday. Jerome Burne, back from the United States, and Roger Hutchinson were recruited to edit a special section covering the days since the magazine's birth from the high tide of the underground to the green grass of its graveyard – *Oz* had just one month and one issue left, and *It* was missing, presumed dead. *Time Out* had colour, it had class, and it had, in another redesign from Pearce Marchbank, the model that lasted into the 1980s. Familiar writers emerged once more. In April 1973 *Red Mole*, *Black Dwarf*'s duller younger brother, had ceased publication, to be replaced by *Red Weekly*, which it was hoped would be more in tune with the times. Out of the new paper came Robin Blackburn, the one-time victimized London School of Economics lecturer, to provide a piece on law and order. From dead *Ink* David Robins wrote on libertarian action and the growth of claimants' unions. Chris Rowley, with no *It* and little *Oz*, wrote on ecology. Eamonn McCann, the 1968 civil rights activist, wrote on Northern Ireland. David Widgery, meanwhile, sifted the wreckage of the underground for incriminating evidence.

'At the core of the shabby myths and collective dishonesties of the underground was the belief that the class struggle had had it', he wrote, 'that the workers had been hopelessly bribed, bamboozled, and betrayed and now the revolution was up to the *New Left Review*, Mick Farren, and the Pantherettes.' But instead, he suggested, the working class had moved. 'Sooner or later one side will inflict a lasting defeat on the other.' Perhaps if he had put 'and' instead of 'or' he would have caught more precisely what was to happen during the next fifteen years. As it was he returned to the theme in his final piece for *Oz* at the end of October that year. 'Despite the protestations of democracy', he wrote of the underground. 'it was just another central London gang and it is fairly hard to interest people who aren't nutters in a political perspective which consists mainly of dodging police truncheons.'

Such activity was indeed painful, more so than reading books. In the anniversary *Time Out* Jerry Palmer, who had been within the underground milieu since university days in Southampton in the early 1960s, surveyed the volumes that counted during the times of *Time Out*. Amongst them he cited the French Marxist philosopher Louis Althusser's *Reading Capital* as his favourite. For the newcomers to left politics from the 1960s and the 1970s it was the flavour of the times, the stuff of those *7 Days* and *Capital* reading groups in flats across north and south London, in Leeds and Sheffield, Cambridge and Oxford. Those who didn't fall under the spell of the left groups, and some that did, embraced Althusser's brand of Marxism. Marxist critics, from the Trotskyists to the emigrés from the 1956 Communist Party like Edward Thompson, complained that it offered theory, thinking about thinking, as a form of practice, perfectly tailored for a middle-class elite's arrogance and passivity, a mode of rationalizing their impotence in the face of bitter struggles going on around them.

Palmer's other choice provided the other side of the coin. It was General Frank Kitson's *Low Intensity Operations*. Kitson, the former British Army supremo in Northern Ireland, became favoured reading for those on the left who suspected that a coup lay at the back of some of their rulers' minds. Others dismissed such ideas as fantasy, even on the left, but there were straws in the wind. There had been, after all, the recently published diaries of the former head of the *Mirror* group, Cecil King, who had, it seemed, passed many an arid lunch date in the late 1960s with the great and good, discussing ways of ousting Harold Wilson and hinting of doing so by some military-based coup. The seizure of power of most relevance to King had been that which ousted him from the *Mirror* in 1968, but there was other evidence then, and later, that such ideas weren't just paranoia.

There were the odd little incidents. By 1973 *Spare Rib* was well enough established for *The Times* to send a reporter round to Newburgh Street to interview Marsha Rowe. The Australian explained that the magazine wasn't *just* for women, but for all oppressed groups. It wasn't much more than a throwaway line, from an editor building the paper. A couple of days after it appeared she was rung by *The Times* journalist. Wasn't it funny, she was told, the Home Office had just rung the paper and made queries about Rowe? She didn't find it very funny, and even less so when, a couple of days later, a notice that she had two weeks to leave Britain came through from the Home Office. In 1971 the scandalous editor of *Oz*, Neville, had such a ruling thrown out, but by 1973 the editor of *Spare Rib* didn't find the process so simple. She contacted her old Australian ally from the *Oz* trial, Geoff Robertson, and he in turn contacted John Mortimer. Through the winter months of 1973 and early 1974 she fought on, but the authorities were unrelenting; despite postponements, she was going to have to leave.

They were strange times. Between March 1973 and February 1974 around fifty bombs had gone off in mainland Britain, the product of the Provisional IRA's campaign. In September 1973 a bomb had exploded at Chelsea Barracks, in December a car-bomb outside the Home Office injured fifty-four people. But most significantly of all, as 1973 gave way to 1974, the miners' overtime ban was beginning to cripple British industry and pose a direct challenge to the survival of the Heath Government.

In February 1974 came the crisis election, and the departure of Edward Heath from 10 Downing Street. Within days Rowe received another communication from the Home Office. The order to make her leave the country had been rescinded. Instead she was given residency status.

To the baffled, battered survivors of the intellectual left and the underground, the *Time Out* February 1974 Election cover seemed appropriate. It depicted a boxer-shorted blindfolded Edward Heath under the strap 'Tanks for the Memories'. Inside David Jenkins and Duncan Campbell provided the script for a 'rock opera' on the subject.

They did things differently in Australia. In December 1972 Gough Whitlam's Labour Party had been returned to power after more than two decades in the wilderness. One of Whitlam's first actions had been a raid on the Australian security services. The country was clearly becoming an interesting location again.

Back in Sydney, no longer the sleepy little town of 1965, Louise Ferrier received a call from Richard Neville. Birmingham's ATV wanted to do a documentary on him, and her. He wasn't very keen, but it would pay his air fare and get him some money. Thus his London career ended as it had begun, with the media in pursuit. But no longer was it Londoner's diary, but a television crew, and the venue had changed from Clarendon Road in Notting Hill to the spaces above his native city. The programme was called *A Sense of Freedom* and Neville concluded it by observing: 'I don't think many people could afford the sort of freedom I have, but I do think more people could strike out for it.'

The couple still had two more air tickets for London. They returned together one more time, and stopped off in Bali en route. It was the end of one underground trail.

Four days before the programme's transmission the four convicted members of the Stoke Newington Eight, plus Jake Prescott, had their appeals rejected. Lord Justice Widgery's only concession was to harmonize the sentences at ten years apiece. In July the Angry Brigade itself got a place in the media sun, with the BBC's documentary interpretation of the group's actions.

As the interstices of the underground had subsided, the media had indeed taken increasing interest in its survivors, as they came blinking out into the other world. In February 1973 Sheila Rowbotham's *Women, Resistance and Revolution* was published, a book which continued her project of synthesizing Marxism and feminism, and ranged across 500 years of history and global, contemporary feminism. Alison Fell reviewed it in *Oz*; Michelene

Wandor in *Time Out*. Elsewhere in London Margaret Drabble, the seer of the graduate mums, was working on a new novel. It dealt with the London of the 1970s. The old problems were pushed to one side; in their place was a portrait of the city haunted by the industrial struggles around, the presence of an unseen threat, the crump of the IRA bombs within it. The left, feminist, and underground championing of the night-cleaners campaign had led to a success, of sorts, in August 1972, with the conclusion of a deal between the workers and contractors. By July 1973 May Hobbs had published her own autobiography, *Born To Struggle*, with appropriate interest from the media. A television drama on her life was to follow. Meanwhile Germaine Greer paid the penalty for the success of *The Female Eunuch*. Having bought herself a house in *Oz*'s traditional village, Notting Hill, she found it promptly taken over by squatters. They complained of the middle-class affluent invasion of the neighbourhood.

In Trinidad another Notting Hill habitué, Michael Abdul Malik, was fighting against a death sentence that had followed conviction for the murder of Joseph Skerritt. In London his allies continued to campaign against his execution. And Malik, with that talent that remained within him throughout his strange, contradictory career, won new supporters. The American feminist Kate Millett came over to add her support to his struggle. So too did the Chicago Eight defence lawyer, William Kunstler. He got short shrift from some. 'Malik', Darcus Howe of *Race Today* told Kunstler, 'was denounced by the revolutionary movement in Trinidad. He was lined up with government ministers and he was doing land deals with them.' In the spring of 1974 Malik went to the gallows in Port of Spain. In London his old colleagues from *It*, Bill Levy and John Michell, published 'A Souvenir Programme for the Official Hanging of Michael Abdul Malik'.

At the same time the bookshop that had harboured the underground vanished as well. Better Books, where the young Miles had met Ginsberg in 1965, where the 'Better Books Writers' Nights' had been staged in the early 1960s, where Jeff Nuttall and others had organized the 1965 'sTigma' exhibition, was finally closed. It had never really recovered from its 1965 sale by Tony Godwin to Collins. In 1969 the publishers had sold the premises to John Calder and, that early backer of *It*, Victor Herbert. Calder put in £8,000 but the shop continued to lose money, with rumours of rampant theft being at the heart of the problem. Indica had been gone four years, it was left to Compendium to hold the fort for the London literary avant-garde.

With *It* and *Oz* gone, and *Spare Rib*, *Gay News*, *et al*. providing few writing opportunities, the male writers had problems finding outlets – and money. For people like Jonathon Green the situation was particularly galling. In the United States, he noted, underground writers had little difficulty being swallowed up by the mainstream press, in its diversity, its eclecticism. No such luck in the old country: 'my CV – had I had one – would have been completely meaningless', he observes. 'As far as Fleet Street was concerned I'd never done *anything*. I was writing 20,000 words a week for *Friends* and it was *great* and it ruined me for ever, because it ruined me for editing.'

It left Green, and others, in the curious situation of having to hustle for money from skin mags. While his one-time partner Rosie Boycott worked for feminism and *Spare Rib*, Green hit the typewriter, anonymously, for its diametric opposite. Roger Hutchinson, after a period working with Jerome Burne on *Time Out*, post-fifth anniversary, quit the magazine. The pressure of the previous two years was, he reflected, finally getting to him. Over in Holland a very rich pornographer wanted to produce a European version of an upmarket American pornographic magazine. Edward Barker followed Hutchinson to Breda in Holland. 'We made', notes Hutchinson, 'stacks of money, for doing very little.'

Chapter 18

Kings of kung fu

In 1974 Roger Hutchinson returned to London with his stacks of money, renewed contacts, and wondered what to do next. One day the phone rang. 'Are you the editor of *It*?' asked a female voice down the line. 'I *was*', he replied. He explained how the paper had died. A couple of days later the woman called back. 'Can you come down to Apple?' she asked. 'I have something for you.' It was most peculiar, Hutchinson thought, as he set off for Savile Row. He had no idea what was supposed to be happening. He went into the grand foyer of the one-time alternative business empire of the disbanded Beatles. The woman came down the stairs and gave him an envelope. 'This is from John Lennon', she explained. 'It is given to you on the condition that you mustn't tell anybody.'

He didn't. The cheque was for £1,000, and still in 1974 quite enough to get *It* back into publication, a lot more than a print bill. Lennon, the man who had met Yoko Ono at Indica back in 1966, had remained a reader of the underground press during the ensuing years, as in Britain and the United States it slowly crumbled. In late 1973 he had realized that, while his subscription to *It* hadn't run out, the paper wasn't arriving. Hence the inquiries and hence the cheque.

Hutchinson had been kicking his heels and sharing a flat in the Portobello Road with *It*'s first typesetter, Caroline McKechnie, and Edward Barker and his girlfriend. With no underground left, McKechnie was typesetting the perpetual survivor, *Private Eye*. They rented an office just down the road from the old *Frendz* premises. John Carding, Hutchinson, McKechnie, and Barker set to work. It wouldn't be a bi-weekly anymore, they decided, but a monthly, and this time it would be a part-time operation. Others from the old group were called back. Jonathon Green produced an issue with Richard Adams and Don Atyeo; they were big, and, thinks Hutchinson, they were good – a hobby, and a labour of love.

After three issues the love affair ended. Distribution and cheques as usual presented a problem, and Hutchinson and co. had no desire to go back down the path of interminable arguments and rip-offs with printers. Ironically once again the printers were in Banbury. 'It was good old Woodrow Wyatt', says Hutchinson. Thus the underground finally ended with the very printer who, in the late

1960s, had abandoned *Oz* after the complaints from his own subsequent employer, the *News of the World*. 'We dealt with one of the company's salesmen who obviously thought that getting the contract was an incredible feather in his cap. 'He used to come and pick up the boards himself. Invariably we didn't use to get it finished until an hour before it was supposed to be on the presses. He would arrive in Portobello Road at six in the morning and drive me and Edward to Banbury and take us for a company lunch.'

The lunches, the contract, and *It* were finished. Except that *It* could never completely die. Like a ghost it haunted the fringes of publishing on into the 1980s. The following year, indeed, an *It* appeared, subtitled 'Free Nation News' for the 'People's Free Festival in Watchfield'. By the late 1970s an indignant Felix Dennis was being pressured for money to revive *It* by a group of new devotees. Dennis had done well out of the underground, it was his turn to put something back. The, by now affluent, entrepreneur turned down the suggestion.

For Richard Adams, and for Dennis, 1973 and 1974 had been dispiriting years. While Elliott's *Time Out* flourished Dennis had concentrated at H. Bunch on his string of adult/underground comic books. There had been *Sin City: Tales of Urban Paranoia*, *View from the Void*, and *Rock 'n' Roll Madness*. The latter had been sold on the line '*Rolling Stone* eat your heart out.' But Wenner, over in California, was unlikely to be doing any such thing. By then the paper, across the United States, had established through rock music and politics a grip on the middle-class young that only *Time Out* in the tiny world of London could attempt to match. And, post-movement, it was, with writers like Greil Marcus and Hunter Thompson, achieving the balance between music criticism and political journalism that was to represent its best years. While *Time Out* went to the Stoke Newington Eight trial, *Rolling Stone* located, via Thompson, a different brand of paranoia in 'Fear and Loathing in Las Vegas', and set the tone for an awful series of plagiarizers.

Adams's career was moving along more modest lines: Pearce Marchbank's new studio in Clerkenwell provided work, so did Dennis and Dick Pountaine in Goodge Street. But Bunch was primarily relying on imports from the American West Coast, on Shelton, Clay Wilson, Richard Crumb. In the same way that *Rolling Stone* could draw on the 'life-style' middle-class rock devotees the American cartoonists could draw on a visual culture learned by young Americans throughout their childhood. It was early days for such a genre in Britain, brought up on the tradition of *Beano*, *Dandy*, *Eagle*, and only recently introduced via the underground to the radical use of cartoon graphics. There were new, innovative English artists, but selling their work proved then more difficult. 'The one comic that broke Bunch's back,' suggests Adams, 'was

Serious Comics by William Rankin. It was absolutely fantastic. But it was too surreal. Fifteen thousand were printed and, I guess, 13,000 were returned.'

Other ideas were floated. Perhaps the old magazine, as *Oz International*, a quarterly, could be revived, with Don Atyeo, Dick Pountaine, and Dennis in London, Martin Sharp and Richard Neville in Australia, Jim Anderson and Jonathan Goodchild in California, and Abbie Hoffman in New York. Work was started on the new magazine. But the project foundered, Neville wasn't keen on giving his name to a magazine where he didn't have direct editorial involvement.

But another different door was about to open and the key that was to open it had turned in July 1973 with the death of a then obscure Chinese-American film actor, Bruce Lee. While Clint Eastwood had gone to Italy to revive a flagging film and television career, Lee had, in the late 1960s and early 1970s, gone to Hong Kong to establish his career, in a succession of cheap kung fu movies, like *Big Boss*.

Mystic peace and love out of Asia had been one of the underground standbys. Now mystic violence provided a financial lifeline for a group out of money and with no particular place to go. Lee's movies had by stealth, through small Chinese film clubs and then local flea pits, begun to take a hold on the imagination of the young of the inner cities. Just before his death his reputation had finally earned him a substantial Hollywood-backed movie, *Enter The Dragon*. The movie baffled and exasperated critics, and, followed soon afterwards by the death of its star, it set the seal on the Bruce Lee myth. It also sucked in incongruous fans. In February 1974 *Time Out*, picking up on the phenomenon, ran a cover feature by Phil Ochs on Bruce Lee. In two days the issue had sold out. There was, for anyone who could do it, a market waiting to be tapped.

Poster magazines weren't new. When *Performance* had been released three years before *Time Out* had run off a quick example of the genre, a big picture of Jagger, plus simple information on the movie. Later a music journalist, Bob Houston, had latched on to the idea, with a proper poster-format magazine, *Pop World*. Aimed at a juvenile market it won few plaudits for design or content, but it sold. And from the production point of view it was a perfect product. Two sides on a single sheet, with full colour photographs that could be provided cheap, or free, from record company promotion departments, and copy that, suggested unkind critics, could have been written – and was certainly read – by 13-year-olds.

One night Dennis, on his way home to his flat in Kingly Street, near Oxford Circus, passed through Leicester Square. 1974 was not a particularly good year for movie audiences, but there was, he noted, a queue stretching round the block for one movie, Bruce Lee's *Enter The Dragon*. He went home, climbed into the bath, and thought. Displacement theory had worked for Archimedes and it worked for the proprietor of Bunch Books. He phoned Adams and Don Atyeo.

There was no money, little time, but an idea. Within around thirty-six hours the first issue of a new poster magazine, *Kung Fu Monthly* was completed. Dennis hadn't seen the movie, but he had seen the queue; his colleagues had seen neither. 'None of us knew about the martial arts', says Adams, 'but it didn't matter that we didn't really know what the bloody hell we were doing. We were dealing with a completely new set of standards and a different readership. I'm afraid we completely sold out, went downmarket, and produced a piece of shit that was so phenomenally successful that it started off Felix's publishing empire.' It also earned Atyeo and Adams the largest fees they'd ever received, and a percentage of the revenue from a man who renamed himself 'Felix Yen' for the occasion, and the magazine. It went on to sell in its English language edition more than 500,000. And Dennis, learning again from the underground, had provided a list of Bruce Lee souvenirs that were available. On *Oz* in its later days mail order had been one of the magazine's standbys. When the monthly was produced none of the souvenirs existed. This was quickly rectified. Soon there was a Bruce Lee pillowslip, a Bruce Lee T-shirt, a Bruce Lee *kit*. Within days the postman was delivering huge sacks of mail; the demand was, it seemed, insatiable. Others, such as Jonathon Green, were called in for the second issue, and Green was rewarded with £60.

'There were three of us', he remembers, 'with three cardboard boxes and sacks of mail. They sat there, going: "Cash, postal orders, cheque, cash, postal order." One realized that times had changed. Times had certainly changed.'

By the autumn Green briefly returned to the pages of *Time Out* as 'Jo Na Thon' Green, to chart Dennis's bizarre change of fortune. By then further contracts and advances for Bruce Lee books were flooding in, and Dennis still hadn't seen a kung fu movie.

Kung Fu Monthly came out, rescued several rocky bank accounts, and left Adams, and others, with qualms, but it also provided a regular £200 for six or eight hours work a month. It was a long way from being fed with grapefruit all those years before in the offices of *Ink*. 'They wrote themselves, they designed themselves, and they sold themselves', he observes, 'and, for a while, I sold my soul. But having gone through the underground press on £20 a week and peanuts this was just money, and I'd never seen that kind before. Neither had anybody else.'

The book, with Dennis, Atyeo, and Adams, *Bruce Lee: King of Kung Fu*, quickly followed. Others within the old underground worked on similar projects. And, for two years, Adams stuck with Bunch. The company had taken off; Andrew Fisher, Dick Pountaine, Don Atyeo, Felix Dennis, and Sally Croft formed a partnership to produce *Kung Fu Monthly*, and to work on other projects and make enough money to finally achieve that underground dream, and the dream of good capitalists everywhere: self-sufficiency, with the possibility, perhaps, of retirement. Poster magazines had to be taken to the United States, to Europe, Australasia. . .

Problems set in, competition, corporate carve-ups, but the central empire continued to thrive. With no underground, but a reserve army of designers, writers, photographers, and illustrators with nowhere to go but *Time Out* and Felix Dennis, the possibilities were there, and via Dennis they were taken.

But, eventually, for Adams it became just too much. Bruce Lee had been the beginning, but others followed, an abortive Olympics guide, poster magazines on Lee and David Cassidy, *Jaws*, and then Noelle Gordon and the staff and saga of the Midlands motel, *Crossroads*. Adams found himself interviewing and photographing the crew and cast of the production; he found himself sucked into the office politics of the production, found himself en route to Guildford to visit its star, Ms Gordon, while in residence at her health farm. There he would hear tales of her life, her holidays in the Caribbean, the problems of stardom. . .

It was Birmingham again, back to the city where he had set out, full of hope, for the London of *Oz*, *It*, and *Ink* back in the late 1960s. But now it was the mid 1970s and, while the money was better, Britain's second city was the same, or worse. His old friends from the underground, Mick Farren, Chris Rowley, Roger Hutchinson, they too were involved in producing the magazines. The atmosphere, thought Adams, and the lengths he was having to go to to support himself, were too much. 'Birmingham', he recalls, 'was the last straw.'

And he wasn't altogether happy about his cut from the project, and his wife wasn't too happy about the project, full stop. Adams pulled his share out of the company and took his royalties to the United States, as Wilcock, without money, had done all those years before. In San Francisco he stayed with Jonathan Goodchild, and then returned. Another venture followed for those left. Open Head Press drew back Haynes, Greer, and Levy, but the era, for Adams, was finally over.

Chapter 19

Ghost town

'There can', Bill Henderson told me, 'never be another Beatles. Look at the kind of money it takes to take a band on the road these days. Look at them. The Pink Floyd; Queen; Emerson Lake and Palmer; even Rod Stewart. And as for Abba, they're big, but its a different audience. Small-scale rock means pubs.'

Henderson was the music editor of a new fortnightly paper, *Street Life*, the year was 1975, and I was its news editor. The tall, laconic Scot was, of course, right. There would never be another Beatles, but within a year there would be something else. Punk: untrained musicians, loud noise, lyrics certain to *épater le bourgeois*, and massive British and American sales for what some liked to see as the final revenge – from another teen generation – of the hippies.

In 1965 *Time* magazine had featured swinging London; in 1975 a May cover showed a very different city, and very different inhabitants. Long after the Vietnam Solidarity Campaign had sunk into obscurity and Grosvenor Square had settled back into tranquillity *Time* featured nine smiling young Vietnamese, Kalashnikovs poised under the flag of the National Liberation Front of South Vietnam. 'Hanoi's Triumph' was the strapline. Long after the Tet Offensive the NLF had finally made it, but already the war, in western minds, was fading into history, leaving the Vietnamese to pick up the pieces.

And the underground too. In 1975 the way forward, it seemed, was professionalism. *Street Life* was to have learnt the lessons of the old underground. As *Rolling Stone* had built its empire on music, so *Street Life* would chart its development on the same grid. And money was available, £180,000 filitered in via the Island Records company to set the magazine up. It wasn't a bad paper and, in the language of the times, its production values were good. It utilized professional hi-tech computer setting down at Portsmouth and Sunderland Printers in Portsmouth. It had full colour printing that put the old underground to shame, and it had some good writers. It mixed its upmarket rock coverage with political news, cultural news, even an attempt at a national listings section.

By the spring of 1976 the offices were occupied by the chapel, the money had been exhausted, and the magazine was, give or take a few acrimonious exchanges between the staff and the proprietors, dead. Those two great rocks of the underground – distribution and advertising – had claimed another victim. And the times were different. The large affluent potential readership didn't exist, or, if it did, it was perfectly happy with the one paper still inexorably sucking in London readers, *Time Out*, and the still buoyant *NME*, flourishing on the residue of writers from the old underground and unknowingly in for a further boom with the arrival of punk.

The birth of *Street Life* had perturbed another survivor of the underground press. David Clark in the late 1960s and early 1970s had been a main mover in the Manchester underground/alternative paper scene. By 1975 he was persuaded that there was a market for a new radical paper, linking in with the struggles covered locally by the still surviving community papers like the *Islington Gutter Press*, but providing nationally the kind of coverage that the *Time Out* news department was specializing in. And, further, it would have a consistent, radical cutting edge absent from that magazine.

Meetings continued through the winter of 1975–6 and a dummy was produced in 1975. Money was not easy to find. The economic crisis could still filter down to the world of small magazines, and the benefactors who had opened their wallets for *Black Dwarf* and *7 Days* were now long gone, or even tighter with their money. And, as one sympathizer pointed out at an early fund-raising meeting, the problem was that more and more of the old cadre had other things on their mind – like children, like mortgages. Yet a system was evolved to deal with the problem, a network of 'founding subscribers' was established to set the magazine up, and yielded by its launch in 1976 around £1,680 – some £23,000 less than its founders had originally hoped for. Clark remained the magazine's primary inspiration in its early days, but the *Leveller*, as it was called, remained plagued by problems of internal organization, distribution, and sales.

Both *Street Life*, with its comparatively generous funding, and, over a longer period, the *Leveller*, could not find that place in the market. There were radicals, there were those interested in cultural politics. There was not, however, a tide behind them, as there had been a decade before.

In the mid 1970s there were other tides. Alongside punk came a new spate of fanzines, using graphics crudely, innovatively in a way that echoed the experiments of the underground, while rejecting any connection with those dim, distant, and doubtless bombed-out hippies. Five years is a millennium in youth culture.

And, as the Labour Government faltered, and the National Front grew, so too, out of punk, out of the Trotskyist left – and some of the survivors of the underground, like David Widgery – grew Rock Against Racism, and its paper, *Temporary Hoarding*. An indigenous movement had been created, with reference not to

Vietnam, or France, but to the Britain of that dreary decade.

Time Out was there to report it. And *Time Out* was now, even in the eyes of the mass London market a magazine with a substantial affluent readership. The paper, still uneasily balanced between its radicalism and its hip capitalism, continued its expansion. In 1978 preparations were made to celebrate the tenth anniversary of its first publication. By then the offices in Gray's Inn Road had been abandoned. In their place new premises had been found in Covent Garden.

It was an area going through changes. The market porters of Sue Small's times at *It* had begun to pull out. Community action had ensured that plans to demolish the area – as the fruit and vegetable traders decamped south of the river – were thwarted. Instead the first trickle of the new shops and boutiques that were to flourish in the 1980s had begun to appear.

Down the road in King Street, from where the Perfumed Garden and the Electric Garden had run their *Oz* benefits in the 1960s and early 1970s, came a new venue: the Rock Garden offered hamburgers instead, with some light punk in the basement. And *Time Out*'s new offices reflected the change in its status too. Located in Southampton Street, just off the Strand and five minutes' walk from the Endell Street *It* offices which Tony Elliott had visited in 1968, the new offices had once been the home of a clutch of women's magazines. Indeed *Time Out*'s floor had once housed another symbol of the 1960s, *Nova*, designed to be the first of a new wave of women's magazines, and dead by the 1970s. The new premises seemed to be inspired by the Washington *Post* of 'All the President's Men', or *Architectural Design*.

And it had another new editor. Back at Keele in the 1960s one of Elliott's fellow students had been John Fordham. By the end of the 1960s he found himself making the occasional contribution to the bi-weekly. A jazz aficionado at a time when the world was full of the Grateful Dead he was soon established as the magazine's jazz correspondent. By the early 1970s he shared briefly, with John Lloyd, the post of features editor. Later in the decade he became assistant editor, and by 1978 he was installed in the new offices as editor. With him were many of the old guard from the early 1970s, but also present was a new wave, suspicious of Elliott in some cases, suspicious of the countervailing power of the newsroom in others, but all benefiting from a magazine that couldn't, it seemed, go wrong.

But it did, with irritating regularity. There was no special celebration issue of the tenth anniversary. Instead there was a strike. But in its aftermath the sales of the weekly continued to rise. By 1980 they had passed 80,000 and were made up of a slice of Londoners with more money to spend, more time to pass than almost any other in the city. They were the children of 1968 and after, coming not into the milennium, but into the benefits of a university degree, or shrewd moves in the changing 1970s job market.

And the paper, apart from being rich, remained controversial. A succession of news stories on Britain's secret state, on the location of post-nuclear war fall-out shelters, from the *New Statesman* stringer, Duncan Campbell, the deportation of the magazine's American newsroom staffer Mark Hosenball, the arraignment of news reporter Crispin Aubrey, with Campbell and John Berry, had ensured that. It was a state of affairs that both impressed and exasperated *Time Out*'s proprietor. Elliott was very much a child of the 1960s, but he had always been an affluent child, moving from a middle-class home, through university, and into the almost immediate success of *Time Out*. In that, he didn't differ greatly from many of his employees. The difference was that some of them, rather than embracing the classless anyone-can-make-it ethos that one section of the post-underground had followed – including Elliott – remained doggedly committed to a version of the radical tradition of 1968.

Or so *they* thought. For Elliott it wasn't about roots in the 1960s. 'It was about', he argues, 'a change of character of some of the people in the mid 1970s.' The battles of the 1970s hardened positions. Outside Southampton Street, the boom and the flowering of that earlier decade had passed, and the concept of 'doing your own thing' could no longer be shared. Doing your own thing as an entrepreneur was very different from doing your own thing as an employee.

The staff's radicalism permeated the magazine's structure. Outside a small management group all staff were paid equal wages. Once *Time Out* had paid what it could, when it could. It was a rough and ready egalitarianism mirroring that of the underground generally, except that even in the early days the payments were likely to be more substantial. By the mid 1970s, with the emergence of the paper above ground, into the full glare of the Department of Health and Social Security's searchlights, and underpinned by a militant, if occasionally unreal, brand of trade unionism, the equal pay structure had been institutionalized.

Amongst its staff the system worked well. As long as the paper continued to expand, wages uniformly went up. And with the kind of money it was beginning to make any resentments between newcomers and the old hands – not that there were many – were easily overcome. It was, it seemed, a supremely rational system, and fair, to the bulk of the employees.

It was less appealing to Elliott. The power of the staff challenged his own, or he believed it did. Many of the battles centred around the redoubtable American mother of the chapel, Mandy Merck –

who had joined as a copy editor in 1974 – and Elliott himself. For sections of the chapel Elliott seemed on occasions to operate as an absentee landlord, occasionally materializing to attempt to issue dictats to the staff. For Elliott, he complained, any attempt to introduce change was met with stonewalling, contempt or indifference. For the staff, there were memories of earlier indiscretions: the flopped *Time Out North West* of the early 1970s, and a later expensive flop with an attempt to produce a *Time Out New York*.

In 1980 Elliott met his old features editor, Neil Lyndon. 'What's happened to all the young people with style and talent?' he asked. It was the kind of question that would both exasperate *Time Out* employees trying to find such worthies, and, on occasions, appal them. 'None of them', he says now, 'were coming to the magazine. Anything that anybody on the streets was beginning to do – which then became the *Face* or *I-D* – was dismissed because it didn't fit the perceived framework of what life was all about.'

Before Christmas 1980 the climate had begun to change. Within the magazine everybody noticed but few cared that much. There had been plenty of ructions before, plenty of arguments; they had all been settled; if another flare-up occurred, well, that one would go the way of all the others.

But the climate outside had changed too. Since the summer of 1979 a new kind of Conservative government had ruled. True, Edward Heath, back in those early struggling days of the magazine, had promised a different kind of Conservatism, but nothing had come of it, except U-turns and defeat at the hands of the miners. But this government, in its fundamentalism, its ruthlessness, was something else. And while there had been plenty on the left to point out the bankruptcy of Labour in the early 1970s its hollowness had been concealed by the disastrous record of the Conservatives, and by the wave of industrial militancy which had, just, edged Harold Wilson back into power. In 1979 it had been seen as the 'winter of discontent', a rising of the lower paid against the Callaghan Government's wages policy that had ousted Labour. In the 1960s and 1970s the left had slammed Labour's inadequacies; by 1979 everybody else agreed. In opposition, the Party had begun a route march to the left as the country began to adjust to the rule of Mrs Thatcher.

These were not concerns that impinged daily on the cloistered life within *Time Out*'s Tower House offices. True, the evidence of the new order was all around. While industry might be losing entire factories under Sir Geoffrey Howe's economic policies, while the level of unemployment might be crawling towards two million, Covent Garden, post-community action was one of the few bright spots in the new Conservative London. The trickle of boutiques, clothes shops, restaurants, and wine bars had become a flood, the new Covent Garden market was opening with more of the same, and, from the fifth floor of Tower House, despite Elliott's forebodings, *Time Out* proclaimed the message of Miles's '24-hour city' of 1967. Consume! Eat! Drink! Be Merry! Go to a rock gig!

It proclaimed another message too. Support the left – in its myriad forms – watch out for the police, and support the poor. It produced *in extremis* the magazine that the women protesters of the 1972 Roundhouse meeting had only dreamed of: rampant consumerism and far left politics. Yet the readers continued to buy it, if not always with enthusiasm, with interest. For every Mick Jagger – who proclaimed that going through the magazine's news section before getting into the listings was like crossing a picket line – there were others who relied on the magazine to provide the city's only radical voice. Thus did the tone of some of the mail the magazine received echo this schizophrenia. Readers denounced its trendy leftism, its consumerism, its anti-sexism, its sexism. It was as if the magazine had become a mirror of that 1968 generation. Holding it up the readers could see their own past, the radical ideas, and ideals; and their own present, the foreign holidays, the new stereo, the expensive restaurant for the following weekend.

The straw in the wind in the winter of 1980 had been an apparently minor issue. Following the failure of *Time Out New York* the chapel had won agreement that any further company expansion, or the takeover or development of new companies, would be considered by the chapel, that consultation would occur. In that winter it became apparent that a new company had indeed been set up, and that no such consultation had taken place. A brisk and furious row ensued; the two sides withdrew to contemplate the new year.

There was plenty to consider. Each year, according to ritual, a new house agreement between the management and staff had to be agreed. Each year the federated chapel – which, almost uniquely in British journalism, allied the three main print unions of the NUJ, SOGAT, and the NGA – would prepare its claim; and each year, after a brisk exchange of pleasantries or recriminations, occasionally accompanied by the threat or reality of industrial action, a deal would be reached. For *Time Out* was still, coasting on the still-rich middle classes, enjoying that luxury of the 1950s and 1960s, effortless expansion.

But just before Christmas came a sudden, strange, jolt. In early December in New York, the man who had met his future wife at Indica, engaged in dialogue with John Hoyland on *Black Dwarf*, become a short-lived revolutionary in the *Red Mole*, and floated the last three issues of *It*, was murdered. It was a Tuesday morning at *Time Out*. The magazine's cover feature had been written, the cover designed by Marchbank had been printed, ready for the issue to hit the presses that night. For the older members of the staff the news of John Lennon's death was shattering. For those below the age of 25 perhaps less so. It proved to be the last hurrah for a fragmenting alliance between two sides of the class of 1968. Elliott provided the finance, John Fordham, Pearce Marchbank, and I began the research. I rang John Hoyland, picked up the correspondence from that long-forgotten feature; the city was scoured for material. That evening, in Pearce Marchbank's studio, a special supplement was compiled. Elliott, his number two Bob Wilson – a one-time habitué of the old *Friends* premises in Portobello Road – typesetter Kathy Munro, with one of the IBM golfball machines that had set the underground and were on the verge of disappearance with the onset of computer setting, Marchbank, Fordham, and myself were there. By ten in the evening the issue was finished. 'It's just like, just like the *old days*', said Wilson. It was, for one evening.

It was also *Time Out*'s first use of colour, and the fastest turn-round of a cover the paper had ever seen. By the following morning the magazine was on sale. Elliott put £5,000 into the special. He got it back. That week's *Time Out* sales rose from 84,000 to 98,000. The magazine had been in the right place at the right time.

But in early 1981 it was different. The chapel wage claim went in as usual, together with the customary moves for improved fringe benefits. The management, as usual, was unhappy about them. But this time the management had a more important demand of its own, that the equal pay system itself should be scrapped, that the staff should agree to the introduction of differentials.

Back in the 1960s Harold Wilson had derided Hugh Gaitskell's push to scrap clause four of the Labour Party's constitution promising to nationalize the means of production, distribution, and exchange. It was like telling the Salvation Army, he had suggested, that there was no salvation. Thus with *Time Out*, except that for the sixty-strong band of more or less willing brothers and sisters on the fifth floor there was salvation – it was called the existing *Time Out* house agreement, and its fruits were delivered in equal portions in bank balances once a month.

By February 1981 the negotiations between the two sides had begun, and the atmosphere, bad from the beginning, was further poisoned – in Elliott's view at least – by a fracas around an advertisement booked by a film company. In the early 1970s Sue Small would have been delighted by an ad total of £2,000 a week. By 1981 the weekly total was pushing beyond £30,000. Indeed rows had broken out between editorial and advertising on just how much advertising could be booked before the magazine's content was completely submerged. A fifty–fifty ratio was agreed upon.

That week the complaint was different. The ad – for Brian de Palma's *Dressed To Kill* – was considered by many on the staff to be a depiction of male violence against women, complete with a menacing stranger poised at the door while a half-dressed woman stood in front view. The dispute, with editors, advertising manager, and proprietor locked in tortuous negotiation, ended with the ad – despite attempts at compromise – being ditched. For Elliott this was an intolerable interference. For the staff – including the writer – it was an exasperating failure to communicate. Memos circulated for weeks afterwards, attempting to evolve a trouble-free system. Elliott never noticed, and continued to regard the incident as one of bland refusal by the staff, outraged innocence from management. The argument about the new company, the film ad, and now the house agreement, coupled with a sporadic work-to-rule tactic by the staff concentrated management's minds.

And in the outside world, in London, the long-ago predictions of those inhabitants of the Garden, the Gate, the Grove, and the Farm suddenly came true. Instead of street-fighting freaks battling it out in a post-hippy metropolis, it was the young, working-class blacks and whites of Brixton who that spring erupted on the streets. It was the kind of event – as with Lennon's death the previous Christmas – that *Time Out* was uniquely qualified to handle, and via Duncan Campbell, far from the ad agencies of the 1960s, and the *Frendz* and *It* of the early 1970s, it did so. The Angry Brigade's bombs, the free festival fantasies, the reports of blazing Watts in the late 1960s had finally hit a resonance in London. It was a curious, and disturbing realization. It was also a story – as that long hot summer of street battles against the police, the city, the government, the decade, broke out – that *Time Out* would be ideally qualified to report.

But it never did so. By late April the magazine's marriage between the two souls of 1968 was finally moving towards divorce. A strike broke out. Piece by piece the chapel's claim was being whittled away, but on one point there was no room for compromise – the equal pay system had to remain.

The two sides didn't enter the dispute with any great enthusiasm, but both were committed, and both suffered from sufficient misconceptions to ensure a protracted battle. For Elliott the dispute was a product of that tightly knit, politically motivated group of men and women who, once separated from the loyal *Time Out* staff, would soon be revealed for the paper tigers they were. For the staff Elliott's success would effectively spell the end of their power within the paper, and the equal pay system was the one part of their radicalism they weren't prepared to abandon. 'If necessary', said theatre editor Steve Grant, 'we should stay out for *three weeks* to win this dispute.'

If Elliott was confident that a month without money would break the staff, they, on the other hand, were confident that once his cash-flow had been cut off – the term had moved from a few financial whizzkids of the early 1970s into popular parlance within the building by then – he would soon come running for a settlement. But there was always the risk, it was suggested, that management might try a lock-out. Thus the middle classes embraced their Gramscian inspirations. The offices were occupied, as of early May 1981. Sleeping bags arrived amidst the potted plants, felt carpets, and stereos. Rotas were organized. Meetings occupied the time of the occupiers. The management, glaring at their tormentors from over the potted palms, brooded. Then in came their own ultimate deterrent: some baffled, proletarian security men, or bouncers, who shared the office, and, from across the desks, the occupation.

It was a serious situation, it was an exciting situation, it was a farcical situation. Long discussions between the two sides went on into the early hours, but, increasingly, the two sides' conversations were with each other. One or two members of the staff suggested that perhaps now was the time to consider a new way of settling the dispute, to break away, and set up a new magazine. The staff had, during the past fifteen years, proved that they could run a magazine, why did they need a Tony Elliott? One or two other members of the staff suggested that the federated chapel might be unreasonable, that perhaps some sort of settlement should be made with the management. They were, in May 1981, a tiny minority. The vast majority of the staff were content to let the strike run until victory. And the three unions, nationally, had backed the dispute, despite the NGA's reservations about equal pay and lack of grading. It meant that efforts by the management to produce any bootleg edition of *Time Out* were doomed.

Pressure within the offices grew. Elliott went to the courts to get the staff evicted. Eventually the staff quit the building and took up residence at the Drill Hall, a fringe theatre off Tottenham Court Road. The staff were sacked, but this meant little, since it was a tactic used before. Negotiations dragged fitfully on. And the staff tried a new tactic. Since they were on strike they couldn't sell a newspaper, but they could give away a strike sheet. Thus they produced a broadsheet. It was called *Not Time Out* and featured the distinctive logo that Marchbank had designed back in 1970. The broadsheet was an immediate success.

If *Time Out*'s success had been built on its listings, the culture it had detailed had, in its turn, become dependent on the magazine. The summer of 1981 was becoming a bleak one for the fringe theatre, without the magazine, and *Not Time Out*, which featured listings amongst its reports on the strike, was an immediate success. And a pitch of '*Not Time Out*, free! Donations welcome!' meant that the paper more than paid for itself. On Saturday afternoons £40 or £50 could be taken in Portobello Road, where once *Hustler*, *Oz*, *Frendz*, and *It* were the alternatives on sale.

It wasn't a development that particularly pleased Elliott, and what particularly irritated him was the use of 'Time Out' within the title. But, unknown to the staff, as he issued a writ to restrain them from using it, he had a problem. Once more the ghosts of the early 1970s appeared.

Marchbank's last redesign for *Time Out* after the fifth anniversary had been the definitive one, still used by the paper in 1981. And the cover logo which he had designed in 1970 was still in use. The problem that the proprietor had, as he moved against the staff that summer, was that his solicitors indicated that the designer – rather than the magazine – might have the copyright. The logo, which had stamped the magazine's mark on the city, and which Elliott, wisely, has consistently refused to have revamped, had been designed, in a hurry, one Sunday afternoon. And when Marchbank had produced it he had assumed it was going to be temporary. 'It was supposed to look like an out-of-focus neon sign', he explained.

After the strike broke out Marchbank who, as a freelance designer, had no commitment to either side – took a holiday in Dorset. One day he found a message to call a Mr Elliott. While he was doing so, in London, the staff of the magazine were contemplating their defence against their employer's action to restrain them from the use of the logo, which, they assumed, was his copyright.

In Dorset Marchbank took a walk to the local post office. He had no 'phone at his holiday cottage. He rang. 'Pearce', said the voice at the other end, Elliott sounded embarrassed, 'My lawyer thinks you own the *Time Out* logo copyright. I want you to write me a letter now saying you're giving it to me.'

Marchbank contemplated the suggestion. With the logo, *Time Out* was, he decided, rather more valuable than it was without, a difference of, he suspected, around £100,000 should its founder decide to sell. And his own financial situation at the time was dire. 'I will do no such thing', he replied. 'You can have it, sure, but how much is it worth to you? I want £2,000 for it.'

'What? £2,000! How can you do this to me?' asked Elliott. 'After all the things I've done for you!'

Marchbank laughed. The conversation terminated. And Marchbank returned to London. But by now the other man – with Elliott and Howard Marks – who had done well out of the underground and its aftermath was taking an interest in the market that *Time Out* had opened up, and now, off the streets, was losing.

Richard Branson had experimented in the late 1960s and early 1970s with a national magazine, *Student*. Despite diligent effort it remained unfashionable, unloved, and largely unread, and flopped. But Branson's mail-order record business had expanded by the early 1970s into the recording business. Aided by Mike Oldfield's

'Tubular Bells', which was perfectly timed to catch the post-hippy wave of quack mysticism, his empire had expanded, the Virgin Records business had mushroomed, and Branson had become, comfortably, a millionaire. But one thing that he didn't have – and Elliott did – was a zappy, go-ahead periodical hitting home on the affluent young of London. There was no better time, reasoned the Virgin team, to move into the market; thus plans and glossy brochures for a new magazine were prepared.

By August it was announced. *Event* was going to be new. With full colour, a clued-up writing team, a massive advertising campaign, and, avoiding the mistakes of *Inside London* eight years before, Pearce Marchbank as designer. The news didn't cheer Elliott, and it didn't cheer the striking staff of *Time Out* either. As a going-away present Marchbank presented the logo – or any claim he might have on it – to Elliott.

Time Out's art director since the days when Marchbank had quit back in the early 1970s had been Carol Warren. By August she, in common with the rest of her colleagues, had been on strike for three months. Money was running low, extremely low. 'This strike', she observed, 'is getting like the First World War. No one knew what they were getting into, and none of us know how to get out of it.' It was true. The assumption that Elliott's cash-flow would dry up proved to be ill-founded. *Time Out*'s overheads – with few staff salaries or printing bills – were declining, and money for earlier issues was still coming in. The operation could be kept ticking over. Conversely Elliott's assumption that the strike would crumble after a few days, or weeks, was ill-founded, together with his belief that it was the product of a few plotters leading worthy cart-horses. A few strikers were still expressing their conviction that a return to work had to occur, and as soon as possible, but they didn't know how, or indeed when. And a few others with increasing conviction argued that a new magazine – the co-operative dreamed of in the early 1970s – had to be started. But for the bulk of the staff there was no alternative but more time in the trenches, or, to be precise, the basement of the Drill Hall, inking out, amidst petrol-based fumes, the *Time Out* logo from *Not Time Out* and thus creating yet another new magazine, *Not . . .*

Branson's move changed the situation. Perhaps the strike could continue until Christmas. Perhaps. But would the unions, nationally, remain solid? Or would they begin to urge a deal? After all, equal pay was an oddity, an eccentric variant on normal business practice. Yet it wasn't to the staff. It had become the benchmark of their commitment, to each other, to the magazine, to the strike, and to what they believed in. After ten increasingly affluent years the strikers were finally being forced to pick up the tab, and they did so. As the sporadic negotiations spluttered on more and more of their original claim was whittled away, but one aspect remained unchanged – the commitment to equal pay. But if *Event* was coming on to the streets that autumn then both sides could be wiped out in the ensuing eruption.

Since the beginning of the strike a group had met to plan finances. The threat of *Event* changed its function, and the mood of the bulk of the strikers. If the strike couldn't be won, in the foreseeable future, then perhaps the idea of an alternative magazine wasn't so daft after all. Once again, nothing, it seemed, could stop the idea now the time had come. But the plan, in its turn, regrouped the strikers. It increased the desire of some to settle with Elliott – and fuelled their suspicion that a new paper had been the idea all along – while others such as the former mother-of-the-chapel, Mandy Merck, fought against either settling, or setting up the alternative. The strike had to be won.

But the committee extended its feelers to the *New Statesman*. Its publishing manager, Johnny Johnston, was consulted on the prospects for a new paper. Eventually it was decided to call a meeting. But, with the probability of a leak to Elliott of the plan, the staff divided. The meeting called to debate the issue did not include all of the strikers. Its organizers concluded that some of the staff committed to a return would not accept the idea anyway. It was a small group, but the move injected a divisive note into a strike which, although beginning to splinter, had been remarkably cohesive and amicable in its internal dealings. With one exception, the meeting decided to go ahead with the magazine. Subsequently the issue was debated within the entire staff. By around forty votes to seven the decision was taken to set up a new paper. It was a curious occasion; what poison had begun to circulate within the group, in the meeting's aftermath dissolved, temporarily at least. The two groups wished each other well, with a third group – those planning a shift to *Event* – completing the process.

The forty had unique advantages. They had worked with each other, they knew, unlike their predecessors ten and fifteen years before, how to put together a magazine, and they even had an editor, since John Fordham had decided, nine years after writing a paper denouncing the idea of a co-operative at *Time Out*, to quit Tower House and join the breakaway.

The forty also had the common problem of the previous decade – no money. And to set up a paper to rival *Time Out* would, it was estimated, cost upwards of £350,000, and the finance had to be raised within a month, since *Time Out*, with the strike over, was planning to republish in mid September, and *Event* was to hit the streets in early October.

Thus began a frenetic and bizarre series of meetings. Finance corporations were approached, promised much, and delivered nothing. Curious entrepreneurs were met in back rooms and, on one occasion, in the arrival room at London airport, where a northern vegetable magnate again promised much, and delivered nothing. The atmosphere varied between brief spurts of elation, prolonged periods of fear, and considerable periods of gloom.

That spring the Greater London Council elections returned a Labour administration. Within a day a new leader, Ken Livingstone, had been elected. The new, radical GLC was committed, it said, to generating new business. The new magazine was, said its hopeful founders, going to be just that. By dint of considerable effort and negotiation a commercial loan from the GLC's trade and industries committee was obtained, for £80,000, with an option – never drawn – for a further £20,000. But what about the remaining funding? The £350,000 talked about had become a fantasy, but the strike had engendered substantial London-wide support. Enough people could be found to invest in and make loans to the project. Thus a further £100,000 was raised, half shares, half loans. Few making the money over could have expected to have seen any of it back.

A title was a more enjoyable problem. *Time Out* had taken its title from a Dave Brubeck LP. The new magazine's staff considered various possibilities, 'City Lights', 'Limelight', 'Metropolis', and eventually settled on a suggestion from a regular freelancer, Liz Heron – *City Limits*.

Offices were found in Islington, not a noted location for radical magazines, but large enough, and reminiscent indeed of the old *Time Out* offices in Gray's Inn Road. The staff, and new recruits, moved in. A designer was appointed: David King, the veteran of the old *Sunday Times Magazine*, *Town*, and *Workers Press*. The internal design staff chose themselves, largely veterans of *Time Out* – like Carol Warren – and including, in people like Judy Groves and Claudine Meissner, people whose track records went back to *Ink*, *Oz*, *It*, *Frendz*.

The wheel had come almost full circle when, on 6 October 1981, the first issue of *City Limits* was completed. It was five months to the day, and hour (4 p.m.) – since the start of the *Time Out* occupation. And although few of the staff, if any, thought of it, the birth of the paper marked a further stage of the dialectic. The underground of a decade before had been born in chaotic egalitarianism and had, with one exception, withered and died. Now *Time Out*, the survivor, had generated its own antithesis, *City Limits*.

Four years, and many traumas, later *City Limits* moved offices to Clerkenwell, to larger and more opulent surroundings, with the GLC loan – and £30,000 of interest – repaid. The old offices in 313 Upper Street were promptly squatted by a group of young libertarians. Amongst them was a group trying to get a new paper on the road. It wasn't really a new paper, however, but a revival of an old one. It was called *It*.

Chapter 20

Aftermath

Off Holborn, on the edge of Covent Garden, are the offices of *i-D* magazine, in one of those Victorian conversions so much a part of 1980s Britain and of that part of central London in particular. Its co-publisher is Tony Elliott and he prefers the quiet scruffiness of the premises to those of *Time Out*, further into Covent Garden.

He gestures at a stack of publications on his desk, the *Time Out* shopping, eating, student guides; a copy of *i-D*; some *Time Out* Filofax inserts. 'It was never going to work', he says, talking of the strike of 1981. 'All these things we do now I wanted to do in 1976, 1977, but the staff then were dismissive of guides.'

The staff would disagree, but no matter. Tony Elliott, as he has spectacularly proved over twenty years, is a great master of lists, and he draws up another one. It is of the current alternative magazines on sale; *i-D* is there, so is *The Face*, the monthly that made a style of style. 'What is going on now is a lot similar to what was going on in the 1960s', he suggests. 'People have things to say, so they make publications happen. The driving force of both eras is a wish to produce print because it's a very accessible medium. What's the difference?'

The political element is missing, he agrees. Amidst the fashion shots and the gossip, the record reviews and the advertisements there is little need to talk of protest. Paris is again fashion shows not May Events. Berkeley is square and a square. And Grosvenor Square a place for American visas not America's Vietnam. So we get different magazines. The alternatives offer an ante-chamber to the palace of the glossies – style, grace, and class only slightly skewed from the world of *Harpers*, *Vogue*, and *Elle*. Reflecting the times the magazines preach acceptance not dissent and offer tips on jumping the queue to *everybody*.

Nor is it a desperately new phenomenon. Asked to define *Time Out*'s market position in 1980 – at the dawn of the Thatcher era – a sizeable chunk of its readership already placed it firmly in that world of the glossies, much to the chagrin of its pre-strike radical staff members. Wasn't the underground press similar? Weren't the pages of *Oz* and *It* crammed with the protests of the dispossessed north of Watford and south of the Thames? The metropolis has always been a magnet, and no more so than in the 1960s, but the essence of those 1960s protestations was that, while in that city they believed a cultural revolution was taking place, in their own locality they were meeting overwhelming resistance. How, they asked, do we change it here? And the change was the development of a counter-culture, not the building of an ante-chamber. And for those who came to the city there was an ideology – if not the reality – of a community of the young, the non-conformist, the rebels. Squatting might be a necessity, it could also be seen as a political act. Today it is a necessity, it evokes pathos rather than politics.

In the 1960s they scored. In the 1980s they beg and they know it.

'The underground press', says John Wilcock, 'was everybody, not just the people who wrote it.' Often it seemed everybody *did* write it. 'The words "do it again" were never heard on the underground press', says Pearce Marchbank. 'It was a sort of public access to the print that sometimes worked and sometimes didn't. People were producing the most prodigious amount of work. But the only way you could produce a good magazine was when people who had access were relatively limited.'

Or a *consistently* good magazine. The underground press produced some of the worst-written, bombed-out, unresearched copy then seen. But sometimes, in London and elsewhere, a paper took flight, journalistically, stylistically, pictorially. More often than not it subsided into a hedgerow – or bedsit – by the following issue.

Public access and the ideology of the time could give the writing an immediacy, and an openness. When Sue Small reported on Phun City in *Mole Express* she was passing a message from a front, farcical or otherwise, to other members of a community, which in Manchester could be numbered in the hundreds and probably in the thousands, and that community took in ideas.

'Just as the pot trail helped me overcome national boundaries', says Richard Neville, 'so the underground encouraged global thinking. And to have a vision of the future is a very important evolutionary process, and although that vision wasn't achieved at that time I think the vision has been transmuted and will keep on popping up again and again.'

'Timothy Leary said in Golden Gate Park that acid "gets you out of your box man". Everybody has to get out of their box sometime', says Wilcock. 'At that time we were very vulnerable to some very interesting ideas that were being put in our head. Like we're altogether in the jungle.'

Despite the rhetoric of the time the acid wasn't the essential ingredient, as many of the survivors now concede. 'The greatest criticism you can make of the underground press was that it heightened people's expectations in a pretty irresponsible way', says Mark Williams. 'There were a lot of seriously deranged people whose brains had been eaten away by LSD who never recovered, or drifted into smack.'

But Wilcock's key point remains: Within the underground press was a flurry of contradictory ideas fighting their way out of their boxes, and into brains ready to receive them. The papers 'grew out of a movement which had no reflection in the popular press and had new technology on its side. Today the Sunday supplements and *everybody* has new technology. Some of the ideas of the underground were modest verging on the banal, the 24-hour city; some were positively harmful – kill yourself a Trafalgar Square pigeon, make pie, cook, consume, and, as a reader pointed out, poison yourself with DDT. Some were the media's first encounter with the issues of the years that followed: feminism, gay and lesbian sexuality, ecology, Northern Ireland, the politics of psychiatry.

The popular press, tabloid and heavy, took a long time getting out of the 1950s and earlier. That in 1956 the Angry Young Men could have caused such a stir with such modest proposals, or lack of proposals, is a comment on the aridity of the times. 'The underground coincided with the time when it was very badly needed to get the word out to the people who'd just run the Second World War and been through the McCarthyite period', notes Wilcock of its birth in the United States.

But having established the first bases, a flood of new recruits came in, the children of the long post-war boom which was to keep the movement afloat until it subsided in the early 1970s. In the early 1960s there were the papers of the post-1956 New Left, there were the little poetry magazines, the inheritors of Charlie Parker, the white British sound of black American rhythm and blues. A meeting ground was CND. In Britain in 1967, with *Oz* and *It* in existence alongside the birth of a new left-wing press, there came the Summer of Love by import, and, indigenously, but drawing on American, Continental, and Third World influences, the Dialectics of Liberation. Barriers between hedonism and orthodox radical politics began to crumble, a free market in ideas emerged. Briefly politics and psychiatry were taken seriously by people who didn't want to take anything seriously, and the pigeon-holing of left politics – worker/student/intellectual, gloomy good times versus hard work – began to crumble.

Which didn't mean that antagonisms crumbled, but that people who before and later could dismiss each other were forced into proximity, on the rival papers, on the street, the events. In 1968 the process climaxed for good and ill; radical politics had the examples of the Tet offensive, Paris, and Prague to draw on, and became briefly part of mass youth culture. The Rolling Stones' 'Sympathy for the Devil' took its inspiration from Marianne Faithfull's reading of the Russian surrealist novel of the 1930s, *The Master and*

Margarita. Their 'Street Fighting Man' had more obvious derivations. 'I saw Mick Jagger at Grosvenor Square', recalls Pearce Marchbank, 'and then lo and behold, next month out came the record.'

Youth culture is ephemeral, and the participants soon took their own paths again. Yet things could not be the same. From the 1950s the mass production of students from relatively unprivileged backgrounds was and remained essential to the system's regeneration. Growing up with expansion, they expected expansiveness and weren't put off when it was refused. Thus they stumbled into that mansion of dreams, experiments, crack-pottedness, and innovation, once the domain of a few within an upper-class counter-culture. Where once there had been Byron and Shelley, the decade trippers wandered through the halls, tried out the doors, searched for keys. The great art was absent, but then they didn't stay very long.

But some interconnections had been made. The rediscovery of Marxism in that time emphasized self-activity, not the monolithic state of Stalinism. It found the new left activists of the time pitching for grassroots organization; partly because the bureaucracies were impregnably dominated by the old left orthodoxies, but crucially because they believed it was right. And that orientation did have echoes of the most apolitical hippies professed desire to 'do their own thing'.

It went further, the young working-class man who had accompanied Sheila Rowbotham to Paris in 1960 was a prototype of another model of the 1960s. Through hippiedom came a route into an intellectual world, through its poetry, its music, and its ideas. Via papers like *It* and *Oz* the avant-garde was exposed to new eyes, whether it be Ezra Pound or William Burroughs, Germaine Greer or Simone de Beauvoir, Aleister Crowley or Leon Trotsky.

The underground press was also the medium by which another life-style could be lived, then. Women were to complain that the left promised liberation after the revolution, and they wanted it now. In the 1960s, when radical governments had promised something and apparently delivered nothing, the counter-culture had offered the vision of a post-revolutionary *then*. It was its appeal and its downfall, since communal and communistic visions were one thing; attempts to live them something else. In revolutions dual power is a passing phase, and the welfare state kids of the times assumed that change, like most things they encountered, came easy.

The opposition didn't. Today the May Events tend to be written off as a student affair. They weren't, they involved millions of people, and they rocked the French state. No such upheaval challenged Britain's rulers in that year, but the paranoia that surrounded the build-up to the great Vietnam protest march of that autumn was not merely a product of the mainstream media, it seeped into the state's consciousness. That it was an anticlimax was a relief to them, and also a useful warning. 'In the very early days, 1967–8 I did believe for a while that it was going to spread over all the world and augur in a new society', says Dick Pountaine of the pre-May 1968 underground. 'Then for a while I did believe in actual political revolution; that only lasted for another year.'

For others it went on longer. People were always arriving within the underground press, staying for a weekend, a month, a year, and departing, but there were waves. There had been the wave of the early 1960s, another larger group sucked in during 1967, and the politicization of 1968. By that time some of the early pioneers – like the Americans of *It* – were beginning to drift away. Others came in, from politicization or from the cultural energy being generated. 'When I was at art school the energy of certain people like Hoppy (John Hopkins) was fantastic', says Marchbank. For some of the late arrivals politics was everything, for others a tiresome distraction from the business of enjoying yourself.

For both those groups the idea of freedom, doing what they wanted, was important. To the establishment such a phenomenon was an irritant to be confronted occasionally at festivals, on the streets, in the Old Bailey, but containable. A cultural revolt had taken place, but it hadn't, it seemed, triggered any other forces. 'Occasionally you'd meet shop stewards at conferences who were interested in the underground press', says David Widgery, 'or got stoned, or were interested in radical music. That was always very fruitful. Otherwise there wasn't much apparent link between the workers' struggle and this – psychedelic flowering. The former was pragmatic and fairly empirical, predominantly concerned with money and making excuses for Harold Wilson. The latter was almost wholly an imported problem, which is what made the "off the pigs" rhetoric so flimsy.'

By 1970 the need to make excuses for Harold Wilson had passed with his government. In its place came a new militancy which swept the rug from under the Conservatives' feet, but also eroded the underground's base. 'Our paranoia', says David Robins, 'was right.' In place of exhortations in the underground press to explore new life-styles came exhortations to defend them; in place of Situationist projects in Better Books' basement came bombs in Biba; and in place of blurred underground consensus came sharply defined groups and loose coalitions. Under it all the boom had subsided, the strike wave had accelerated, and the recession had begun.

'All these issues were beginning to strain at the fragile centre of the underground press', says John Lloyd. 'And it was beginning to end anyway. People were going off into hard drugs, others going into communes, some were just growing up and out of it, others were going into groups like the International Socialists which were growing strongly at the time, and were taking exactly that kind of person who had come in during 1968. And the American tributary began to dry up.'

The other factor was the women's movement, which, Widgery had suggested, finally wrecked the underground. Michelene Wandor disagrees. 'By the early 1970s there were so many other things going on. Artists were becoming more politicized, and politics were going out on the streets *more*. The involvement in the class struggle in the early 1970s contributed as much. And it wasn't so much that the women upped and left and the men couldn't boil their eggs on their own. No way, it was just part of the new politics of which many women were a part. Paradoxically, a lot of women from the underground were not involved. It was the women *from* the women's liberation movement who were. So if the underground press and the underground dwindled it was because *men* stopped doing it. There would always have been the women to do the typing, look at now.'

The underground press, its alumni agree, changed the direction of their lives. It turned ad trainees into journalists, journalists into TV stars, it provided a background of rough and ready expertise and, as Sue Small says, if you could survive *It*, you could survive anything. But, for some, memories can be dispiriting. 'If you are going to be cynical you will say that all the underground press did was tell people what was on', says Dick Pountaine. 'All the rest was just hot air. Its lasting effects have been in cosmetic areas like graphic design and perhaps in journalistic prose style.'

Some learnt in reaction to it. 'It had no roots', says Phil Kelly, 'some people drifted off, some people were pure entrepreneurs. But I learned lessons from *Time Out* that meant for the next ten years I was a union activist.'

As divine revelation leads to dogmatic cults, so some manifestations of underground culture, considered radical at the time, changed their meaning in the intervening years. Thus the supposedly progressive and loud rock of the late 1960s turned into the heavy metal of the 1980s, with the mysticism giving way to pulp science fiction, the sexual freedom to braggadocio, and its devotees from the supposedly liberated to the actively repressed. The nudity of the underground was also progressive, in its way, yet it took another Australian/American, Rupert Murdoch, to mass market it as pure titillation. In the 1960s the young dropped out, in the 1980s they are dropped out. Two decades ago drugs were supposedly a tool to heighten reality, and offer visions of the future, in the 1980s they are an escape from the present, and a replacement for the future. Across the decades the lost army of travellers still makes its pilgrimages to Glastonbury.

So what survived? The right have few doubts. 'The revolting students of the 1960s are the revolting teachers of today', wrote Colin Welch in the *Spectator*, 'reproducing themselves by teaching as received wisdom what they furiously asserted against the wisdom received from their own teachers.' If he's right, it has been an uphill battle against a nostalgia that delights in other pasts, whether the Victorian era of politicians, or the 1950s iconography of popular culture. One offers heroic individuals striving through industry to prove that the road to heaven is paved with bad intentions, the other loners grooming their way to non-conformity.

There is also a smaller but thriving 1960s nostalgia industry, draining the politics, the poetry, the drugs, and leaving the tunes and the clothes – safe, sanitized and meaningless. And one ghost makes sporadic attempts to again take on a material form, but *It* can never really live again, for its support system, its atmosphere, are past.

But the issues raised by the underground press in all its forms, *It*, *Moul Express*, *Friends*, *Grass Eye*, *Black Dwarf*, *Ink*, *Oz*, *7 Days*, even *Gandalf's Garden*, were never resolved. The arguments about self-activity, about the failures of reform, the limitations of conventional politics, the need to step outside an alienated system, were never refuted. History filed them for future reference.

Some of the points raised by that press, and that movement have been consulted in the interim. It is a minor irony that the Greater London Council of the early 1980s drew on some of the lessons, and some of the people of the counter-culture. An irony because its most visible representative, Ken Livingstone, was joining the Labour Party in 1968 at the very moment when the majority of his contemporaries were moving out. Later he would see many of them back in again, together with feminism, decentralization, festivals in parks, lesbian and gay rights, co-operatives and other fragments of that movement of ten years before. The GLC bureaucracy may have done little for their vitality, since metropolitan-organized festivals of the oppressed seemed a contradiction in terms, but the echoes remained. And thus the likes of Sheila Rowbotham found themselves within the GLC's Popular Planning Unit at County Hall after ten years of writing and organizing. Again Rowbotham was working on a paper attempting to link those disparate socialist, trade union, and feminist endeavours and dreams. Its name, *Jobs For A Change*, lacked the panache of *Black Dwarf* yet her motivations were not dissimilar, even if the radical change of society had yielded to the more mundane project of small reforms, small changes, building from the base, beyond the fragments.

Seventeen years on from *Friends* Alan Marcuson edits a connoisseurs' magazine about carpets and rugs in Kilburn. 'Maybe I am just a South African playboy', he says, 'for me it was perhaps the difference between commitment and involvement, like the difference between bacon and eggs. The chicken is involved, but the pig is *committed*. I was involved.'

Perhaps Richard Neville was too, but he retains an affection for its achievements. 'Some grew rich. Some grew wiser. Some have fallen dead as junkies. Some have suffered. But it *was* a period of intellectual ferment. It was a compost heap.'

John Wilcock is still on the road, still recording, reporting on the world from the outside, and still waiting. 'People devise the ideas and then somebody publishes them', he says. 'There are always these ideas, so, in a way, there's always an underground. Andy Warhol's quote about everybody being famous for fifteen minutes has become such a convenient shorthand that nobody really *thinks* about it. How do you *get* to be famous for your fifteen minutes? What I think he meant is that everybody could be, if they chose, genuinely, honestly creative for fifteen minutes. It would do them the world of good.'

Sources

I drew heavily on the underground papers of the 1960s and 1970s in writing this book, specifically on *Idiot International*, *Black Dwarf*, *Friends*, *Frendz*, *Ink*, *Gandalf's Garden*, *Oz*, and *It*. Outside London there were such papers as *Mole Express*, *Rap*, *Grass Eye*, the *Liverpool Free Press*, the *Manchester Free Press*, *Grapevine*, *Mother Grumble*, *Inside Out*, the *Aberdeen Free Press*, and *Brighton Voice*. Outside the underground, but very much within the period, were *Time Out*, *Spare Rib*, and *Inside Story*. All were an invaluable source of information and a reflection of the mood of the times. Without Harvester Primary Social Sources microfilms of the press of the times, stored within the British Library, this book would have been almost impossible to put together.

1 Almost tomorrow

The chapter title comes from the Dream Weavers' 1956 British number one, 'It's Almost Tomorrow'. Nicosia's biography of Kerouac is a source for the chapter, as are Widgery's *The Left In Britain*, Peck's *Uncovering the Sixties*, Leamer's *The Paper Revolutionaries*, and Nuttall's *Bomb Culture*.

2 The biggest place in town

The material on Miles in this and subsequent chapters comes from an interview conducted by Russell Southwood, David Morley, and Charles Landry of Comedia. The coverage of the *Lady Chatterley* trial was assisted by Knightley and Kennedy's *An Affair Of State* and Levin's *The Pendulum Years*. The primary source of Jim Haynes's early British career was his autobiography *Thanks For Coming!*. The *Private Eye* coverage was greatly helped by Marnham's history of that magazine. The account of the early history of *Oz* draws on Richard Neville's account in *The Age* (16 April 1983), on Palmer's Trials of *Oz*, on *Ink 8* (9 June 1971), and on Neville's *Playpower*. Hewison's account of the sTigma exhibition in *Too Much* was useful. The early history of Better Books was covered in *Time Out* (12 April 1974). Selerie's published interview with Tom McGrath, and the latter's account in *Peace News* of the Albert Hall poetry reading, were important sources on that subject.

3 Their very own and golden city

Much of the American background in this and other chapters draws on Abe Peck's history of the US underground press. On Britain I drew on Haynes, Marnham, Selerie, Grogan's *Ringolevio*, and Ronnie Davis's history of the San Francisco Mime Troupe. The *It* gathering at the Roundhouse was reported in *It2* (31 October 1966), and covered in Farren and Barker's *Watch Out Kids*.

4 The disturbing world of the flower children

Juliet Mitchell's pioneering essay on feminism appeared in *New Left Review 40*. Harvey Matusow's career in 1950s McCarthyite America is extensively documented in Caute's *The Great Fear*. The material on John Hopkins drew on Miles's recollections and on Maureen Green's *Observer* piece 'Who's who in the underground', republished in *Thanks For Coming!* Another source was Miles and Selerie's interview with McGrath.

5 Dreams and dialectics

The music references in this and other chapters were greatly assisted by Gillett and Frith's *Rock File 4*. Coverage of the Dialectics of Liberation was helped by Widgery's July 1987 *New Society* article on the subject, and his *The Left in Britain*. Sources on the US at that time include Gottlieb and Wolt's *Thinking Big* and Kopkind's *America The Mixed Curse*.

6 New explanations

The material on the Rolling Stones drew on Norman's history of the band. The material on the Situationists drew on their *Totality For Kids*, Widgery's *The Left In Britain*, and Hewison's *Too Much*.

7 Demand the impossible

Tariq Ali's *Streetfighting Years* is important on the times, and on Clive Goodwin. I drew on my own interview in 1970 with D. A. N. Jones. The May Events are graphically covered in Quattrocchi and Nairn's *The Beginning of the End* and Seale and McConville's *French Revolution 1968*. *The Hornsey Affair* is an important source on that battle, as was *It* during that period, and *Time Out* later. The birth of the women's movement is covered in Rowbotham's *Dreams and Dilemmas* – which gathers together much of her contemporary writing during that period – and Mitchell's *Woman's Estate*.

8 The hell of it

Norman's *The Rolling Stones* and Nuttall's *Bomb Culture* were sources. Petrakis's piece on sexuality appeared in *It50* (14 February 1969), and the angry reply in *It52* on 14 March 1969.

9 Friends and enemies

The Genesis Hall Arts Lab battle was covered in *It53* (28 March 1969). Jim Anderson and Felix Dennis's background is dealt with in Palmer's *The Trials of Oz*. My notes of the time were useful for the Isle of Wight. Cockburn and Blackburn's *Student Power* and Widgery's *Left in Britain* are again useful on the politics of the period.

10 The women's room

I drew on my own recollections of the *Idiot* saga, and the report which appeared in *Ink* (1 May 1971). Again Rowbotham's and Mitchell's writings on the women's movement were important, as were Peck's on the struggles around *Rat* and *It77* (9 April 1970).

11 Getting straight

I interviewed Jann Wenner in 1969, which is the source for his view on the ownership of Coca Cola.

12 Shattering the spectacle

Farren covers Phun City in *Watch Out Kids*. Reports at the time appeared in *It85* (13 August 1970), *Friends* (21 August 1970), and *Grass Eye*. Neville's comment on Farren was in *Friends* (2 October 1970). Peck covers the rise of US sex papers, and Haynes deals with *Suck* in *Thanks For Coming!* as did Germaine Greer in *UK Late* (Channel 4) July 1987. The pamphlet *Why Miss World?*, put together by some of the protesters, is an important source on the views of the protagonists. *World In Action* reported on the Angry Brigade on 7 December 1972, and provided a useful insight.

13 Professional problems

Alan Marcuson is quoted from *Time Out* (30 April 1971). Sally Beauman's interview with Eldridge Cleaver appeared in *Ink4* (22 May 1971). The career of Jim McCann and Howard Marks is entertainingly dealt with in

David Leigh's *High Time*, although it is an account with which Alan Marcuson has considerable disagreements.

14 Time of trial

The principal account of the *Oz* trial remains Tony Palmer's book. *Time Out*'s coverage of the Angry Brigade throughout the period is very useful, specifically the chronology provided on 20 August 1971. So too was the *World In Action* on the subject, and the pamphlets produced by the Stoke Newington Eight Defence Committee. *Time Out* covered *7 Days'* launch on 5 November 1971, and I drew on that source. Rosie Boycott's *A Nice Girl Like Me* deals with her role in the creation of *Spare Rib*.

15 We are all angry?

Again *World In Action*, *Time Out*, and the Stoke Newington Eight Defence Group were useful sources. The comments from the latter were from its political statement published early in 1972. The review in *Ink* of *A Clockwork Orange* appeared on 7 January 1972. The 'Responsibility in the Media' Conference was covered in *Frendz* and *Time Out*. Peck's reportage on Wenner is useful.

16 Ribs, rads, and bombs

Oz42 covered the *Spare Rib* planned launch in May 1972, and reported on its party in *Oz43* in the summer. Boycott's *A Nice Girl Like Me* covers that period. The divisions within *Suck* are covered in Haynes's *Thanks For Coming!* and were dealt with on Channel 4's *UK Late* in July 1987 by Germaine Greer, together with the motives for her involvement.

17 Around the corner

The saga of *Inside London* was dealt with in *Time Out* (23 November 1973), as was Michael Abdul Malik's defence by Kunstler and Millett on 23 February 1973, and Bill Levy and John Michell's protest was covered in the magazine on 26 April 1974. On 12 April 1974 it dealt with the death of Better Books. Patrick Marnham's history of *Private Eye* deals with the ill-fated *Scene* of the early 1960s.

18 Kings of kung fu

The amazing success of *Kung Fu Monthly* was covered in *Time Out* (13 December 1974), in a feature by Jonathon Green.

19 Ghost town

To that small group on strike – or resisting it – in the spring and summer of 1981, the hit record of that time, the Specials' 'Ghost Town' seemed peculiarly appropriate, hence the chapter title. Landry *et al.*'s *What a Way to Run a Railroad* was useful on *The Leveller*.

20 Aftermath

David Edgar's 'It wasn't so naff in the sixties after all' (*Guardian*, 7 July 1986) is a vigorous defence of the counter-culture. John Carvel's *Citizen Ken* is illuminating on the background of the former leader of the GLC. Judith Williamson provided valuable insights into the contrasts between then and now.

Bibliography

In charting the developments of those times I drew on many sources, including the following books:

Ali, Tariq (1987) *Streetfighting Years: An Autobiography of the Sixties*, London: Collins.

Boycott, Rosie (1984) *A Nice Girl Like Me: A Story of the Seventies*, London: Chatto and Windus/The Hogarth Press, and (1985) London: Pan.

Carvel, John (1984) *Citizen Ken*, London: Chatto & Windus/The Hogarth Press.

Caute, David (1979) *The Great Fear: The Anti-Communist Purge under Truman and Eisenhower*, New York: Simon & Schuster/Touchstone.

Cockburn, Alexander and Blackburn, Robin (eds) (1969) *Student Power: Problems, Diagnosis, Action*, Harmondsworth, Penguin.

Coleman, Ray (1984), *John Lennon*, London: Sidgewick & Jackson, and (1985) London: Futura.

Davis, R.G. (1975) *The San Francisco Mime Troupe: The First Ten Years*, Pal Alto: Ramparts Press.

Farren, Mick and Barker, Edward (1972) *Watch Out Kids*, London: Open Gate Books.

Fordham, John (1986) *Let's Join Hands and Contact the Living: Ronnie Scott and his Club*, London: Elm Tree Books.

Gillett, Charlie and Frith, Simon (eds) (1976) *Rock File 4*, London: Panther.

Gottlieb, Robert and Wolt, Irene (1977) *Thinking Big: The Story of the Los Angeles Times*, New York: G.P. Putnam's Sons.

Grogan, Emmett (1972) *Ringolevio: A Life Played for Keeps*, London: William Heinemann, and (1974) London: Granada.

Haynes, Jim (1984) *Thanks For Coming! An Autobiography*, London: Faber and Faber.

Hewison, Robert (1986) *Too Much: Art and Society in the Sixties; 1960–75*, London: Methuen.

Hornsey College Of Art, students and staff (1969) *The Hornsey Affair*, Harmondsworth: Penguin.

King, Cecil (1972) *The Cecil King Diary 1965–1970*, London: Cape.

Knightley, Phillip and Kennedy, Caroline (1987) *An Affair of State: The Profumo Affair and the Framing of Stephen Ward*, London: Cape.

Kopkind, Andrew (1969) *America the Mixed Curse*, Harmondsworth: Penguin.

Landry, Charles, Morley, David, Southwood, Russell, Wright, Patrick

(1985) *What a Way to Run a Railroad: An Analysis of Radical Failure*, London: Comedia.

Leamer, Laurence (1972) *The Paper Revolutionaries: The Rise of the Underground Press*, New York: Simon & Schuster.

Leigh, David (1984) *High Time: The Life and Times of Howard Marks*, London: William Heinemann, and (1985) London: Unwin Paperbacks.

Levin Bernard (1977) *The Pendulum Years: Britain and the Sixties*, London: Pan.

Lewis, Roger (1972) *Outlaws of America: The Underground Press and its Context; Notes on a Cultural Revolution*, London: Pelican.

McAuliffe, Kevin Michael (1978) *The Great American Newspaper: The Rise and Fall of the Village Voice*, New York: Charles Scribner's Sons.

Mitchell, Juliet (1971) *Women's Estate*, Harmondsworth: Penguin.

Neville, Richard (1970) *Playpower*, London: Cape, and (1971) London: Paladin.

Newfield, Jack (1967) *A Prophetic Minority: The American New Left*, London: Anthony Blond, and (1966) New York: New American Library.

Nicosia, Gerald (1983) *Memory Babe: A Critical Biography of Jack Kerouac*, New York: Grove Press, and (1986) Harmondsworth: Penguin.

Norman, Philip (1984) *The Stones*, London: Elm Tree Books.

Nuttall, Jeff (1968) *Bomb Culture*, London: McGibbon & Kee.

Palmer, Tony (1971) *The Trials of Oz*, London: Blond & Brigss.

Peck, Abe (1985) *Uncovering the Sixties: The Life and Times of the Underground Press*, New York: Pantheon.

Quattrocchi, Angelo and Nairn, Tom (1968) *The Beginning of the End: France, May 1968*, London: Panther.

Rowbotham, Sheila (1983) *Dreams and Dilemmas: Collected Writings*, London: Virago.

Roszak, Theodore (1970) *The Making of a Counter Culture: Reflections on the Technocratic Society and its Youthful Opposition*, London: Faber & Faber.

Seale, Patrick and McConville, Maureen (1968) *French Revolution 1968*, London: Penguin/Heinemann.

Selerie, Gavin (ed.) (1983) *The Riverside Interviews 6: Tom McGrath*, London: Binnacle Press.

Stoke Newington Eight Defence Group (1971–2) *If You Want Peace Prepare for War, and a Political Statement*.

Thompson, E.P. (1978) *The Poverty of Theory and Other Essays*, Devon: Merlin.

Weiss, Peter (1965) *The Persecution and Assassination of Marat as Performed by the Inmates of the Asylum of Charenton Under the Direction of the Marquis de Sade*, London: John Calder, and (1966) London: Caldcr & Boyars.

Welch, Chris (1972) *Hendrix: A Biography*, London: Ocean Books.

Widgery, David (1986) *Beating Time: Riot 'n' Race 'n' Rock 'n' Roll*, London: Chatto Tigerstripe.

– (1975) *The Left in Britain 1956–70*, Harmondsworth: Penguin.

Index